Continuum

Carla Belanger
Carol Danbrook
Don Deeter
Suzanne Falkeid
Andrew Famiglietti
Terri Hammond
Jack LeSage
Jim Mennie
Ellen Radomski
Todd Romiens
Larry Salekin
Cathy Steele
Marianne Strasser

Rogue Media Inc.
Calgary, Alberta, Canada

Continuum

Editor in Chief:
Jack LeSage

Editors:
Jim Mennie
Ellen Radomski
Marianne Strasser

Editorial Contributions:
Terri Hammond
Larry Salekin

Project Manager: Carla Belanger

Design by: Marianne Strasser R.G.D.
Desktop Publishing by: Laser Graphics Desktop Publishing
Cover by: K Graphics

National Library of Canada Cataloguing in Publication
LeSage, Jack W.
Continuum

Includes index.
ISBN 0-9688975-3-3

1. Mathematics. 2. Finance, Personal. 3. Consumer education.
QA39.3.C66 2002   332.024   C2002-903284-9

Printed and bound in Canada

11 10 09 08 07 06 • 9 8 7 6 5 4

CONTENTS

PUZZLES & PATTERNS — 3

Order of operations — 4

Integers — 8
Integers — 8
Comparing Integers — 11
Combining Integers — 13
Adding Integers - Tiles — 15
Adding Integers - Number Line — 16
Subtracting Integers — 19
Multiplying Integers — 24
Using Technology to Investigate Multiplication — 30
Division and Multiplication — 32
Dividing Integers — 35
Using Integers — 37

Patterns — 39
Recognizing Patterns — 39
Visualizing a Patterning Relationship — 45
Graphing Patterns — 46
Points or Line? — 49

Puzzles — 53
Magic Squares — 53
Number Tricks — 59
Calendar Math — 62

Review — 64

Project- Mathematics and Puzzles — 69

ENTERTAINMENT — 71

Decimals — 72
Rounding — 72
Money Adds Up — 74
Adding &Subtracting Decimals — 76
Spending Money — 80
Multiplying A Decimal — 82
Multiplying by Tens — 85
Multiplying Decimals — 87

Dividing by Tens 90
Dividing Decimals 93

Graphs 96
Reading & Interpreting Graphs 96

Review 113
Project - Entertainment Industry 117

HOME 121

Fractions 122
What is a Fraction? 122
Mixed Numbers & Improper Fractions 126
Equivalent Fractions 133
Adding & Subtracting Fractions 138
Multiplying Fractions 145
Dividing Fractions 151

Measurement 158
Linear Measure 158
Using an Imperial Ruler 158
Adding & Subtracting Imperial Measures 163
Linear Measurement 167
Conversions Between SI and Imperial Units 171
Perimeter 173
Area 176
Working With Area 179
Volume 193
Mass / weight 198

Review 201
Project - Room Design 208

FOOD FARE 211

Equations 212
Solving One-Step Equations 212
One-Step Equations- Problem Solving 219
Verifying Answers to One-Step Equations 223
Solving Two-Step Equations 225

Verifying Answers to Two-Step Equations   232
Problem Solving with Two-Step Equations   234

Ratios, Rates, Percents   239

Ratio   239
Ratios   248
Rate   255
Per Cent   261
Percent Problems   271
Proportions   278

Review   284

Project - Running a Successful Restaurant   290

PERSPECTIVES   295

Angles   296

Constructing & Measuring Angles   296
Angle Relationships   302
Angles in Navigation   308

Circles   312

Circumference of Circles   312
Area of A Circle   319

Review   327

Project - Where's the Cache   330

SPORTS   333

Central Tendencies   334

Sports Statistics   334
Mean, Median, Mode, Range   339
Mean, Median or Mode?   341
Central Tendencies in Sports   343
Track Times   346
Player Evaluation - The +/– Statistic   348

Theorem of Pythagoras   351

Square Roots   351
Theorem of Pythagoras   354
Applying Pythagorean Theorem   355

Review   **360**

Project - Choosing a Community Sports Facility **364**

ADVERTISING   **369**

Pizza   370
Cellular Phones   375
Percent discounts   376
Best Buys   378

Review   **385**

Project - Buying Electronics   **385**

GLOSSARY   **387**

ANSWERS   **395**

INDEX   **430**

ICONS USED IN THIS BOOK

ICON	PURPOSE
Multi-Media	The CD icon indicates that a *complimentary interactive lesson* is found on the CD Rom.
Get Thinking	The light bulb indicates that these questions will encourage students to *draw on their prior knowledge, be resourceful, take initiative in their learning,* and *make real world connections.*
Project	The globe indicates *an appropriate time to work on a section of the final project* and is also a reminder of the *unit destination* (the real world connection).

WELCOME TO THE WORLD OF CONTINUUM!

In this book you will find the mathematics that you will encounter in the world of work and at home.

We have organized the course into seven themes that reflect the world in which you will live.

Good luck!

Carla Belanger
Chinook College

Jack LeSage
Georgian College

Carol Danbrook
Daemen College

Jim Mennie
Consultant

Don Deeter
Chestermere High School

Ellen Radomski
St. Anne High School

Suzanne Falkeid
Crescent Heights High School

Todd Romiens
University of Windsor

Andrew Famiglietti
Georgian College

Larry Salekin
Bert Church High School

Terri Hammond
Dr. Gordon Higgins Junior High School

Cathy Steele
Bishop McNally High School

The authors would like to thank their families for their understanding and support.

We would also like to thank Marianne and Grant Strasser for their desktopping and design talents and for their contributions to the content.
Also appreciated are the contributions in quality control made by Debbie Duvall and Katie Pallos-Haden.

Finally, we would like to thank Carla and Rikk Belanger who made this possible.

1

PUZZLES & PATTERNS

GET THINKING

☐ When reading the story, "The King's Chessboard", by David Birch, how can I use mathematics to predict the outcome?

☐ What mathematical patterns and relationships must I understand to lay floor tiles?

☐ Why would I need to know the order of operations when I am ordering fast food?

☐ What events and objects follow number patterns?

☐ How can I use integers to make sure I put enough money in my overdrawn bank account to cover a payment that is coming out?

AND MENTAL MATH, PROBLEM SOLVING, REASONING, TECHNOLOGY, VISUALIZATION, COMMUNICATION, CONNECTIONS, ESTIMATION

Content

- Integer concepts
- Integer operations
- Order of operations
- Generalize a pattern
- Write expressions & equations to represent patterns
- Read and interpret graphs
- Graph and analyze relations

Meaning and Understanding

Intellectual Curiosity

How is mathematics used in the creation of puzzles, brain teasers, tricks and games?

Why is "the study of patterns and their relationships" a good description of mathematics?

Mathematics and Puzzles

Research the Internet for brain teasers;
present one to a group;
communicate the mathematics behind the puzzle.

Think about the things that you do to get ready for school, for work or for an evening with friends. When you dress in the morning, you use some order of operations that are not mathematical, but the way you dress is an order of operations. You need to put your socks on before you put your shoes on and the same goes for other parts of your clothing.

When you answer the skill-testing question in a contest it is important that you know the order of operations.

Programming of computers requires the use of order of operations.

In mathematics, we use the following convention for the order of operations.

B	rackets	(inner most first)
E	xponents	
D	ivision	
	(or)	(left to right, in the order that they appear)
M	ultiplication	
A	ddition	
	(or)	(left to right, in the order that they appear)
S	ubtraction	

If you look at the first letters of the terms above you will see that they form the "word" BEDMAS.

BEDMAS is an acronym that you can use to help you remember the order of operations.

Example 1:

Solve the following skill–testing question and win a beach holiday!

Use the acronym BEDMAS to help you remember the order of the operations

$$2 \times 3 + 4 \div 2 - 5$$

Think	Ask yourself	In this case
B	Are there any operations inside brackets?	No
E	Are there any exponents?	No
D or	Are there any multiplications or divisions?	Yes, 2×3
M	The multiplication appears first so it is done before the division.	and $4 \div 2$
A	Are there any additions or subtractions?	6+2 then 8–5
S	The addition appears first so it is done before the subtraction.	

Solution:

$$\overset{1}{2 \times 3} + \overset{2}{4 \div 2} - 5$$
$$= \overset{3}{6 + 2} - 5$$
$$= 8 - 5$$

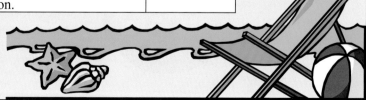

Example 2:

Evaluate: $6^2 - 3 \times 4 \div 2$
Write a complete solution.

Solution:

$6^2 - 3 \times 4 \div 2$
$= 36 - 3 \times 4 \div 2$
$= 36 - 12 \div 2$
$= 36 - 6$
$= 30$

Think	Ask yourself	In this case
B	Are there any operations inside brackets?	No
E	Are there any exponents?	Yes, $6^2 = 6 \times 6$
D or	Are there any multiplications or divisions?	Yes, 3×4 then
M		$12 \div 2$
A	Are there any additions or subtractions?	$36 - 6$
S		

INVESTIGATION

On his way home, Jean Paul picked up burgers for his family.
He ordered 3 cheeseburger combos at $5.49 each, 7 ice cream sundaes at $1.29 each and 4 chicken combos at $5.99 each.

Explain how Jean Paul can calculate the total cost of his order.

Using the order of operations, write an expression for the total cost.

Calculate the total cost before taxes.

Example 3:

Evaluate: $1 + 3^4 - 4 - 5 \times 2(7 - 6)$
Write a complete solution.

Solution:

$1 + 3^4 - 4 - 5 \times 2(7 - 6)$

$= 1 + 3^4 - 4 - 5 \times 2(1)$	*Brackets first*
$= 1 + 81 - 4 - 5 \times 2(1)$	*Exponents next. 3^4 means $3 \times 3 \times 3 \times 3$*
$= 1 + 81 - 4 - 10(1)$	*First Multiplication*
$= 1 + 81 - 4 - 10$	*Second Multiplication*
$= 82 - 4 - 10$	*First Addition*
$= 78 - 10$	*First Subtraction*
$= 68$	

Check your calculator to find out how it handles order of operations.

Sometimes a question may contain calculations with numbers that are very large or difficult to work with.

Most scientific calculators can accommodate the rules for order of operations.
If a calculator is not programmed for the order of operations, you must key in brackets around calculations that need to be done first, or calculate sections according to the rules individually.

Calculate $1 + 2 \times 3$ on your calculator by entering:

If the calculator shows 7 then it can handle the order of operations.

If the calculator shows 9 then it added the 1 and 2 first and so it is not programmed for the order of operations.
If you have a calculator like this then enter:

and you should see 7.

1. Find the error in each calculation.
   Calculate the correct answer.

   a. $4 \times 2 + 3 \times 6$
          $= 4 \times 5 \times 6$
          $= 20 \times 6$
          $= 120$

   b. $30 - 5 \times 3$
          $= 25 \times 3$
          $= 75$

Example: 1, 2, 3, 4 = 5

Solution:
$(1 + 2) \times 3 - 4 = 5$

2. Insert $+, -, \times, \div$ or ( ) to make each sentence true.
   Calculate the value of the left side to check your work.

   a. 43 7 2 = 100   b. 8 9 2 4 = 11

Set up an order of operations expression for the following problems and then solve to find the answer.

3. A garage charges $25 to do an inspection of your vehicle.

   If there is any work to be done on the vehicle the charge is $65 per hour.

   If a mechanic works on a car for 3 hours, what will the total bill be? (Do not include tax.)

4. A grocery store makes up a meat tray consisting of 15 slices of ham, 12 slices of turkey, 21 slices of roast and 25 sausage slices.

   If the store receives 8 orders for this meat tray, how many slices of meat are there in total?

5. A telephone company charges seven cents per minute and also charges a $5.99 monthly fee.
   During the month, Jim used the phone for 190 minutes and Joan used the phone for 90 minutes.

   How much will the total bill be?

6. A group of students wants to order some fast food.

   They decide on a hamburger, fries and a pop each.

   Three students want Double burgers @$3.65 each.

   Two students want Super burgers @$4.79.

   Three students want Super B I G burgers @$5.24.

   Five students want Regular fries @$1.25.

   Three students want Large fries @$1.75.

   They all want medium fountain pop at $1.00.

   Calculate the total cost of the bill, before tax.

7. Write the expression to show that 6 is multiplied by 3 and then 8 is subtracted from the result.
   Calculate the answer.

8. Write the expression to show that 3 and 6 are added and the result is multiplied by 5.
   Calculate the answer.

9. Write the expression for the change received from a fifty–dollar bill after purchasing two packages of golf balls at $23.95 each.
   Calculate the answer.

10. Write the expression to show that 15 is increased by the product of 3 and 6 and then decreased by 10.
    Calculate the answer.

You are now ready to start Step 1 of your project.

INTEGERS

GET THINKING

Have you ever played mini golf?
Explain how integers are used in keeping score.

In mathematics, the + and – signs represent the operations of addition and subtraction. They also represent positive and negative whole numbers that are called **integers**. Integers are used to express opposites. To show ideas about **going up, gain or profit**, the **positive** symbol + is used. To show ideas about **going down or loss**, the **negative** symbol – is used.

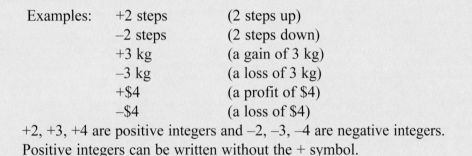

Examples: +2 steps   (2 steps up)
             –2 steps   (2 steps down)
             +3 kg   (a gain of 3 kg)
             –3 kg   (a loss of 3 kg)
             +$4   (a profit of $4)
             –$4   (a loss of $4)

+2, +3, +4 are positive integers and –2, –3, –4 are negative integers.
Positive integers can be written without the + symbol.

Integers can be shown on both horizontal and vertical number lines.

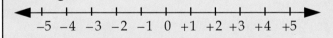

On the horizontal number line, numbers to the **left of zero** are **negative**.
Numbers to the **right of zero** are **positive**.
Zero is an integer that is **neither positive nor negative**.
On the vertical number line, numbers **above zero** are **positive** and numbers **below zero** are **negative**.
Opposite integers are the same distance from zero but are on opposite sides of zero. So they have the **same number with opposite signs**. The opposite of –4 is +4.

Remember:
Integers are always whole numbers.

1. Write an integer to show each of the following.
   - a. 3° C above freezing
   - b. a loss of 10 points
   - c. 70 km above sea level
   - d. a raise of 6%
   - e. 2 floors down
   - f. a deposit of $500
   - g. a gain of 3 kg
   - h. ground level

2. In golf a score of −5 means 5 strokes below par. What would each of the following scores mean in a golf game?
   - a. −7
   - b. −1
   - c. +4
   - d. +9
   - e. 0
   - f. −3
   - g. +8
   - h. −2

3. Write an integer to show:
   - a. 4 less than zero
   - b. 3 more than zero
   - c. 18 more than zero
   - d. 10 less than zero

4. What integer is shown by each location?

a.

b.

5. Integer (−4)   Opposite integer (+4)

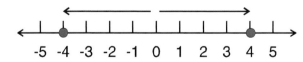

For each integer, draw a number line and draw an arrow to show the opposite of each integer.
   - a. +3
   - b. −6
   - c. +2
   - d. −5

Integers can be compared and ordered by placing them on a number line.
As we move to the right on a number line, the numbers increase.
As we move to the left, they decrease.
If a number is to the right of another number, the first number is said to be
greater than (>) the second number.
If a number is to the left of another number, the number on the left is said to be
less than (<) the other number.

In the diagram above:
    –5 is less than –2. This is written as –5 < –2
    –2 is greater than –5. This is written as –2 > –5
    –5 is less than +1. This is written as –5 < +1
    +1 is greater than –5. This is written as +1 > –5
    –2 is less than +1. This is written as –2 < +1
    +1 is greater than –2. This is written as +1 > –2

PUT INTO PRACTICE

1. Which integer is farther to the right on a number line?
  a. +2 or +4 b. –4 or –3 c. –8 or +5 d. +6 or –6

2. Which integer is farther to the left on a number line?
  a. +9 or +7 b. –3 or –5 c. –9 or –12 d. +2 or –2

3. Which integer in each pair is greater?
  a. –3 or –5 b. +5 or –8 c. –10 or +2 d. +4 or +6

4. Which integer in each pair is smaller?
  a. –2 or –4 b. +3 or –3 c. –7 or +4 d. +1 or –3

5. For each set of integers, identify the largest and the
  smallest integer.
  a. –7, –2, –5   b. +2, –3, –1   c. +3, –5, –3000

6. Write each set of integers in order, from greatest to least.
   a. +7, +9, –3, –2   b. –5, –2, –9 +1   c. –4, –5, –2, –9

7. Write each set of integers in order, from least to greatest.
   a. +6, –5, 0, +2   b. –4, –6, –3, –2

8. Copy and replace ☐ with < or >.
   a. –8 ☐ +1   b. –4 ☐ –7   c. –12 ☐ +1,   d. +3 ☐ +1

9. Which one of the following is true?
   Correct those that are not true.

   a. +6 is less than +4   b. +5 is greater than –3
   c. +2 is less than +1   d. –10 is greater than –4
   e. –2 is greater than 0   f. +1 is less than 0

Substance	Freezing Point
Radon	–71° C
Water	0° C
Mercury	–39° C
Nitrogen	–210° C
Neon	–249° C

10. a. Which of the substances in the table on the left has the lowest freezing point?

    b. Arrange the temperatures in order from lowest to highest.

11. Look at the table on the left.

City	Today's Temperature
Calgary	–6°C
Hong Kong	+16°C
London (England)	+8°C
Montreal	–8°C
Moscow	+1°C
Vancouver	+6°C
Wellington (NZ)	+24°C
Winnipeg	–14°C

   a. Which is the warmest place today?
   b. Which is the coldest?
   c. List the cities in order from the coldest to the warmest.
   d. Which city do you think you would like to be in? Give reasons for your answer.

12. Which of the following integers are less than +3 but greater than –4?

   a. –2   b. +1   c. +5   d. –6   e. 0   f. –12

To help us understand integers we can represent positive and negative numbers using coloured tiles.

There are many patterns involving operations with integers. The tiles will help you to spot these patterns.

We will use red tiles to represent positive integers and white tiles to represent negative integers. One red tile ■ represents +1.

One white tile ☐ represents –1.

One red tile and one white tile together represent zero. I.e., ■ ☐ represent 0.

Two red tiles and two white tiles together also represent zero. ■ ■
☐ ☐

And five red tiles and five white tiles together represent zero.

■ ■ ■ ■ ■
☐ ☐ ☐ ☐ ☐

Each pair of red and white tiles represents +1 and –1 and they combine to represent zero.

This pairing of opposites to represent zero is called the **Zero Principle**.

INVESTIGATION

Combine 5 red tiles and 7 white tiles and state what integer they represent.

■ ■ ■ ■ ■   ➡   ☐ ☐
☐ ☐ ☐ ☐ ☐ ☐ ☐

Explain in writing what you did to find the solution.

Example:

Combine 5 white tiles and 4 red tiles and state what integer they represent.
Write the addition sentence.

Solution:

The 4 white tiles and 4 red tiles together represent 0.
There is 1 white tile left and this represents –1.
(–5) + (+4) = –1

PUT INTO PRACTICE

1. a. Work with a partner.
   You will need red and white tiles and a container for each.
   Draw some red tiles from one of the containers and some white ones from the other container.
   Put them together.
   Record the result of putting them together.
   Return the tiles to the container.
   Repeat this process until you have recorded five different results.
   Have your partner record another five results.

   b. Write the ten integers, in order from least to greatest.

   c. Draw a number line and record the ten integers.

2. What statement can you make about any integer that is to the left of or below another integer on a number line?

3. What statement can you make about any integer that is to the right of or above another integer on a number line?

4. Write an integer that is:
   a. 7 greater than –2   b. 8 less than 0
   c. between –9 and +9   d. 5 units to the left of –8
   e. 5 units to the right of –8

GET THINKING

Do you agree or disagree with the following statements?
a. When adding two positive integers, the result will always be positive.
b. When adding two negative integers, the result will always be negative.
Explain

Example:

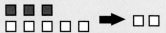

The three red tiles and three white tiles together represent zero. There are 2 white tiles left and they represent –2.

(+3) + (–5) = (–2)

INTERACTIVE LESSONS

PUT INTO PRACTICE

1. Combine the following tiles and write the result as an addition sentence.

   a. 4 reds and 2 whites   b. 4 reds and 6 whites
   c. 3 reds and 2 whites   d. 2 reds and 5 whites
   e. 3 reds and 1 whites   f. 3 reds and 3 whites

2. Write the appropriate addition sentence.
   a. ■■□□□   b. □□□□ ■■■
   c. ■■■■■□   d. ■■□□

3. Represent each set of tiles as an integer.
   Write each addition statement and determine the sum.
   a. 3 reds and 2 whites   b. 3 reds and 4 reds
   c. 2 reds and 4 whites   d. 2 whites and 1 whites

4. Use tiles to add each pair of integers.
   a. 3 + (–2)   b. 5 + (–8)   c. –4 + 4   d. 5 + 3
   e. –2 + (–3)   f. –2 + 4   g. 0 + (–4)   h. –1 + (–2)

5. Write each expression as an addition statement.
   Add:
   a. –6 to +4   b. +3 to –2   c. –5 to –3   d. +4 to +1
   e. +8 to –4   f. –4 to +8   g. –50 to –30   h. –20 to +15

6. Evaluate:
   a. –2 + (+5)   b. –8 + (–7)   c. +16 + (–12)
   d. –4 + (–8)   e. +6 + (+2)   f. +10 + (–15)
   g. –5 + (+5)   h. +6 + (–4)   i. –7 + (–3)
   j. 9 + (+1)   k. –11 + (–99)   l. –17 + (+23)

INVESTIGATION

Use the number line to find the integer at the end of the move.

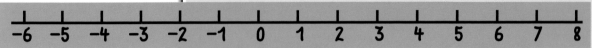

a. Start at +3 and move 4 units to the right.

b. Start at 0 and move 5 units to the left.

c. Start at (−1) and move 3 units to the right.

d. Start at +3 and move 3 units to the left.

Example: Use the number line to calculate: a. +4 + (+3)

Solution:

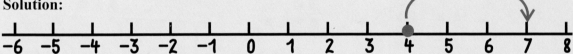

We can see that: +4 + (+3) = +7.

b. +3 + (−5)
Solution:

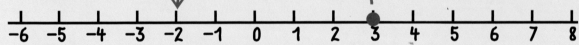

We can see that: +3 + (−5) = −2

PUT INTO PRACTICE

1. Evaluate:
   a. (−2) + (−5)   b. +5 + (−3)   c. (−5) + (+4)

2. Draw a number line to show the sum.
   Write the addition sentence.
   a. +5 + (+1)   b. (−1) + (+8)   c. (−7) + (+3)
   d. (−2) + (−2)   e. (−4) + (−5)   f. (−5) + (−4)

3. Add using a number line.
   a. +7 + (+1)   b. (–5) + (–6)   c. (–4) + (+3)
   d. +2 + (+6)   e. + 10 + (–4)   f. (–4) + (+10)

4. Explain how to add:
   a. two positive numbers   b. two negative numbers
   c. a positive and a negative number

5. Determine each sum.
   a. +5 + (–5)   b. +3 + (–3)   c. +7 + (–7)

   d. +4 + (–4)

   e. State the answer when you add an integer to its opposite.

6. For each of the following questions write an addition sentence and calculate the answer.

   a. The temperature was 0°C and it dropped 3°C then another 2°C.

      Now what is the temperature?

   b. The temperature was 0°C.
      It rose 5°C and then dropped 8°C.

      Now what is the temperature?

   c. A producer had to reduce the graphics of a music video to make it fit on a CD.
      He reduced it by 225 kbytes and then 175 kbytes.

      What was the total reduction?

Profit = Income – Expenses
Loss = Income – Expenses

d. A pop concert had expenses of $45 000 and income of $75 000.
What was the profit or loss?

e. A theatre owner was experimenting with ticket prices. She introduced a Two-Toonie-Tuesday price and the average attendance increased by 70.
She eliminated the policy and the new average attendance decreased by 30.

What was the final effect on the average attendance?

7. A roller coaster car starts at an altitude of 5 m above the ground.
The following changes in height took place:
+20 m, –12 m, –15 m, +30 m.

a. How high above the starting point is the car after these changes?

b. How high above the ground is the car after these changes?

8. Evaluate:
a. $(–3) + (+3) + (+11)$
b. $+1 + (–5) + (+4) + (–6)$
c. $+7 + (–4) + (+6)$
d. $+8 + (–6) + (–4)$
e. $+1 + (+2) + (–6)$
f. $+12 + (–13) + (+7)$
g. $(–9) + (–5) + (–8)$
h. $(1234) + (–5678) + (–1234)$

9. Evaluate:
a. $(–5) – (–3) – (+2)$
b. $(–4) – (–5) – (–1)$
c. $+10 – (–4) – (+12)$
d. $(–2) – (–8) – (+3)$
e. $+20 – (+15) – (–25)$
f. $(–9) – (–9) – 0$
g. $(–13) + (–2) – (–15)$
h. $+100 + (–10) – (–10)$
i. $(–20) – (–5) + (+17)$
j. $+6 + (–8) – (–6) – (+5)$

Remember that when we *added* integers, we *combined* groups of tiles.

To **subtract** integers, we perform the reverse operation by **removing** tiles from a group of tiles.

Example 1:

We have 5 red tiles and are asked to remove 3 red tiles. We have 2 red tiles remaining, so we write the number sentence as $(+5) - (+3) = +2$.

INVESTIGATION

Similarly, we can start with 5 white tiles and remove 3 white tiles and find that we are left with 2 white tiles.

Model this and then write the subtraction sentence.

Example 2:

If we reverse the first example, and try to remove 5 red tiles from 3 red tiles, we have the number sentence

$$(+3) - (+5) = ?.$$

Before you can remove 5 red tiles, you need to have 5 red tiles.

Recall that we can add equal numbers of red and white tiles without changing the integer. So there are many different ways to represent +3.

The simplest way is to use 3 red tiles but you can also use: 4 red tiles and 1 white tile, 5 red tiles and 2 white tiles (i.e. 2 red tiles and 2 white tiles together represent 0), etc.

So we can add 2 red tiles and 2 white tiles to the 3 red tiles.

(By adding equal numbers of red and white tiles, we haven't changed the integer that is represented by the red tiles.)

 OR  OR

We can now remove the 5 red tiles.

 2 white tiles remain.

We write $(+3) - (+5) = -2$.

Example 3:

Now let us try **(+3) – (–5)**.

In order to take away 5 whites we need 5 whites so we can add 5 whites (and therefore 5 reds) to the 3 reds and we still have a model for +3.

Now we can take away the 5 whites.

You can see that the result is +8 and that we can get it by adding the 5 remaining reds to the original 3 reds.

You will notice that in order to **SUBTRACT** 5 **whites** we eventually **ADDED** 5 **reds**.
So another way to think of the subtraction of integers is that we have simply added the opposite.
The number sentence can be written:

$$(+3) - (-5)$$
$$= (+3) + (+5)$$
$$= +8.$$

To model the expression **(–3) – (–8)**, you need to ask how can I take 8 white tiles from 3 white tiles? To remove the 8 white tiles we need 5 more white tiles. So we can add 5 white and 5 red tiles. This does not change the value (–3), but allows us to remove 8 white tiles.

5 red tiles remain.

The number sentence can be written as
or it can be rewritten as an addition statement:

$$(-3) - (-8) = (+5),$$
$$(-3) - (-8)$$
$$= (-3) + (+8)$$
$$= +5.$$

Consider these addition statements and the corresponding subtraction statements that give the same answer.

$(+8) - (+3) = +5$	$(-5) - (-3) = -2$	$(+4) - (-2) = +6$	$(-6) - (+3) = -9$
$(+8) + (-3) = +5$	$(-5) + (+3) = -2$	$(+4) + (+2) = +6$	$(-6) + (-3) = -9$

We can see that the result of **subtracting** an integer is the same as **adding its opposite**.

1. Use tiles to show that

   $(-6) - (+4) = (-6) + (-4)$.

2. Use tiles to do each of these subtraction questions.

   a. 2 red subtract 5 red   b. 3 white subtract 6 white

   c. 4 red subtract 7 white   d. 5 red subtract 6 red

   e. 4 white subtract 2 white   f. 9 red subtract 4 white

   g. 6 red subtract 2 red   h. 8 white subtract 6 red

Subtracting
an integer
is the same as
adding its opposite.
E.g.,
$(-5) - (-2) = (-5) + (+2)$
$= -3$

---

3. For each subtraction statment, write the appropriate addition statment.
   Write the answer to each of the statment.

   a. $(+5) - (+2)$ b. $(-3) - (+6)$ c. $(-6) - (+7)$

   d. $(+7) - (-9)$ e. $(+3) - (+8)$ f. $(-6) - (-1)$

   g. $(-6) - (+6)$ h. $(+6) - (-6)$ i. $(-1.2) - (-1.2)$

   j. $0 - (-2)$ k. $(-4) - (-6)$ l. $(+7) - (-5)$

   m. $(-9) - (+6)$ n. $0 - (+2)$ o. $0 - (2)$

4. Evaluate.

   a. $(+8) - (-5)$ b. $(-3) - (-4)$ c. $(+6) - (-3)$

   d. $(-7) - (+4)$ e. $(+5) - (-5)$ f. $(-9) - (+8)$

   g. $(9) - (+8)$ h. $(-9) - (-8)$ i. $(-109) - (-108)$

   j. $(-8) - (+6)$ k. $0 - (-3)$ l. $(+8) - (+12)$

   m. $(-4) - (-4)$ n. $(+3) - (3)$ o. $(1234) - (1234)$

5. Write each expression below as a subtraction statement and subtract.

   Subtract:
   a. +2 from +6   b. –3 from –4   c. +2 from –8
   d. +6 from +8   e. –3 from –3   f. 0 from –8

6. When subtracting one integer from another, how can you predict when the answer will be: negative?   positive? Use tiles or diagrams to support your answer.

7. Determine which of the following statements is true. Correct any false statements.

   a. When a positive integer is subtracted from a positive integer, the result will always be negative.

   b. When a positive integer is subtracted from a negative integer, the result will always be negative.

   c. When a negative integer is subtracted from a positive integer, the result will always be negative.

   d. When a negative integer is subtracted from a negative integer, the result will always be negative.

8. Use the numbers   1, 2, 3, 4, 5, 6, 7, 8, 9.
   a. Insert + and – signs and ( ) so that they will give an answer of 100.
      E.g., $(123) + 4 - 5 + (67) - 89 = 100$.
      Determine at least two different answers.

   b. Compare your answers with others.

If you have a  button on your calculator you can use it to show negative numbers.

Use your  button to subtract.

For this calculator, the sequence for $(-3) - (-4)$ is:

| C | 3 | ± | − | 4 | ± | = |

On some calculators, the sequence is:

| C | (−) | 3 | − | (−) | 4 | = |

9. Use your calculator to calculate the following:

   a. $(+38) - (-27)$ b. $(-17) - (-68)$ c. $(+42) - (-12)$

   d. $(-57) - (-23)$ e. $(+73) - (-73)$ f. $(-62) - (+47)$

   g. $(-24) - (-24)$ h. $(-124) - (-24)$ i. $(+97) - (-3)$

10. Evaluate:
   a. $(-5) - (-3) - (+2)$ b. $(-4) - (-5) - (-1)$

   c. $+10 - (-4) - (+12)$ d. $(-2) - (-8) - (+3)$

   e. $+20 - (+15) - (-25)$ f. $(-9) - (-9) - 0$

   g. $(-13) + (-2) - (-15)$ h. $+100 + (-10) - (-10)$

   i. $(-20) - (-5) + (+17)$ j. $+6 + (-8) - (-6) - (+5)$

Consider 2 sets of red tiles with 3 red tiles in each set.
We can say that this is 2 groups of 3 red tiles, which can be written as (+2) × (+3).
There are 6 red tiles and they represent the integer +6.

If we consider 2 sets of white tiles with 3 white tiles in each set
we can say that this is 2 groups of 3 white tiles, which can be written as (+2) × (–3).
There are 6 white tiles and they represent the integer –6.

Look again at (+2) × (+3).
Since the 2 is **positive** we can think of
adding 2 groups of 3 red tiles
into a container which gives us 6 red tiles or +6.
So we can think of (+2) × (+3) as **adding** 2 groups of +3.
　　　(+2) × (+3) = +6.

We can then think of (+2) × (–3) as
adding 2 groups of 3 white tiles
into a container and this gives us 6 white tiles or –6.
So we can think of (+2) × (–3) as **adding** 2 groups of –3.
　　　(+2) × (–3) = –6.

To model (–2) × (+3) and (–2) × (–3) notice that the 2 is **negative** and so it is helpful to think of
removing items from a container.
So we can think of (–2) × (+3) as **removing** 2 groups of 3 red tiles from a container.

Before we can remove 2 groups of 3 red tiles from the container we need 2 groups of 3 red tiles in
the container. But there is nothing (0) in the container.
Remember that we can represent 0 by:
1 red tile and 1 white tile, 2 red and 2 white, 3 red and 3 white, etc.

Since we need to remove 2 groups of 3 red tiles, we need to put 6 red tiles (and 6 white tiles) into
the container.

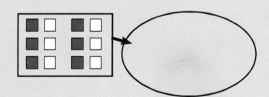

Now, we can remove 2 groups of 3 reds.

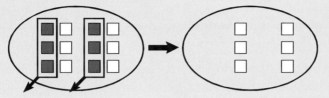

We are left with 6 white tiles or –6.

This can be written as $(–2) × (+3) = (–6).$

We can represent $(–2) × (–3)$ using the same method.

Since we are multiplying –3 by a negative number (–2) we want to remove 2 groups of –3.

We need to remove 6 whites.

We place 6 zeroes into the container.

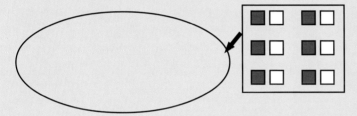

We remove 2 groups of 3 white tiles.

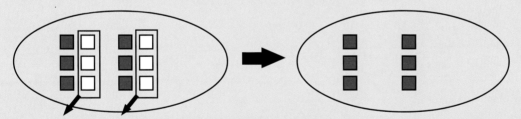

By removing 2 groups of 3 white tiles, we are left with 6 red tiles in the container or +6.

Using tiles, we have discovered that:

$(+2) × (+3) = +6;$ $(–2) × (–3) = +6;$ $(+2) × (–3) = –6;$ $(–2) × (+3) = –6.$

Another way we can determine the products of integers is to examine patterns.

To determine the product of a positive integer and a negative integer, study the following pattern.

$$+3 \times +3 = +9$$
$$+3 \times +2 = +6$$
$$+3 \times +1 = +3$$
$$+3 \times 0 = 0$$

The pattern shows us that the products are decreasing by 3 and so the next product will be 3 less than 0.

So
$$+3 \times -1 = -3$$
$$+3 \times -2 = -6$$
$$+3 \times -3 = -9$$

Write a sentence to explain what this pattern shows us about multiplying integers.

These results can be used to demonstrate the product of a negative integer and a negative integer.

Study the pattern that emerges.

$$-3 \times +3 = -9$$
$$-3 \times +2 = -6$$
$$-3 \times +1 = -3$$
$$-3 \times 0 = 0$$

The pattern shows the products increasing by 3.

$$-3 \times -1 = +3$$
$$-3 \times -2 = +6$$
$$-3 \times -3 = +9$$

Write a sentence to explain what this pattern shows us about multiplying integers.

1. Work with a partner and tiles to complete the table using the blackline master provided.

   The first one has been done as an example.

QUESTION	TILE PICTURE	PRODUCT
$(+5) \times (+1)$	▪▪▪▪▪	+5
$(+5) \times (-1)$		
$(-5) \times (-1)$		
$(-3) \times (+1)$		
$(-3) \times 0$		

2 Work with a partner and and tiles to complete a copy of the table above. Look for patterns.

I.	II.
$(+4) \times (+3) =$	$(-5) \times (+3) =$
$(+4) \times (+2) =$	$(-5) \times (+2) =$
$(+4) \times (+1) =$	$(-5) \times (+1) =$
$(+4) \times 0 \;\; =$	$(-5) \times 0 \;\; =$
$(+4) \times (-1) =$	$(-5) \times (-1) =$
$(+4) \times (-2) =$	$(-5) \times (-2) =$
$(+4) \times (-3) =$	$(-5) \times (-3) =$

3. Complete the following statements.
   When a positive number is multiplied by a positive number the answer is ____.
   When a positive number is multiplied by a negative number the answer is ____.
   When a negative number is multiplied by a positive number the answer is ____.
   When a negative number is multiplied by a negative number the answer is ____.
   When two numbers with the same sign are multiplied the product is ____.
   When two numbers with opposite signs are multiplied the product is____.

4. Decide whether the product is positive negative or zero and then calculate the product.

   a. $-2 \times (+6)$ b. $3 \times (-4)$ c. $-1 \times (-2)$
   d. $-4 \times (-4)$ e. $-5 \times (-2)$ f. -1×0
   g. 1×0 h. -12×2 i. $-7 \times (-3)$

Example 1: Evaluate $-2 \times (-3) \times [(-1) \times (-1)] \times [(-1) \times (-1)] \times [(-1) \times (-1)] \times (-1)$.

Discussion: If we ignore the signs then the product is 6.
Notice that when we multiply two negative numbers we get a positive answer.
There are four pairs of: a negative number times a negative number.
So those four pairs will give a positive answer.
When we multiply this positive answer by the last negative number we get a negative answer.
So the important thing is whether there is an odd number or even number of negative factors.

Solution: There are 9 negative factors.
$-2 \times (-3) \times (-1) \times (-1) \times (-1) \times (-1) \times (-1) \times (-1) \times (-1) = -6$
Notice: because there is an odd number of negative numbers, the answer is negative.

Example 2: Evaluate $-2 \times -3 \times +1 \times -1 \times -1 \times -1 \times -1 \times -1 \times -1$.

Solution: There are 8 negative factors.
$-2 \times (-3) \times (+1) \times (-1) \times (-1) \times (-1) \times (-1) \times (-1) \times (-1) = +6$.
Notice: because there is an even number of negative numbers, the answer is positive.

Remember that 0 times any number is 0.

$$6 \times 0 \times 1$$
$$= 0 \times 1$$
$$= 0$$

5. State whether the product will be positive, zero or negative.
   a. $-3 \times (-5) \times (-6)$ b. -6×0
   c. $0 \times (-8)$ d. $-8 \times (-4) \times 0$
   e. $-7 \times 3 \times (-12)$ f. $-1 \times (-1) \times (-1)$
   g. $-1 \times (-1) \times (-1) \times (-1)$ h. $+2 \times 0$
   i. $-3 \times (-4) \times (+5)$ j. $-2 \times (-3) \times (-4)$
   k. $-3 \times (-2) \times (-1)$ l. $-1 \times (-1) \times (-1) \times (-1) \times (-1)$
   m. $-4 \times (-3) \times (-2) \times (-1) \times 0 \times (+1) \times 2 \times 3 \times 4$
   n. $1234 \times (-5.678) \times 9^2 \times 0$

6. Determine whether each of the statements is true or false.
   If it is true write an example to illustrate it.
   If it is false correct it.

   a. The product of a negative integer and a positive integer is always positive.

   b. The product of a positive integer and a positive integer is always positive.

   c. The product of two negative integers is always positive.

   d. The product of an even number of negative integers is a negative integer.

   e. The product of an odd number of negative integers is a negative integer.

7. Write the products in order from least to greatest.

   a. $(+2)(-6)$ b. $(-8)(+3)$ c. $(+5)(-6)$

   d. $(-3)(+8)$ e. $(-1000)(0)$

8. Determine the values of a, b, c, d, e, f, g.

   Complete a copy of the following multiplication chart.

×	a	b	c	d	e	f	g
2	−6						
−2		+4					
4			−4				
−4				0	−4		
6						+12	
−6							−18

Use the clues.
To calculate a we need to think
"$2 \times$ what $= -6$".

PUT INTO PRACTICE

1. Use your calculator to investigate the following.
    a. Multiply a positive integer by an integer that is:
        i. negative   ii. positive   iii. zero
    b. Multiply a negative integer by an integer that is:
        i. negative   ii. positive   iii. zero

2. Predict whether the product of each question will be positive or negative.
    Use your calculator to check your prediction and calculate the answer.

    a. $(-15) \times 8$ b. $19 \times (-10)$ c. $(-17) \times (-5)$
    d. $(-43) \times (20)$ e. $(-70) \times (-18)$ f. $(+33) \times (-30)$
    g. $14 \times (-62)$ h. $(-13) \times 14$ i. $(+17) \times (-17)$
    j. $(-21) \times (16)$ k. $(-25) \times (-18)$

3. Predict the value of each and then check using the power button $\boxed{x^y}$ on your calculator.

    a. $(-1)^2$ b. $(-1)^3$ c. $(-1)^4$
    d. $(-1)^5$ e. $(-1)^{1234}$ f. $(-1)^{2003}$

> Remember that $(-a)^6 = -a \times -a \times -a \times -a \times -a \times -a.$

4. A spreadsheet can be used to explore the patterns when two integers are multiplied.
    You will need to start a new document in a spreadsheet program.
    Input any positive integer into cell A1.
    Copy this number into all of the column A cells down to cell A21.
    Now, input any 2-digit positive integer into cell B1.
    In cell B2, input the formula =B1 + 1 and copy this formula into all the B cells down to B21.
    In cell C1, input the formula =A1*B1, and copy this formula into all of the C cells down to cell C21.
    Explain what the formula in each cell does.

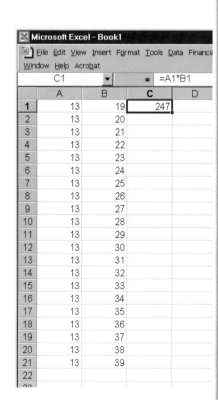

5. Input any negative integer into cell A1.
   Copy this number into all the column A cells down to cell A21.
   Now, input any 2-digit positive integer into cell B1.
   In cell B2, input the formula =B1 + 1 and copy this formula into all the B cells down to B21.
   In cell C1, input the formula =A1*B1, and copy this formula into all the C cells down to cell C21.

6. Input any positive integer into cell A1.
   Copy this number into all the column A cells down to cell A21.
   Now, input any 2-digit negative integer into cell B1.
   In cell B2, input the formula =B1 + 1 and copy this formula into all the B cells down to B21.
   In cell C1, input the formula =A1*B1, and copy this formula into all the C cells down to cell C21.

7. Input any negative integer into cell A1.
   Copy this number into all the column A cells down to cell A21.
   Now, input any 2-digit negative integer into cell B1.
   In cell B2, input the formula =B1 + 1 and copy this formula into all the B cells down to B21.
   In cell C1, input the formula =A1*B1, and copy this formula into all the C cells down to cell C21.

8. Describe the sign of the integer in column C if:
   a. the integer in A is positive and the integer in B is:
      i. negative   ii. positive   iii. zero
   b. the integer in A is negative and the integer in B is:
      i. negative   ii. positive   iii. zero

We can use red and white algebra tiles to model the division of integers.
If we examine the division sentence 6 ÷ 2, we are being asked to divide 6 red tiles into 2 equal groups.
Another way is to look at the inverse relationship and ask ourselves,
"2 groups of how many will equal 6?"
Or, 2 × ? = 6.

There are 3 red tiles in each group, so the quotient is +3.

Similarly, we can look at –6 ÷ 2 and know that we are being asked to divide 6 white tiles into 2 equal groups.

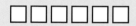 

The quotient is 3 white tiles or -3.

- A **positive** number **divided by** a **positive** number is a **positive** number [(+) ÷ (+) = (+)].
- A **negative** number **divided by** a **positive** number is a **negative** number [(–) ÷ (+) = (–)].

Notice that you could change the ÷ sign, in the two statements above, to a × sign and the statements are still true.

PUT INTO PRACTICE

1. Complete a copy of the table. The first one is done for you.

Tile Picture	Division Statement	Result
■■■■ ■■■■	(+8) ÷ (+2)	+4
■■ ■■ ■■		
■ ■ ■		
□ □ □		
□□ □□ □□		
□□□□ □□□□		

2. Use the results from your chart above to state what the sign of the quotient (answer) will be when you divide:
   a. a positive number by a positive number

   b. a negative number by a positive number.

3. You noticed in the chart that a positive number divided by a positive number results in a positive quotient and that a negative number divided by a positive number results in a negative answer.

   (+) ÷ (+) = (+) and (−) ÷ (+) = (−)

   a. Compare this to the results in multiplying a positive number by a positive number and a negative number by a positive number.

   b. What might you expect the results to be when:
      i.   a positive number is divided by a negative number
      ii. a negative number is divided by a negative number?

Division is the inverse operation of multiplication.

If we multiply two numbers to get a product, we can use division to find a missing factor if we know the product.

Example:

If we multiply 2 by 3 to get 6, we can divide 6 by 3 to get 2.

$2 \times 3 = 6 \quad$ so $\quad 6 \div 3 = 2$.

4. a. Use a calculator to calculate
       3×2.6789
       Then divide the answer by 2.6789.

    b. What is the effect of multiplying by a number and then dividing by the same number?

5. Predict the answer.
   a. I started with 3 multiplied by a positive number and then divided by that same number.
   b. I started with 3 multiplied by a negative number and then divided by that same number.
   c. I started with –3 multiplied by a positive number and then divided by that same number.
   d. I started with –3 multiplied by a negative number and then divided by that same number.

Start with 3, multiply it by 11 and then divide the answer by 11.
If you record the division part of this sequence you will write
$(+33) \div (+11) = (+3)$.

6. a. Start with 3 multiply by 11 then divide by 11. Record the division result.
   b. Start with 3 multiply by –11 then divide by –11. Record the division result.
   c. Start with –3 multiply by 11 then divide by 11. Record the division result.
   d. Start with –3 multiply by –11 then divide by –11. Record the division result.

7. Use your calculator.
   a. Enter 3 multiply by a positive 4-digit number then divide by the same number. Record your answer.
   b. Enter 3 multiply by a negative 4-digit number then divide by the same number. Record your answer
   c. Enter –3 multiply by a positive 4-digit number then divide by the same number. Record your answer
   d. Enter –3 multiply by a negative 4-digit number then divide by the same number. Record your answer

8. Predict the sign of the quotient when you divide:
   a. A positive number by a positive number
   b. A negative number by a positive number
   c. A positive number by a negative number
   d. A negative number by a negative number.

Since division is the inverse operation of multiplication, we can use the patterns we developed for the multiplication of integers and apply them to division. Through an investigation of the patterns that occur when multiplying integers, we discovered that:

a. the product of a positive number and a positive number is always a positive number;
b. the product of a negative and a negative is always positive;
c. the product of a positive and a negative is always negative;
d. the product of a negative and a positive is always negative.

The same pattern that applies to the multiplication of integers, can be applied to the division of integers:

- **the quotient of two positive integers is positive**
- **the quotient of two negative integers is positive**
- **the quotient of two integers with opposite signs is negative**

Examples.
a) $(+12) \div (+4) = +3$, b) $(-12) \div (-4) = +3$, c) $(-12) \div (+4) = -3$, d) $(+12) \div (-4) = -3$.
Check these on your calculator.

In examples a) and b) the signs are the same, and the quotient is positive.
In examples c) and d) the signs are opposite and the quotient is negative.

PUT INTO PRACTICE

Product is the answer when you multiply. Quotient is the answer when you divide.

$$(+) \div (+) = (+)$$

$$(-) \div (-) = (+)$$

$$(+) \div (-) = (-)$$

$$(-) \div (+) = (-)$$

1. Evaluate the following.
   Check your answers using multiplication.
   E.g., $(+6) \div (+2) = +3$. Check: $(+2) \times (+3) = +6$.
   a. $(+15) \div (+5)$ b. $(-50) \div (-10)$ c. $(-12) \div (+3)$
   d. $(+24) \div (-4)$ e. $(-66) \div (-11)$ f. $(-27) \div (-3)$
   g. $(-1) \div (-1)$ h. $(+1) \div (-1)$ i. $(-1) \div (+1)$

2. For the following questions, decide whether the quotient is negative or positive.
   Then calculate the answer.
   a. $(+8) \div (-2)$ b. $(+16) \div (+2)$ c. $(-14) \div (-7)$
   d. $(-24) \div (+3)$ e. $(-25) \div (-5)$ f. $(+18) \div (-3)$
   g. $(-99) \div (-99)$ h. $(999) \div (-999)$ i. $(-999) \div 999$

3. Evaluate the following.
   Check your answers using multiplication.
   a. $(+25) \div (+5)$ b. $(-50) \div (-10)$ c. $(-12) \div (+3)$
   d. $(+24) \div (-4)$ e. $(-66) \div (-11)$ f. $(-27) \div (-3)$

E.g. $(+6) \div (+2) = +3$.
Check: $(+2) \times (+3) = +6$.

4. Do the following divisions.
   Round the answers to No. 4k and l, to 3 decimal places.

   a. $\dfrac{+15}{+5}$ b. $\dfrac{+36}{-6}$ c. $\dfrac{-48}{-6}$

   d. $\dfrac{-55}{+5}$ e. $\dfrac{+42}{-7}$ f. $\dfrac{-27}{-9}$

   g. $(-14) \div (+2)$ h. $(-32) \div (-8)$ i. $(-64) \div (-8)$

   j. $(-39) \div (+3)$ k. $(-123) \div 456$ l. $7890 \div (-123)$

   m. $0 \div 1234$ n. $0 \div (-5678)$

   o. $1.2345 \div (-1.2345)$ p. $(-5.6789) \div 5.6789$

5. a. Explain how you know whether the quotient will be negative or positive when dividing two integers.

   b. What will the quotient be when any non-zero integer is divided by its opposite?

   c. What is the quotient when you divide 0 by a negative number?

The opposite of 5 is –5.

The opposite of –7 is 7.

6. Calculate the missing integer.
   a. $(+8) \div \square = (-2)$ b. $\square \div (+4) = (-6)$

   c. $(-33) \div \square = (+11)$ d. $(+72) \div (+6) = \square$

   e. $(+49) \div \square = (+7)$ f. $\square \div (-7) = (+8)$

   g. $(-36) \div \square = (+2)$ h. $(-8) \div (-4) = \square$

PUT INTO PRACTICE

a. Remember to include the number of empty seats.

b. We know that 100 seats gives a profit and that 55 seats leads to a loss. We can "guess and test".

1. A small 200-seat movie theatre makes a profit of $5 for each seat that is occupied during the showing of a movie and loses $2 for every seat that is empty.

   a. Calculate the profit or loss for each when the number of occupied seats is:

      i. 150   ii. 40   iii. 100   iv. 55   v. 200   vi. 1.

   b. How many seats must be occupied for a profit to be made?

2. Jeri and Luke go on a hot air balloon ride. It is descending at a rate of 190 m/min.

   How much higher was the balloon 6 minutes ago?

3. At an outdoor concert the air temperature was –14°C. The wind was blowing at a speed of 15 km/h. This made the temperature feel like –19°C.

   How many degrees does the "temperature" change because of the wind chill?

4. An independent filmmaker lost $1200/day because the lead performer had the flu. She was ill for 5 days.

   How much money was lost?

From (°C)	To (°C)	Change (°C)
–4	5	
5	–10	
–10	–15	
–15	–7	

5. Waqas and his family have gone to the mountains for a weekend of skiing and relaxing.
    The chart on the left shows how the weather changed while they were on holidays.

    a. Calculate the temperature changes.

    b. Calculate the sum of the numbers in the Change column.

    c. Calculate the change between the first and last temperatures.

6. Zachary sold stocks in his new family entertainment complex, Zack's Place.
    The chart shows the changes in his stock over a week.

    a. Calculate the missing values in a copy of the table below.

Day	Opening Price ($)	Closing Price ($)	Daily Change ($)
Mon	23	21	
Tues	21	24	
Wed		52	
Thurs		19	
Fri		21	

    b. Calculate the sum of the numbers in the Daily Change column.

    c. Calculate the change from Monday morning to Friday afternoon.

PATTERNS

RECOGNIZING PATTERNS

Patterns occur in a wide variety of situations that we see every day such as wallpaper, floor tiles and carpeting designs, knitting, quilting, and even in nature.

Mathematically patterns help us determine relationships between sets of numbers or objects. Once we determine the relationship we can extend a given pattern. In laboratories, scientists look for patterns in their experiments to be able to generalize results of a new drug or therapy treatment. Encoders and decoders use patterns to decipher coded messages.

There are three steps in our study of patterns.
1. **Recognize that there is a pattern**
2. **Extend the pattern**
3. **Describe the pattern in a general way.**

Literature Link:
The King's Chessboard
by David Birch

INVESTIGATION

Here are a series of plant stands.

Number of Plant Stands	Number of Legs
1	4
2	8
3	12

a. Describe any patterns you see.

b. How many legs would there be for four plant stands? For five?
   Hint:
   If there were 4 plant stands, there would be four more legs than are on the three plant stands.

c. Generalize the pattern.

Hint:
In order to generalize the pattern, it is necessary to connect the two columns written in the table in an algebraic way.
In this case,
The number of legs = 4 × the number of plant stands.
If we let "the number of legs" be L and "the number of plant stands" be P then
$L = 4P$
Whenever a generalized rule is written with letters representing parts of the rule, we have an algebraic expression. The **letter** that **represents a value** is called a **variable**.

The equation $L = 4P$ allows us to calculate the number of legs for any number of plant stands without completing a table, one plant stand at a time.

d. Use the rule to calculate the number of legs when there are 72 plant stands.

Hint:
To determine the number of legs for 72 plant stands using the generalized algebraic expression you must replace the variable representing the number of plant stands with the number 72.
This process of **replacing a variable with a value** is called **substitution**.
$L = 4P$ algebraic expression
$L = 4(72)$ substitution

e. Use the rule to calculate the number of plant stands when there are 244 legs.

Hint:
To determine the number of plant stands for 244 legs, the variable for the number of legs is replaced by the value 244.

244 is substituted for L.
         $L = 4P$ algebraic expression
         $244 = 4P$ substitution (To solve, think "4 times what gives 244?")

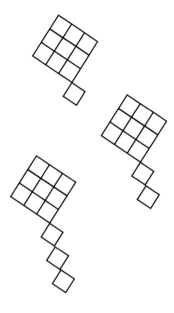

1. A kite with 1 square for its tail has 10 squares.

    A kite with 2 squares for its tail has 11 squares.

    A kite with 3 squares in its tail has 12 squares.

    a. Copy and complete the following table to find out
        how many squares it takes to build a kite with 10
        squares in its tail.

Squares in Tail (t)	Squares in All (a)
1	10
2	11
3	12
...	...
10	?

    b. Write the relationship between "squares in the tail"
        and "squares in all" in words.
    c. Write the relationship between squares in the tail, t,
        and the squares in all, a, algebraically.
    d. Use the expression to calculate the number of squares
        needed to build the kites with the following number of
        squares in the tail. Show the substitution and the
        answer.
        i. 12   ii. 23   iii. 40
    e. Use the expression to calculate the number of squares
        in the tail if the kite uses the following number of
        squares in all. Show the substitution and the answer.
        i. 113   ii. 45   iii. 172

$$a = (12) + 9$$

$$113 = t + 9$$

2. If you are setting up a hall for a graduation dinner you need to decide how to organise the tables.

This table seats 4.

These tables together seat 6.

a. Complete and copy the table below

Extend the table to include up to 8 tables joined together.

Number of Tables (t)	Number of People Seated (p)
1	4
2	6
3	8
4	?

b. One more table means two more people.
You could try: "The number of people is twice the number of tables."
That is not quite right but you can add something to make it work.

b. Write the relationship between the "number of tables" and the "number of people seated" in words.

c. Look at your answer to b.
Replace "the number of people" with *p*.
Replace "the number of tables" with *t*.
Replace "is" with =.

c. Write the relationship of the number of tables, *t*, and the number of people seated, *p*, in algebraic form.

d. Use the expression to calculate the number of people seated when the number of tables used is given.
Show the substitution and the answer.
i. 15   ii. 37   iii. 112

e. Use the expression to calculate the number tables needed to seat the number of people given.
Show the substitution and the answer.
i. 48   ii. 30   iii. 94

3. You can see that you can make one triangle with three toothpicks.
   You need five toothpicks to make two triangles.

   a. How many toothpicks are needed for 4, 5 and 6 triangles? Use a copy of the table below.

Number of Triangles (t)	Number of Toothpicks (n)
1	3
2	5
3	7
4	?
5	?
6	?

   b. Write the relationship between the "number of triangles" and the "number of toothpicks" in words.

   c. Write the relationship in number of triangles, t, and the number of toothpicks, n, in algebraic form.

   d. Use the expression to calculate the number of toothpicks when the following number of triangles has been built. Show the substitution and the answer.
      i. 19   ii. 34   iii. 213

   e. Use the expression to calculate the number of triangles that can be built when the given number of toothpicks is used. Show the substitution and the answer.
      i. 57   ii. 191   iii. 75

4. Carl is building a stairway to his daughter's playhouse.

For one step, he needs one brick

For 2 steps, he needs 3 bricks

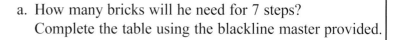

and for 3 steps he needs 6 bricks.

a. How many bricks will he need for 7 steps?
   Complete the table using the blackline master provided.

Number of Steps (s)	Number of Bricks (b)
1	1
2	3
3	6
7	?

b. Describe the patterns that you see.

c. How many bricks will he need for 17 steps?

d. Make a graph showing the relationship between the number of bricks and the number of steps.
   Do the points lie in a straight line?

5. Triangular numbers can be shown by the number of dots required to make an equilateral triangle.
   On the left you see the first three triangular numbers (1, 3, 6).

   a. Draw the next triangular number and state the number of dots.

   b. How many dots will there be in the fifth triangular number?
      Draw it.

PUT INTO PRACTICE

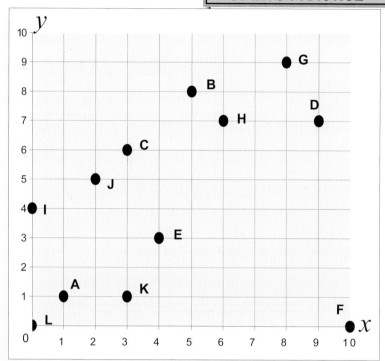

The graph is in the first quadrant of the coordinate plane.

Points on the coordinate plane are named using ordered pairs, (x,y), where the first number is along the x-axis or horizontal axis, and the second number is located along the y-axis or vertical axis.

a. What are the coordinates for the following points?

   i. A   ii. F   iii. K   iv. G   v. C

b. What is the letter of the point with the ordered pair listed below?

   i. (3,1)   ii. (5,8)   iii. (2,5)

   iv. (9,7)   v. (10,0)   vi. (0,0)

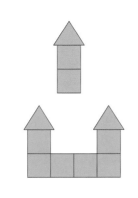

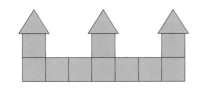

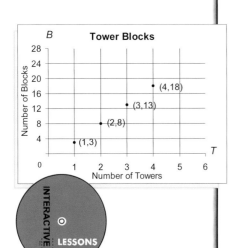

How many blocks do you need to build a castle wall with 6 towers?

Complete the table using the blackline master provided.

Number of Towers	Number of Blocks
1	3
2	8
3	13
4	?
5	?
6	?

Recognizing that to get the next number of blocks in this pattern we add 5 to the previous number, leads us to the fact that we need 28 blocks for a castle wall with 6 towers.

The general relationship is:
The number of blocks = 5 times the number of towers minus 2.

or algebraically

$$B = 5\,T - 2$$

The values in the table are ordered pairs that make the relation true and can be written in the format of ordered pairs:
(1,3), (2,8), (3,13), (4,18).

Since they are ordered pairs, they can be graphed on the coordinate plane to show what the relation looks like.

You can see that if the dots were joined, they would form a straight line.
We call the relationship linear.

Visualizing the line extending beyond the ordered pairs shown also allows you to predict values past the ones actually graphed.

Use the graph to predict the number of blocks used for six towers.

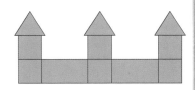

1. a. Complete the table using the blackline master provided.

Number of Towers	Number of Blocks
1	3
2	7
3	11
4	?
5	?
6	?

b. What are the ordered pairs suggested by the table of values?

c. Define the relationship between the number of towers and the number of blocks, in words.

d. Define the relationship using an algebraic expression.

e. Draw the graph of the relation on a coordinate plane. If the points were joined, would they form a straight line?

f. Use the graph to predict how many blocks are needed for 10 towers.

g. Use the algebraic expression to calculate the number of blocks for 10 towers.
   Show your substitution and the answer.

d. Start with:
    $B = \Box \, T - 1$.
    Replace $\Box$ with a number.

2. How many towers are in a 36–block wall?
    Complete the table using the blackline master provided.

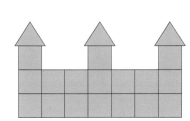

Number of Towers	Number of Blocks
1	4
2	12
3	20
4	?
5	?
6	?

3. Suppose there were 10 people at a party and everyone shook hands with everyone else.
How many handshakes would there be?
A graph can help you see a pattern.

If there was 1 person, there would be 0 handshakes.
With 2 people there would be 1 handshake.
How many handshakes with 3 people? 4 people? 5 people?

   a. Complete the chart using the blackline master provided.

People	Shakes
1	0
2	1
3	3
4	6
5	?
6	?
…	…
10	?

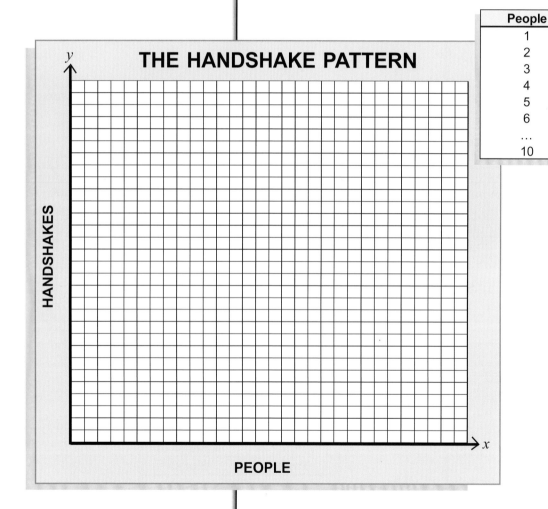

THE HANDSHAKE PATTERN

HANDSHAKES

PEOPLE

   b. Graph the ordered pairs.

   c. Is this a linear relationship?

So far you have only plotted points which have not been joined together with a line.
This is because **the values along the horizontal axis are whole numbers**.
If you can include values between the whole numbers, then you will be able to draw a line through the points.

Here's a problem that highlights the difference.

INVESTIGATION

1. Mitchell got a job at Easy Phone cellular phone company. He will be paid $20.00 per day plus $8.50 for every new customer he signs up for long distance calling. The following table shows Mitchell's potential income where c represents the number of sales and $e represents earnings.

c	0	1	2	3	...
e	20	28.5	37	45.5	...

Complete a copy of the table above.

What is the relationship (algebraic equation) that defines Mitchell's earnings?

Hint:
Mitchell gets paid $8.50 per customer so we can try multiplying the number of customers by $8.50 and comparing the answer to the corresponding answer in the table.

What pattern can you find?

What is the algebraic equation that shows this pattern?

b. Complete a copy of the table below and extend it for three more values.

Make a graph to show the relationship.

c	4	5	6
e			

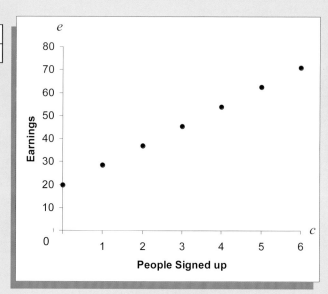

c. Will you join the points on the graph?
Explain.

Example 1:

An empty 10 L can has a mass of 5 kg. When it is filled with melon juice, the mass is 35 kg. Plot the mass of the can and juice in relation to the volume in the can.

Solution:

The volume of juice in the can may have fractional or decimal values up to 10 L. Therefore we can join the points with a straight line.

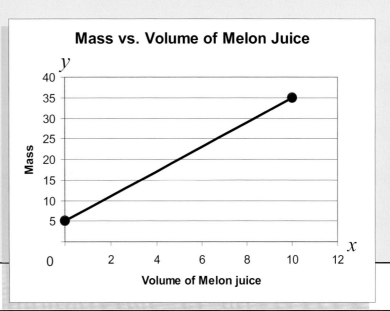

Mass vs. Volume of Melon Juice

Volume of Melon juice

Time (min)	Charge ($)
0	20
10	40
20	60
30	80
40	100

1. Carol Lightfeather owns a cell phone.
   The table on the left shows the costs of the plan based on the time used.
   Draw a graph of the relationship.

   a. Can you join the points?
      Explain.

   b. If Carol uses her phone for 25 minutes in one month, how much would she be charged?

   c. If Carol used her phone for 45 minutes in one month what would her phone bill be?

   d. If Carol's bill for one month was $50, how long did she talk on the phone?

   e. Explain in words how the phone company charges Carol for her calls.

Number Of Melons	Mass (kg)
0	
1	
2	
10	

Real World Project

You are now ready to start Step 2 of your project.

2. An empty fruit crate has a mass of 5 kg.
   When it is full with 10 melons it has a mass of 35 kg.

   a. Calculate the mass of one melon.

   b. What is the relationship (algebraic equation) that defines the mass of the crate of fruit?

   c. Complete the table using the blackline master provided.

   d. Plot the mass of the fruit crate in relation to the number of melons that it has in it.

   e. Should you join the points on the graph? Explain your answer.

3. a. Nigel sells souvenirs at the Stampeder's football games. He earns $15.00 per game and $3.00 for each souvenir he sells. State the relationship between Nigel's salary (W) and the number of souvenirs he sells (S) as an algebraic equation.

   b. How would the equation change if he earned $3.00 for every 2 souvenirs he sold?

4. An adult fare on the Rapid City transit system is a. The student fare is K. The chart shows the numbers of passengers on the two early morning trains:

Train	Adults	Students
#1	20	16
#2	12	24

Write an equation for the total fare collected on both trains.

PUZZLES

MAGIC SQUARES

INVESTIGATION

Magic squares can be developed using patterns.

8	1	6
3	5	7
4	9	2

15 __ __ __

1. a. Copy the magic square in your notebook and calculate the sum of each column. The first one is done for you.

    b. Calculate the sum of each row.

    c. Calculate the sum of the two diagonals.

    d. What do you notice?

    e. Copy and complete:
        The magic sum is ☐ times the number in the middle cell.

This is an example of a 3 by 3 magic addition square.
The sums of all rows, columns and diagonals is the same.
The magic sum is 3 times the number in the middle cell.

2. a. Check to see if this is a magic addition square.

17	24	1	8	15
23	5	7	14	16
4	6	13	20	22
10	12	19	21	3
11	18	25	2	9

    b. Copy and complete:
        The magic sum is ☐ times the number in the middle cell.

1.

8	1	6
3	5	7
4	9	2

In this square the numbers are: 1, 2, 3, 4, 5, 6, 7, 8 and 9.
This sequence of number starts at 1 and goes up by 1.

a. Start with 2 and go up 3 at a time.
List the first nine numbers.

b. Make a square and place the first number (2) where
the **1** is in the square above.
Place the second number (5) where the **2** is in the
square above.
Continue until you have placed all nine numbers in
the squares marked: **1, 2, 3, …, 9**.

c. Check to see if it is a magic square.

d. How does the magic sum compare to the number in
the middle cell?

2. a. Write another sequence of nine numbers that increase
by the same amount each time.
(Pick a start number and pick a number to add each
time.)

b. Create your own 3 by 3 magic addition square with
these numbers.

c. Have another student check to see if it is a magic
addition square.
Have this person check the connection between the
magic sum and the number in the middle cell.

2, 5, ...

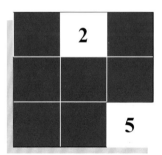

ALGEBRA CONNECTION

Consider a sequence that starts with any number *n* and increases 1 at a time.

Represent *n* by ▭ and 1 by ■.

So *n* + 1 is represented by ▭ ■.

And *n* + 2 is represented by ▭ ■ ■,

n + 3 is represented by ▭ ■ ■ ■.

The magic addition square will look like this.

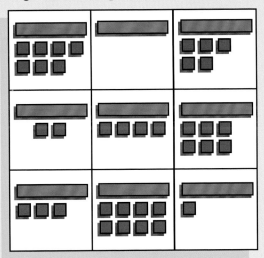

The sum of the first column is:

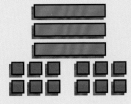

Check the sum of the rows, diagonals and the other columns.

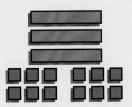

represents 3 *n*'s and 12 ones.
This can be written as 3*n* + 12.

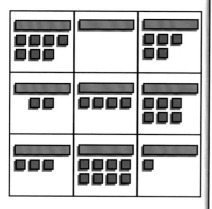

Calculate the magic sum first.

3. a. Make a copy of the magic addition square on the left but replace the models with n's and numbers. The first one is done for you.

$n+7$

b. Write the sum of each column, row and diagonal and write the answer.

E.g., the first column is:
$$\begin{array}{r} n + 7 \\ n + 2 \\ \underline{n + 3} \\ 3n + 12. \end{array}$$

4. Here is in incomplete magic addition square. Copy and complete the square.

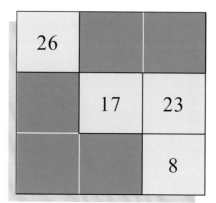

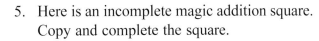

5. Here is an incomplete magic addition square.
   Copy and complete the square.

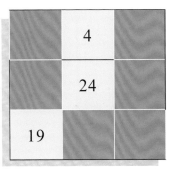

The magic sum of the 3 × 3 magic square is 3 times the middle number.

6. a. Create an incomplete magic addition square and solve it.

   b. Give it to your partner to solve.

7. Check this square to see if it is a magic addition square.

128	1	32
4	16	64
8	256	2

8. Look at the square in No. 7.
   Could it be a magic multiplication square?

   a. Multiply the three numbers in the first column.

   b. Multiply the three numbers in the second column.

   c. Compare the two products.

   d. Check the rows, diagonals and the other column to see if this is a magic multiplication square.

The numbers in No.7 are: 1, 2, 4, 8, 16, 32, 64, 128 and 256.
I.e., the sequence starts with 1 and each term is multiplied by 2.

2, 6, ...

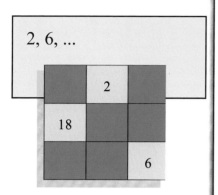

Calculate the magic product first.

9. a. Start with 2 and multiply by 3 each time to create nine numbers.

b. Put these numbers in a magic multiplication square.

c. Calculate the magic product.

10. a. Create your own 3 by 3 magic multiplication square.

b. Have another student check to see if it is a magic multiplication square.

11. Here is in incomplete magic multiplication square.

Copy and complete the square.

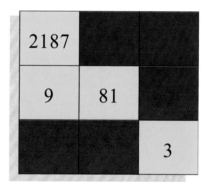

12. a. Create an incomplete magic multiplication square and solve it.

b. Give it to your partner to solve.

Algebra can be used to help us solve card tricks, dice games and other number tricks.

INVESTIGATION

Think of a number.

a. Multiply your number by 3.

b. Add 9 to the result.

c. Divide by 3.

d. Subtract 2.

e. Subtract your original number.

f. Compare your answer with others.

How does this trick work?

We can explain this number trick by using algebra.

ALGEBRA CONNECTION

Because you could have picked ANY number, call the number you picked "*x*"
Now follow the steps:

a) $3x$ *3 times as many*

b) $3x + 9$ *Add 9 (ones).*

c) $(3x + 9) \div 3$ *Divide into 3 equal groups*

$= x + 3$

d) $x + 3 - 2$ *Subtract 2 (ones).*

$= x + 1$

e) $x + 1 - x$ *Subtract the original number*

$= 1$

> The result will always be 1, no matter what number you choose to start with.

1. Think of a number.
   a. Add 3 to your number.

   b. Multiply by 2.

   c. Subtract 2.

   d. Divide by 2.

   e. Subtract your original number.

   f. Compare your answer with others.

   g. Explain how this number trick works.

2. Here's another number trick.
   Think of a number
   Add 17
   Double your result
   Subtract 4
   Double this result
   Add 20
   Divide by 4
   Subtract 20
   Subtract your original number
   Compare your answer with others.
   Explain how this number trick works.

3. Ms Nastasiuk likes to challenge her class.
   She told the students to turn to the following page.
   It is between 50 and 100.
   The page number is a perfect square.
   The sum of the digits of the page number is also a perfect square.

   What is the page number?

Look at the shaded 2 by 2 array of numbers in the calendar.

1	2	3	4	5	6	7
8	9	10	11	12	13	14
15	16	17	18	19	20	21
22	23	24	25	26	27	28
29	30	31				

Notice that 9 is 1 more than 8. I.e., $9 = 8 + 1$.
And, $16 = 15 + 1$.

8	9
15	16

The horizontal pattern seems to be "add 1".

PUT INTO PRACTICE

1. a. What is the vertical pattern in the 2 by 2 array?

   b. What do you notice about the diagonal sums in the 2 by 2 array?

2. a. Pick another 2 by 2 array of numbers.
      Check for horizontal, vertical or diagonal patterns.

   b. Explain the patterns to another student.

How does the diagonal sum compare to the middle number?

3. a. Pick a 3 by 3 array of numbers and look for patterns.

   b. Explain the patterns to another student.

4.

	16	

This is a section from a calendar.

What is the sum of the diagonals?

5.

		1	2	3	4	5
6	7	8	9	10	11	12
13	14	15	16	17	18	19
20	21	22	23	24	25	26
27	28	29	30	31		

a. Pick a 4 by 4 array and look for patterns.

b. Explain any pattern that you have found to another student.

Real World Project

You are now ready to start Step 3 of your Project.

ORDER OF OPERATIONS

Evaluate the following:

1.   a. $25 - (17 - 4)$ b. $(36 - 9) - 20$

     c. $24 - (7 + 6)$ d. $(83 - 64) + 5$

2.   a. $9(4) + 7$ b. $5(2) + 12$

     c. $7(8) - 5 + 6 \times 3$ d. $10 + 45 \times 5 - 4(7)$

3.   a. $34 - 7(4 - 2)^2$ b. $6^2 + 9(5 + 8)$

PATTERNS

4. You have just won a three–minute shopping spree at a local shopping centre.
   You are allowed to gather up the following items up to a maximum of $400.

   > Jeans regular price: $49.99 are discounted by $4.99.
   > T–shirts regular price: $19.99 are discounted by $4.99.
   > Cross trainer shoes regular price: $69.99 are discounted by $34.99.

   If you go over or below $400 you will only receive a small consolation prize.

   If you get exactly $400, you will win an all expenses paid holiday to Mexico.

   How many of each item should you grab in order to get to $400?
   You have to choose at least one of each item.

5. Long-Foi made the following pictures with circles and triangles.

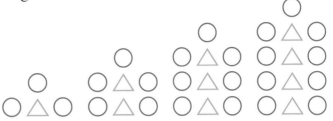

a. He started making a chart to show the number of circles and triangles in each picture.

Complete a copy of the table below.

Picture	Number of Circles	Number of Triangles
1	3	1
2	5	2
3		
4		

b. Write a mathematical sentence to show the relationship between the number of circles and the number of triangles.

c. Make models or pictures to verify your answers.

d. How many circles would you need in a picture with 12 triangles?

e. How can you verify the answer?

f. Substitute numbers in your sentence for each picture.

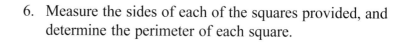

6. Measure the sides of each of the squares provided, and determine the perimeter of each square.

   a. Make a graph by plotting the length of the sides on the horizontal axis and the perimeters on the vertical axis. (Make a table of values.)

   b. Describe the pattern in the graph.

   c. From the results of this graph, make a rule for finding the perimeter of a square.

   d. Explain how you could verify your rule.

ALGEBRAIC THINKING

7. Write the following in algebraic terms.

   a. A number divided by 9 gives 10.

   b. Seven is added to 4 times a number to give 51.

   c. Subtracting 4 from the product of a number and 6 gives 20.

8. Match the equation with the correct statement.
   a. $2n - 1 = 7$ A. A number increased by 6 equals 14.

   b. $x \div 3 = 5$ B. A number multiplied by 2 equals 11.

   c. $2y = 11$ C. Twice a number subtract 1 gives 7.

   d. $t + 6 = 14$ D. A number divided by 3 equals 5.

9. The number of dollars in a savings account is determined by the equation
   Amount = 1025 + 35n
   where n is the number of years the money is left in the financial institution.

   a. Calculate the amount in the savings account if the money has been in the account for 12 years.

   b. Explain your solution in a.

   c. Make up a similar problem and solve it.

   d. Give it to another student to solve.

10. An expression for the mass of two cans and five bearings is $2c + 5b$.

    Calculate the total mass, if each can has a mass, (c), of 200 g and each bearing has a mass, (b), of 75 g.

11. A formula for the perimeter of a rectangle is
    $P = 2l + 2w$.

    Calculate the perimeter when l is 8 cm and w is 6 cm.

INTEGERS

12. Choose the greatest number and the least number.
    a. −1, −10, 9, 0   b. 0, −5, 1, −100

    c. −100, −1000, −1, −10

13. Evaluate:
    a. $(+6) + (-3)$ b. $(+6) - (-3)$ c. $(+6) \times (-3)$
    d. $(+6) \div (-3)$ e. $(-8) + (-2)$ f. $(-8) - (-2)$
    g. $(-8) \times (-2)$ h. $(-8) \div (-2)$ i. $(-12) + 4$
    j. $(-12) - 4$ k. $(-12) \times 4$ l. $(-12) \div 4$

14. Calculate the profit or loss for these following concerts.
    Use a negative number to show a loss.
    Complete a copy of the table below.

Concert	Income ($)	Expenses ($)	Profit/Loss ($)
A	1234	567	
B	567	1234	
C	123 456 789	123 456 789	

15. The profit or loss for three consecutive nights of a
    variety concert were: −$51, −$42, +$154.

    Calculate the total profit or loss.

16. One share in Marchards Inc. showed a change of −$1.50.

    What was the total change in the value of 123 shares?

PROJECT

MATHEMATICS AND PUZZLES

STEP 1: RESEARCH

- Research the Internet to find several sites that offer Brain Teasers, Puzzles and Mathematics Games. (Hint: Enter "Mathematics Puzzles" into a search engine).
- Look for a site that offers math puzzles, games, problems, etc. that are appropriate for high school students.
  Decide on specific criteria with your teacher before you go searching.

- Submit the URL and explain the reason why you thought this was the best site for high school students who want to use mathematics to solve puzzles.

STEP 2: WORK WITH A PARTNER

- Next, select a brain teaser, puzzle or game from your chosen site.
  Bring a copy to class and try it with a partner.

- Together with your partner, assess the difficulty level of the puzzle.
  Do you think this activity is challenging, yet fairly straightforward?
  Once you both have a puzzle that you think is appropriate for your fellow students, submit it.

- Write out a detailed solution or solutions.
  Prepare hints to help people.
  You are ready to present.

STEP 3: PRESENT

- Present your problem or puzzle to a larger group.
  Be sure that everyone has a copy of the puzzle to work on.
  Be prepared to offer hints to help people.

- When the time limit is up, explain the solution and the mathematics that is behind it.

ENTERTAINMENT

AND MENTAL MATH, PROBLEM SOLVING, REASONING, TECHNOLOGY, VISUALIZATION, COMMUNICATION, CONNECTIONS, ESTIMATION

Content

- Apply arithmetic operations on decimals and illustrate their use in solving problems.
- Use estimation strategies to check calculations.
- Read and interpret graphs.
- Collect, display, and analyze data.

Meaning and Understanding

Intellectual Curiosity

How can mathematics address many of the issues found in the entertainment world?

Real World Project

The Entertainment Industry

Choose a topic to research in the entertainment world; investigate it; design a survey to collect data; analyze data; construct graphs to display information; present your project.

DECIMALS

In the world of entertainment people use decimals all the time. Designers, work crews and entertainers have to be able to measure and calculate using decimals and everyone has to be able to deal with small and large sums of money.

Example 1:

A is at 3.4 in the first diagram.
Look at the second ruler and state whether A is closer to 3 or to 4.

A is at 3.4 and 3.4 is closer to 3 than to 4.

3.4 rounded to the nearest whole number is 3.

INVESTIGATION

B is at 3.6. and is closer to ☐.

So 3.6 rounds to ☐.

C is at _ and it is half way between ☐ and ☐.
In this case we round up to ☐.

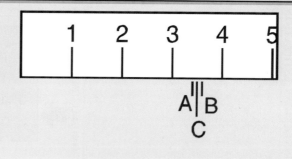

PUT INTO PRACTICE

1. Round each of the following numbers to the nearest whole number.

   a. 3.1   b. 3.9   c. 3.2   d. 3.3
   e. 3.7   f. 3.8   g. 3.0   h. 4.0

2. Round each of the following numbers to the nearest whole number.

   a. 12.1   b. 12.9   c. 12.5   d. 103.2
   e. 103.6   f. 103.5   g. 1003. 3   h. 1003.4

INTERACTIVE LESSONS

You can use the same kind of reasoning to round numbers to the nearest 10 or hundred.

Notice that 34 is between 30 and 40 and that it is closer to 30 so we can say that 34 rounds to 30, correct to the nearest ten.

3.4 rounded to the nearest whole number is 3 and 34 rounded to the nearest 10 is 30.

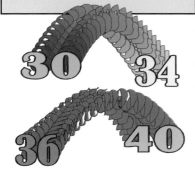

3. Round each of the following numbers to the nearest 10.
   a. 31   b. 39   c. 32   d. 33   e. 37   f. 38

   g. 30   h. 40   i. 35   j. 31.1   k. 31.9   l. 34.9

   m. 35.1   n. 32.99   o. 35.01   p. 91   q. 95   r. 99

4. Round each of the following numbers to the nearest whole number.
   a. 12.1   b. 12.9   c. 12.5   d. 103.2

   e. 103.6   f. 103.5   g. 1003. 3 h. 14.9

   i. 15   j. 15.1   k. 14.8   l. 14.5

5. Round each of the numbers in No.4 to the nearest 10.

340 rounded to the nearest 100 is 300.

340 is between 300 and 400 and is closer to 300.

6. Round each of the following numbers to the nearest 100.
   a. 349   b. 350   c. 351   d. 50

   e. 939   f. 999   g. 999.1   h. 349.99

7. Round each of the numbers to the nearest 10.
   a. 649   b. 650   c. 651   d. 649.99

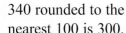

You are now ready to start Step 1 of your project.

Example 1:   Add $3 and 50¢.

Solution: 50¢ = $.50.

So $3 and 50¢ = $3 + $.50 = $3.50.

It would be wrong to say that $3 + $.50 = $53!

One way to avoid this problem when you are doing more complicated questions is to make sure that you add dollars to dollars and cents to cents.

Example 2:   Add: a. $2.96 and $4.73   b. $20, $1.96, $4.73 and $0.40

Solution:

a.
$$\begin{array}{r} \overset{1}{\$2.96} \\ \underline{\$4.73} \\ \$7.69 \end{array}$$

b.
$$\begin{array}{r} \overset{2}{\$20.00} \\ \$\ 1.96 \\ \$\ 4.73 \\ \underline{\$\ 0.40} \\ \$27.09 \end{array}$$

6 hundredths + 3 hundredths = 9 hundredths.

9 tenths + 7 tenths = 16 tenths.

16 tenths becomes 1 whole and 6 tenths.

This 1 whole + 2 wholes + 4 wholes = 7 wholes.

6 hundredths + 3 hundredths = 9 hundredths.

9 tenths + 7 tenths + 4 tenths= 20 tenths.

20 tenths becomes 2 wholes and 0 tenths.

This 2 wholes + 1 whole + 4 wholes = 7 wholes.

The easiest way to add dollars to dollars and cents to cents is to make sure that you keep the decimal points directly under each other.

PUT INTO PRACTICE

1.   Without using a calculator, complete the following additions.

a.	b.	c.	d.
$3.50	$12.50	$7.04	$ 3.96
$2.85	$ 3.65	$2.95	$ 8.24
+$4.60	+$ 9.24	+$1.01	+$11.36

2. Without using a calculator, complete the following subtractions.

    a. $8.69   b. $5.83   c. $19.16   d. $26.32
        −$3.24   −$3.67   −$14.58   −$25.49

3. In the following questions estimate the answer by rounding the numbers to the nearest $1 and adding or subtracting mentally.

    a. $5.61   b. $2.79   c. $9.31
        −$3.48 $4.35 $2.24
                        +$3.12   +$3.11

    d. $3.86   e. $7.04   f. $8.17
        −$1.32   −$3.42   −$5.62

4. Without using a calculator, do each question in No. 3. Use your estimates from No. 3 to check whether your answers are reasonable.

5. Estimate the answer for each question by rounding to the nearest dollar.
    a. $1.96 + $4.73   b. $39.95 − $19.80

    c. $2.81 + $12.96 + $1.07   d. $36.49 − $22.75

6. Calculate the sum of the prices on each group of tickets.
    a.

    b.

Reminder

To calculate the sum of decimal numbers without a calculator, arrange the digits in columns according to their place values. Remember to line up the decimal points in each number.

Write 3.5 as 3.50 to show that there are zero hundredths.

Example1:

Samantha measures distances of 3.5 m and 9.27 m on the stage.

Add the distances and check to see if your answer is reasonable.

Solution:

First

Estimate an answer.

3.5 rounds to 4
9.27 rounds to 9
The answer should be close to 4 + 9 = 13.

Second

Do the calculation.

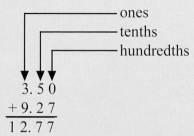

$$
\begin{array}{r}
3.50 \\
+\ 9.27 \\
\hline
12.77
\end{array}
$$

Third

Is the answer reasonable?

12.77 is reasonably close to 13.
Yes.

Subtract 2.34 from 8.4 and check whether or not your answer is reasonable.

Hint:

First

8.4 rounds to ☐.

2.34 rounds to ☐.

An estimate of the answer is ☐.

Second

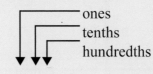

ones
tenths
hundredths

$$8.\overset{3}{\cancel{4}}\overset{1}{0}$$
$$-\ 2.3\ 4$$

4 tenths becomes 3 tenths and 10 hundredths

Write 8.4 as 8.40.

Third

Is the answer reasonable?

☐ is reasonably close to my estimate of ☐.

PUT INTO PRACTICE

1. Without using a calculator, add or subtract the following decimals.

a. 0.40	b. 0.80	c. 4.30	d. 3.70	e. 8.21	f. 5.60
+0.50	−0.20	−0.60	+0.55	+3.90	−0.90

g. 0.4	h. 0.8	i. 4.3	j. 3.7	k. 8.21	l. 5.6
+0.5	−0.2	−0.6	+0.55	+3.9	−0.9

2. For each question:
    Estimate an answer.
    Calculate the answer.
    Check that your answer is reasonable.

a. 17.28 +32.61	b. 64.9 −43.6	c. 42.25 −18.27	d. 184.9 + 30.65

e. 194.6 − 76.48	f. 47.06 172.3 +289.79	g. 100 − 99.36	h. 589.6 17.35 +608.15

3. Calculate the answer to each question.

a. 4.76 + 9.87   b. 75.5 – 64.6   c. 102.7 + 91.83

d. 79.22 – 37.33   e. 84.6 – 67.75   f. 2.094 + 6.88

g. 14 – 0.15   h. 2.375 – 1.008   i. 17.83 + 12.381

j. 3.6 – 2.035   k. 6.11 – 4.999

l. 28 + 2.445 + 3.09

4. Read each of the following problems carefully.
   Solve each one, making sure to organize and show the steps of each solution.
   Be sure to make a final statement to answer the problem.

   a. The height of a small spruce tree was 0.9 m.
      In the next few years it grew 1.8 m.
      What is the height of the tree now?

   b. Jade bought four books when she was preparing for her role in a play.
      Three of the books cost $4.98, $1.02, and $2.10.
      The total GST on her purchase was $0.68.

      If Jade received no change from a $10 bill, what was the cost of the fourth book?

   c. Sheri has a paper route.
      In two weeks she collected $156.10 from her customers.
      She paid the Sun $93.66 for the newspapers.

      How much money did she keep?

   d. The Laszcz's are going to buy bowling balls.
      The stated diameter of a bowling ball is 21.725 cm.
      The league allows balls whose diameters are within 0.25 cm of that diameter.

      What are the largest and smallest diameters allowed?

   e. Ling bought two equally priced CD's and a poster priced at $11.95.
      Before tax, the total price was $49.93.

      Explain why the price of each CD must have been less than $20.
      What was the price of each CD to the nearest dollar?

When you are buying something in a store the amounts are usually scanned into a machine at the checkout and the calculations are done for you.

It is important to be able to estimate the total cost of your items.

You can then be sure that you have enough money and that no mistakes have been made by the cashier.

When you buy from a catalogue or price list you usually have to do your own accurate calculations.

PUT INTO PRACTICE

Andre went to an OddJob concert.
He liked the group so much that he picked up their catalogue on the way out of the stadium.
On the left are some of the items in the catalogue.

1. Which costs more?
   a. two posters or one T-shirt
   b. CD or two hats

2. How much more does the sweatshirt cost than the T-shirt?

3. Charlene bought four posters.

   What was her total cost before tax?

4. The catalogue company is advertising a "We pay the tax" sale.
   You have $100 to buy items for your room.

   What combination of items would you buy to use as much of the $100 as possible?

5. Which would you buy: four T-shirts or one sweatshirt? Explain your decision.

COPYRIGHT © 2002   Rogue Media Inc.

Example 1: Kelsey bought three mood bulbs, that cost $0.78 each, for the drama production.
Calculate the cost.

0.78
0.78
0.78

Solution: 3 × $0.78 = $2.34

The cost of these three mood bulbs was $2.34.

Example 2: Raine wants to decorate the school stage with the school colours.
She decides to make five school ribbons, each 1.3 m long.
How much ribbon does she need?

1.3
1.3
1.3
1.3
1.3
6.5

Solution: 5 × 1.3 m = 6.5 m

She needs 6.5 m of ribbon.

Example 3: One light in a track-light unit has a mass of 0.25 kg.
Calculate the mass of seven lights.

0.25
0.25
0.25
0.25
0.25
0.25
0.25
1.75

Solution: 7 × 0.25 kg = 1.75 kg

The mass of seven lights is 1.75 kg.

INVESTIGATION

1. In Example 1:

   a. How many decimal places are in $0.78?

   b. How many decimal places are in $2.34?

   c. Compare the number of decimal places in $0.78 and in the answer ($2.34).

2. In Example 2:
   a. State the number of decimal places in 1.3 m.

   b. State the number of decimal places in 6.5 m.

   c. Compare the number of decimal places in 1.3 m and in the answer (6.5 m).

3. Explain how you know how many decimal places will be in the answer when you multiply a decimal number by a whole number.

Example 4:

The rental company has three red carpets, each 4.8 m long.
What is the maximum length of walkway that can be made using the three carpets?

Step 1. Round the numbers: $4.8 \times 3 \doteq 5 \times 3$. $\doteq$ means "is approximately equal to"

Step 2. Estimate the product: 15.

Step 3. Multiply the numbers, ignoring the decimals

$$
\begin{array}{r}
4.8 \\
\times\ 3 \\
\hline
1\,4\,4
\end{array}
$$

Step 4. Place the decimal point in the answer (14.4)*.

   The maximum length is 14.4 m.

   * There are two ways to know where the decimal point goes.
   The estimate is 15 so the correct answer will be 14.4.
   OR
   There is one decimal place in the question so there should be one decimal place in the answer.

1. Estimate an answer for each.
   a. 6.3×3 b. 14.2×4 c. 4×23.2 d. 5×12.7

   e. 0.84×6 f. 3.07×8 g. 7×1.92 h. 9×0.801

   i. 0.802×5 j. 0.103×9 k. 7×1.86 l. 9×0.809

2. Do each of the multiplications in No.1 without a calculator.
   Compare your answers with your estimates.

3. Jerrod volunteered 12 hours on stage sets.
   The amateur theatre group would have paid $5.90/h for this.

   How much did they save?

4. The local music group decided to give a sticker to everyone who comes to the concert.
   The supplier agrees to supply the stickers at $5.19/roll instead of the usual $5.69/roll.

   a. How much did the group pay for 12 rolls?
      How much did they save?

   b. The group decided that they need another 4 rolls.
      How much should they pay?

   c. What is the total cost and the total amount saved?

   d. How many extra rolls can they buy with the amount saved?

5. The drama club needed to raise money and so they organized a tour of the homes in the area.
   The cost of a pass was: Adults $8.25 and Students $5.75.

   Calculate the cost for:
   a. 120 adults.   b. 25 students.

   c. 240 adults and 130 students.

INVESTIGATION

1. Use your calculator to find the following products.

A	B	C
$1000 \times 5 = \underline{\quad}$	$1000 \times 0.3 = \underline{\quad}$	$1000 \times 0.24 = \underline{\quad}$
$100 \times 5 = \underline{\quad}$	$100 \times 0.3 = \underline{\quad}$	$100 \times 0.24 = \underline{\quad}$
$10 \times 5 = \underline{\quad}$	$10 \times 0.3 = \underline{\quad}$	$10 \times 0.24 = \underline{\quad}$
$1 \times 5 = \underline{\quad}$	$1 \times 0.3 = \underline{\quad}$	$1 \times 0.24 = \underline{\quad}$
$0.1 \times 5 = \underline{\quad}$	$0.1 \times 0.3 = \underline{\quad}$	$0.1 \times 0.24 = \underline{\quad}$
$0.01 \times 5 = \underline{\quad}$	$0.01 \times 0.3 = \underline{\quad}$	$0.01 \times 0.24 = \underline{\quad}$
$0.001 \times 5 = \underline{\quad}$	$0.001 \times 0.3 = \underline{\quad}$	$0.001 \times 0.24 = \underline{\quad}$

Look at the 5 after you have entered it on the calculator.
Notice that the 5 has a decimal point after it even though you do not need to enter it.

Use your results to answer the following questions.

2. If a number is multiplied by 10, 100, 1000 … ,

   a. does the number get larger or smaller?

   b. in which direction does the decimal point move?

   c. what is the connection between the number of 0's and the number of places that the decimal point moves?

3. If a number is multiplied by 0.1, 0.01, 0.001 …. ,
   a. does the number get larger or smaller?

   b. in which direction does the decimal point move?

   c. what is the connection between the number of decimal places and the number of places that the decimal point moves?

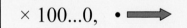

$\times \ 100...0, \quad \bullet \longrightarrow$

$\times \ 0.00...1, \quad \longleftarrow \bullet$

When you multiply by a number that is of the form 1 with a series of 0's, then the decimal point moves **that number of places** to the **right**.

Example 1

$1.2 \times 100\,000 = 120\,000.$ 5   0's   1.2 0 0 0 0.

When you multiply by a number that is of the form: a decimal point, a series of 0's and 1, then the decimal point moves **that number of places** to the **left**.

Example 2

$1.2 \times 0.000\,001 = 0.000\,001\,2.$ 6 decimal places   .0 0 0 0 0 1.2

PUT INTO PRACTICE

1. Answer the following questions without using a calculator.
   a. 1000×0.5 b. 6.48×10 c. 0.416×100

   d. 0.73×1000 e. 100×30.4 f. 1.004×1000

2. Do the following questions without using a calculator.
   a. 4×0.01 b. 34×0.001 c. 6.2×0.1

   d. 0.01×128 e. 0.1×7.4 f. 1.8×0.001

   g. 0.88×0.1 h. 0.4×0.01 i. 0.03×0.1

   j. 0.96×0.001 k. 0.01×0.7 l. 0.001×0.36

3. A printer charges \$0.04/page.
   A student charges \$0.05/flyer to distribute them to other students.

   Calculate the cost of printing and delivering the following numbers of 1-page flyers.

   a. 100   b. 1000   c. 10 000

4. Each glass has 0.1 L of juice.
   Calculate the total amount of juice in 23 glasses.

Example 1:   Multiply 1.36 by 2.9.

Step 1. Estimate: $1 \times 3 = 3$.

Step 2. Multiply:

$$
\begin{array}{r}
1.36 \quad \text{-> } \textbf{2} \text{ decimal places} \\
\times\, 2.9 \quad \text{-> } \textbf{1} \text{ decimal place} \\
\hline
1224 \\
2720 \\
\hline
\end{array}
$$

Step 3. Insert the decimal point: 3.944 -> **3** decimal places

The estimate is 3 and so the decimal has to go between the 3 and the 9.

Notice that the number of decimal places in the answer is equal to the sum of the numbers of decimal places in the factors.

To determine the number of decimal places in the product count the number of decimal places in both factors.

That is the number of decimal places that you will have in the product.

INVESTIGATION

Multiply: 4.3×2.6

Step 1. Estimate: ☐.

Step 2. Multiply the numbers without worrying about the decimals.

$$
\begin{array}{r}
4.3 \quad \square \text{ decimal place} \\
\times 2.6 \quad \square \text{ decimal place} \\
\hline
258 \quad \text{Multiply by 6.} \\
860 \quad \text{Multiply by 20.} \\
\hline
\end{array}
$$

Step 3. Now insert the decimal point. 11.18 ☐ decimal places

Step 4: Does the answer agree with the estimate? ☐.

$4.3 \times 2.6 =$ ☐.

Multiplying decimals is similar to multiplying whole numbers. Estimate the answer first.

Example 2:   13.6   **1** decimal place
              ×0.29   **2** decimal places
            ─────
             1224
             2720
            ─────
            3.944   **3** decimal places

> The number of decimal places in the answer is equal to the sum of the number of decimal places in the original question.

PUT INTO PRACTICE

1. Rewrite the answer with the decimal point in the correct place.

   a.   13.123456789
                ×0.8
        ─────────────
        104987654312

   b.   6.5123456789
               ×0.47
        ─────────────
        3060802469083

   c.   14.831234567
               ×0.17
        ─────────────
        252130987639

   d.   209.61234567
              × 4.06
        ─────────────
        8510261234202

2. Without a calculator, determine which of the following questions will have a product greater than 50.
   a. 11.8×6.4 b. 65×0.25 c. 10.84×0.95

   d. 11.76×7.47 e. 7.07×6.71 f. 65.8×32.6

3. Estimate an answer for each of these questions.

   a.   3.6
          ×2.4
        ─────

   b. 5.7
        ×2.5
      ─────

   c. 0.46
        ×2.3
      ─────

   d.   8.3
          ×3.7
        ─────

   e. 2.4
        ×1.6
      ─────

   f. 0.27
        ×2.1
      ─────

4. Estimate an answer for each of these questions.
   a. 2.3×1.9 b. 3.2×3.2 c. 1.84×2.2

   d. 3.4×0.43 e. 0.04×8.3 f. 0.87×2.3.

5. Calculate an answer for each of the questions in No. 4.

6. Each riser of a set of steps is 22.8 cm.
   Each tread is 30.1 cm.

   Calculate the height and the depth of the set of steps.

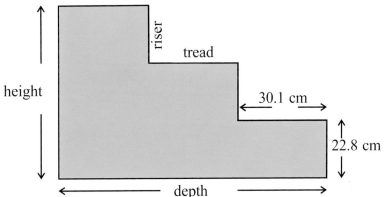

7. Calculate the cost of 3.4 m of ribbon when it costs:

   a. $2.30/m   b. $2.07/m   c. $1.84/m

INVESTIGATION

1. Complete the tables using the blackline master provided. Use your calculator to complete the following patterns.

A	
3 ÷ 1000	= __
3 ÷ 100	= __
3 ÷ 10	= __
3 ÷ 1	= __
3 ÷ 0.1	= __
3 ÷ 0.01	= __
3 ÷ 0.001	= __

B	
1.2 ÷ 1000	= __
1.2 ÷ 100	= __
1.2 ÷ 10	= __
1.2 ÷ 1	= __
1.2 ÷ 0.1	= __
1.2 ÷ 0.01	= __
1.2 ÷ 0.001	= __

2. If a number is divided by 10, 100, 1000 …

   a. Does the number get larger or smaller?

   b. In which direction does the decimal point move?

   c. What is the connection between the number of 0's in the divisor and the number of places that the decimal point moves?

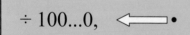

÷ 100...0, ⟵•

3. If a number is divided by 0.1, 0.01, 0.001 ….

   a. Does the number get larger or smaller?

   b. In which direction does the decimal point appear to move?

   c. What is the connection between the number of decimal places in the divisor and the number of places that the decimal point appears to move?

÷ 0.00...1, •⟹

When you divide by a number that is of the form 1 with a series of 0's, then the decimal point moves **that number of places** to the **left**.

Example 1:

$1.2 \div 1000 = 0.0012.$ 3   0's $0.0\overset{\frown}{0}\overset{\frown}{1}.2$

When you divide by a number that is of the form: a decimal point, a series of 0's and then 1, then the decimal point moves **that number of places** to the **right**.

Example 2:

$1.2 \div 0.0001 = 12\ 000.$ 4 decimal places, $1.2\overset{\frown}{0}\overset{\frown}{0}\overset{\frown}{0}0.$

PUT INTO PRACTICE

1. Calculate the following:

    a. i. $5 \div 10$ ii. 5×0.1

    b. i. $5 \div 100$ ii. 5×0.01

    c. i. $5 \div 1000$ ii. 5×0.001

2. What is the relationship between **dividing** by 10, 100, 1000, … and **multiplying** by 0.1, 0.01, 0.001, …?

3. Calculate the following:

    a. i. $5 \div 0.1$ ii. 5×10

    b. i. $5 \div 0.01$ ii. 5×100

    c. i. $5 \div 0.001$ ii. 5×1000

4. What is the relationship between **dividing** by 0.1, 0.01, 0.001 …. and **multiplying** by 10, 100, 1000 … ?

5. Evaluate:
   a. $27 \div 100$ b. $35 \div 1000$ c. $4 \div 1000$

   d. $587 \div 10$ e. $697 \div 100$ f. $304 \div 10$

6. Evaluate:
   a. $64 \div 0.1$ b. $7 \div 0.001$ c. $683 \div 0.01$

   d. $40 \div 0.01$ e. $67 \div 0.001$ f. $37 \div 0.1$

7. Evaluate:
   a. $41.32 \div 100$ b. $219.5 \div 1000$ c. $1.92 \div 0.1$

   d. $0.495 \div 0.01$ e. $82 \div 0.001$ f. $0.8 \div 0.01$

8. Which question has the smallest answer?
   Which one has the largest answer?
   Explain your answers.

   a. $3.581\ 234\ 567\ 89 \div 0.1$

   b. $3.581\ 234\ 567\ 89 \div 100$

   c. $3.581\ 234\ 567\ 89 \div 0.01$

   d. $3.581\ 234\ 567\ 89 \div 1000$

   e. $3.581\ 234\ 567\ 89 \div 10$

   f. $3.581\ 234\ 567\ 89 \div 0.001$

INVESTIGATION

At a garage sale, Spencer bought four Beatles posters for $26.

1a. Estimate the cost of one poster.
Hint: Pick a number close to 26 that is a multiple of 4.

1b. Calculate the cost of a poster without a calculator.

1c. Calculate the cost of a poster with a calculator.

$$
\begin{array}{r}
\;\;\;\;\cdot \\
4\overline{)26.00} \\
\underline{24} \\
20 \\
\underline{20} \\
0
\end{array}
$$

Hint: Use the sequence: $\boxed{Cl}\ \boxed{2}\ \boxed{6}\ \boxed{\div}\ \boxed{4}\ \boxed{=}$

The unit cost is $\boxed{}$.

Check: Is this close to your estimated cost?

Example 1:

The drama club sold souvenir tiles.   Six tiles cost $12.72.

a. Estimate the cost of one tile.
Solution:
Use $12 for the cost because it is divisible by 6.
$12 \div 6 = 2$.
The cost of one tile is a little more than $2.

b. Calculate the cost of a tile without a calculator.
Solution:

$$
\begin{array}{r}
2.12 \\
6\overline{)12.72}
\end{array}
$$

The unit cost is $2.12.
Check: Is this close to your estimated cost?

c. Calculate the cost of a tile with a calculator.
Solution:
$12.72 \div 6 = 2.12$
Use the sequence: $\boxed{Cl}\ \boxed{1}\ \boxed{2}\ \boxed{\cdot}\ \boxed{7}\ \boxed{2}\ \boxed{\div}\ \boxed{6}\ \boxed{=}$

The cost of a tile is $2.12.

1. Estimate an answer for each.
   a. 13.2 ÷ 4   b. 37.5 ÷ 3   c. 4.8 ÷ 6

   d. 87.65 ÷ 5   e. 50.4 ÷ 6   f. 46.5 ÷ 6

2. Compare your estimates with others and discuss any differences.

3. Without a calculator, calculate the answer for each part of No. 1.

4. Four students paid $23 to rent some videos. How much did each pay?

5. George charged $49.20 for 8 h of repairs to the stage. What was his rate per hour?

6. Omar bought five posters for $56.25. What was the cost of each poster?

Get Thinking

How do your estimates help you know if your answer is correct?

Example 2:

Jacques has to cover the back of a stage that is 12.96 m wide.
The panels are each 2.4 m wide.

How many panels does he need?

Solution:

To estimate, use 12 and 2 because 12 is divisible by 2.
12 ÷ 2 = 6
We expect an answer of about 6.

12.96 ÷ 2.4 = 5.4   `Cl 1 2 . 9 6 ÷ 2 . 4 =`

He needs 6 panels (5 full panels and a part panel).

7. Kori charged $223.44 for working 28.5 h on changing the garage into a rehearsal space for the Johnny D and the Mathcats group.

   Calculate her hourly wage.

8. Tish and two friends spent $10.20 on popcorn and $28.60 for admission.
   They shared the costs equally.

   Calculate the cost for each.

9. The special edition of the magazine *"The Concert of Your Dreams"* sold for $4.25 a copy and 295 136 copies were sold.

   Calculate the total revenue.

10. The height of the stage is 2.52 m.
    Each step in a staircase is 0.21 m high.

    Calculate the number of steps.

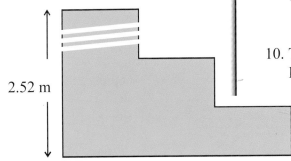

2.52 m

0.21 m

Real World Project

You are now ready to start Step 2 of your project.

GRAPHS

The entertainment industry relies on the data found in graphs to make future predictions about the marketplace and to determine how much money should be budgeted for production costs.

READING & INTERPRETING GRAPHS

1. **Movie Dollars**

   The Motion Picture industry involves huge sums of money. How do you think the money is spent?

   Some of the costs involved in making a movie are:

   Purchase of a **story**
   Director's fee
   Cost of building or preparing **sets**
   Actors' salaries
   Cost of buying, making or renting **costumes**
   Studio **rental**
   Film purchase, processing and editing
   Rental of equipment, food services, locations.

   a. Work with a partner to arrange these costs in order from greatest to least.

   b. Why did you make those decisions?

   c. Compare your order with other groups. Discuss major differences.

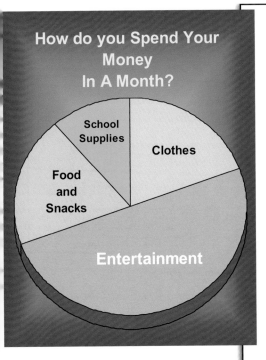

How do you Spend Your Money In A Month?

School Supplies

Clothes

Food and Snacks

Entertainment

2. **How Do You Spend Your Money in a Month?**
Andrew earned $50 in a month and this circle graph shows how Andrew spent his money.

 a. What fraction of his money did he spend on entertainment?

 b. How much money did he spend on entertainment?

 c. Which two sectors of the graph seem to be the same size?

 d. How much money did he spend on school supplies?

 e. How much money was spent on clothes and on food and snacks?

3. **How Did Andrew Spend His Entertainment Dollars?**

 This incomplete graph shows how Andrew spent his entertainment money for a year.

 a. Copy the graph and label it to show the following information.
 Concerts: $100   Movies: $75   Rentals: $50
 CD's: $50   Video Games: $25

 b. What was the total amount spent?

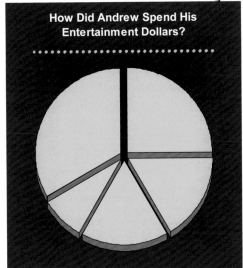

How Did Andrew Spend His Entertainment Dollars?

4. **Let the Music Play**

A class survey was taken to identify students' favourite performers.

Students were allowed to vote for two groups or people.

Here are the results.

	Tally	Frequency
Paul Brandt	~~IIII~~ II	7
Diana Krall	~~IIII~~ IIII	9
Breach of Trust	~~IIII~~ I	6
Blue Rodeo	~~IIII~~ ~~IIII~~ I	11
54-40	~~IIII~~ ~~IIII~~ IIII	14
The Wilkinsons	~~IIII~~	5
Nickleback	~~IIII~~ III	8

Frequency

is the number of times that a person was chosen.

a. How many votes were recorded?

b. Who got the most votes?

c. Who got the least number of votes?

d. If each person used his or her two votes, how many people voted?

5. Use technology to draw a circle graph to show the results of the class survey on favourite bands.

GLENNS ORKESTER

Bands	Frequency
Paul Brandt	7
Diana Krall	9
Breach of Trust	6
Blue Rodeo	11
54-40	14
The Wilkinsons	5
Nickleback	8
Total	60

1. Using the blackline master provided, create information to complete three of the graphs below.
   Remember that each graph must have a title, labels and scales.

a.

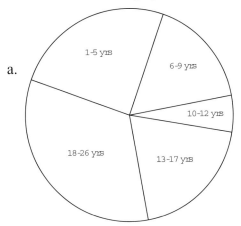

b.

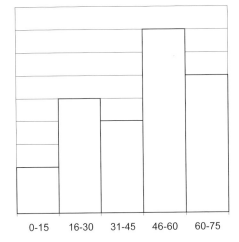

c.

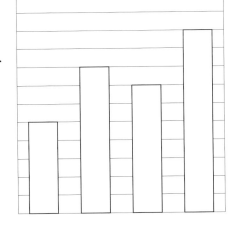

d.

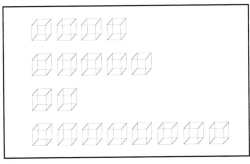

e.

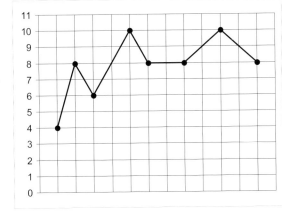

Remember we have to be sensitive to the feelings of others when we ask questions in a survey.

2. a. Decide on an entertainment question you would like to ask your classmates.
        You may ask questions such as:
        "Which three Canadian performers would you like to see in person?"
        "Which 10 Canadian performers do you think are the most talented?"

    b. Carry out the survey.
        Make sure that your question is not biased.
        I.e., Don't ask a question like: "Wouldn't you like to see _____ in person?"

    c. Make a tally and a graph to show your results

    d. Compare your graph to those of others in your class. Be sure to save your results as you may wish to use them in your project.

You may wish to consider the following important questions:

• Are the performers worth the money they are paid?
• Should they be paid more or less?
• How much more or less?
• Should they be paid according to the "good" they do for others?

100 GRAPHS

People who attended came from the following locations.

Place	Distance From Regina (km)	Number Attending
Medicine Hat	471	36
Saskatoon	257	55
Wild Horse	553	4
Chief Mountain	772	5
Three Hills	782	8
Swan Hills	814	10
Ponoka	849	8
Wetaskiwin	885	7
Slave Lake	1041	11
Grande Cache	1226	6
Pincher Creek	1274	9
Fairview	1348	12
High Level	1568	7
Vancouver	1720	35

A **histogram** is the graph of a **frequency distribution**.
The intervals are marked on the horizontal axis and they must represent **equal intervals**.

3. The 1999 National Aboriginal Achievement Awards were held in Regina.

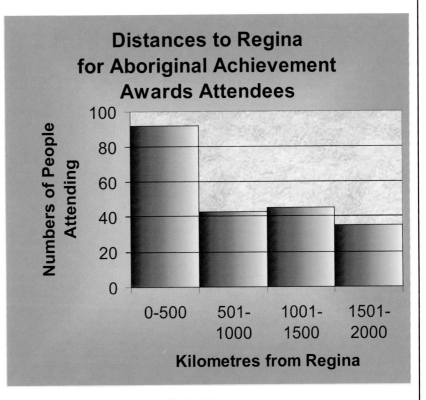

This type of graph is called a histogram.

It shows information about the distances traveled by the people who attended the ceremony.

a. How is it different from a bar graph?

b. How is it organized?

c. Which distance category is most frequent?

d. How could the information be used?

e. What useful information is not shown?

Get Thinking!

4. Over the years there have been many awards given in different categories.
This circle graph shows the awards given.

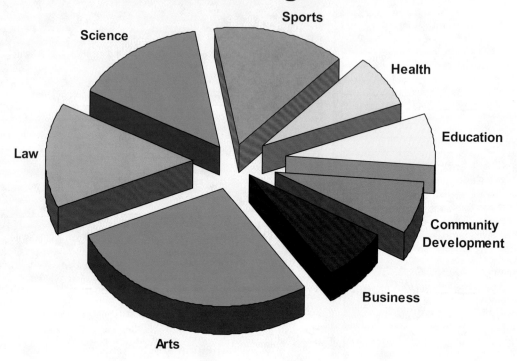

National Aboriginal Achievement Awards Categories

a. In which category were most awards given?

b. Which category had the second highest number of awards?

5. A group of students was surveyed to see which National Aboriginal Achievement Award they would most like to win.

This is a tally of their preferences.

	Tally	Frequency
Arts	⊬⊬ ||||	9
Business	|||	3
Community Development	||	2
Education	||||	4
Health	|||	3
Law	⊬⊬ |	6
Science	||||	4
Sports	⊬⊬	5

a. How many people were surveyed?

b. Which award did most people want to win?

c. Which category is as popular as business?

d. Which award has the same number as science?

e. How many wanted to win an award in law?

CANADIAN ABORIGINAL FESTIVAL

Which Award Would You Want?

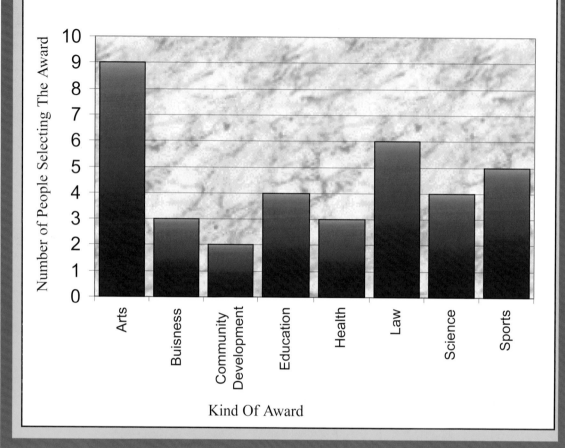

Number of People Selecting The Award

Kind Of Award

Arts · Buisness · Community Development · Education · Health · Law · Science · Sports

6. This graph shows the same information as the tally.

   a. How does it show the information differently?

   b. Carry out a similar survey in your class or group.

   c. Make a graph either by hand or using technology and compare it to the graph shown above.

   d. How is it the same? How is it different?

7. Make a graph.

    a. Research another local, national or international awards show.

    b. Make a graph to display some of the information that interests you.

8. The following pictograph shows the kinds of music a certain radio station plays in an afternoon.

    a. What does each musical note represent?

    b. Why is this an effective graph to show the information?

What Music Does CKCV Play In An Afternoon?

Blues	♪ ♪ ♪ ♪
Country/Western	♪ ♪ ♩
Folk Traditional	♪ ♪ ♪ ♪ ♪
Jazz	♪ ♪ ♪
Rap & Hip Hop	♪ ♪ ♪ ♪ ♪ ♩
Rock & Pop	♪ ♪ ♪ ♪

♪ = 2 playings of the kind of music

♩ = 1 playing of the kind of music

9. Choose five types of music to use in a survey.

MUSIC GENRES

Alternative	**Blues/ R&B**	**Calypso**
Celtic/East Coast	**Classical**	**Classic Rock**
Country/Western	**Electronica/Dance**	**Folk Traditional**
French/Acadian	**Gospel**	**Industrial**
Jazz	**Metal/Heavy**	**Opera**
Punk/Hardcore	**Rap & Hip – Hop**	**Reggae**
Rock and Pop	**Ska**	**Steelband**
World		

a. Design a questionnaire to use with your classmates or friends.

b. Carry out the survey to find out the music preferences of your classmates or friends.

c. Make a pictograph to show your results. Don't forget to include a title and other relevant information.

d. Compare your results to that of another group. Why might your results be different?

10. This double bar graph shows which award shows members of a class would like to host.

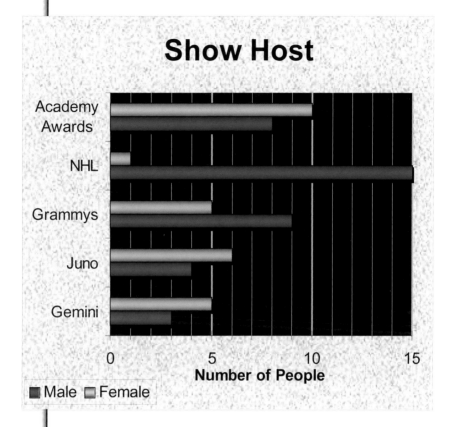

a. Why is a double bar graph an effective way to show the information?

b. How many people were questioned?

c. If you surveyed people you know, would the results be similar? Explain.

d. Construct a similar question about award shows and make your own double bar graph to display the information.

11. Here is another question from the world of entertainment for you to consider:

What kind of entertainer do you most admire, or would you like to be?

A Sample of Canadian Entertainers

A comedian like Martin Short?   **A TV star like Michael J. Fox?**

A singer like Diana Krall?   **A songwriter like Paul Brandt?**

A sports star like Wayne Gretzky?   **Add your own.**

Survey your class to find out their preferences and present the information in a graph of your choice.

12. This is a circle graph showing how money is usually spent on making movies in Canada.

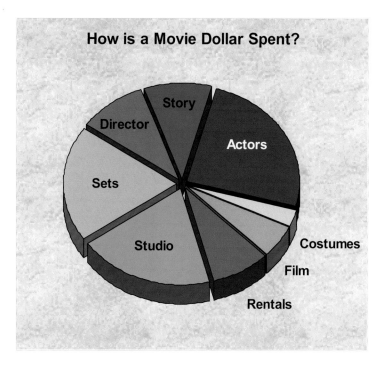

How is a Movie Dollar Spent?

Story
Director
Actors
Sets
Studio
Costumes
Film
Rentals

a. Which categories spent about the same amount?

b. Why do you think this is true?

c. About how much would the actors be paid if the movie budget is 10 million dollars?

d. How do you think it is decided which actors are paid the most?

e. Do you think this a fair or an unfair practice?

f. Comment on any surprising categories in the graph.

g. Why is a circle graph an effective way to communicate this information?

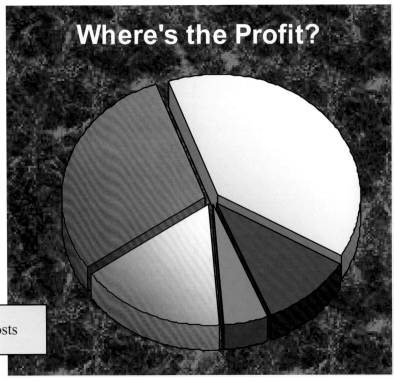

Where's the Profit?

Profit = Total Income − Total Costs

Real World Project

This might be an area for you to consider further research for your project. You could investigate the costs and profits for another area of the entertainment industry.

13. How Does a Movie Make a Profit?

This graph can show how most of the money is spent on a movie.

The sections are:
Production costs
Distribution costs
Cost of making copies of the film
for distribution
Administration and Taxes
Profit.

a. Copy the graph and label it as you think it might be sectioned.

b. Compare your labeling with those of another person in the class.
Discuss any major differences.

Ages of Canadian Moviegoers

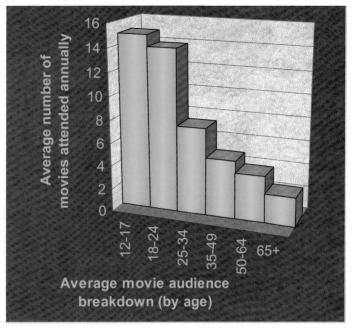

14. The graph above gives data about the ages of Canadian moviegoers.

    a. What other information is shown besides the ages of the moviegoers?

    b. Which age group attends the most movies?

    c. Which age groups attend the fewest?

    d. Explain why you are, or are not, surprised by this information.

    e. How would this compare to a multi-aged group that you know of, or can survey?
Give reasons for your answer.

    f. Conduct a survey in your class to find out how often your classmates see movies.
Decide whether or not you will include videos, pay per view or TV movies.

Average World Movie Admission Prices

Cost in US Dollars

(Countries from top to bottom: Japan, Switzerland, Germany, France, Australia, Canada, Brazil, UK, Russia, Hong Kong, US, Singapore, South Africa)

15. This bar graph shows comparative movie admission costs in different parts of the world.

   a. Which countries have the highest ticket prices?

   b. Which have the lowest?

   c. Is this what you expected or is it surprising? Explain your answer.

   d. What other costs are involved if you have a "night out at the movies"?

   e. Make a graph showing all the expenses you have paid.

Real World Project

You are now ready to start Step 3 of your project.

REVIEW

These questions will help you check whether or not you have mastered the concepts in this unit.

It is perfectly all right to look back in this book for help in finding the answers to the questions.

As you do the questions be sure to think of how you can use decimals and graphing in your project.

DECIMALS

> Line up the decimal points.

1. Estimate the following sums:
   a. $6.3 + 3.8$ b. $24.96 + 0.43$ c. $0.987 + 5.632$

   d. $23.05 + 21$ e. $198 + 0.385$ f. $0.5 + 6.9254$

   g. $0.6240 + 7844$ h. $0.6253 + 7844$ i. $0.6943 + 7844$

2. Find the answer for each part of No. 1.
   Do not use a calculator.
   Check. Are your answers close to your estimates?

3. Subtract:

a.	b.	c.	d.
6.8	6.3	16.3	16.3
-4.3	-4.8	-4.9	-9.4

   e. $26.9 - 15.5$ f. $26.4 - 15.5$ g. $26.3 - 16.5$

> The number of decimal places in the product is equal to the sum of the numbers of decimal places in the factors.

4. Copy the questions and answers.
   Correctly place the decimal point in each of the answers.
   a. $16.7 \times 4 = 668$ b. $52.85 \times 3.1 = 163835$

   c. $425 \times 4.98 = 211650$ d. $0.256 \times 0.21 = 5376$

5. Estimate the following products:
   a. 365×4.98 b. 16.8×4.3 c. 144×19.98

   d. 2.15×0.3 e. 0.236×84.5 f. 19.65×0.985

   g. 23.94×16.89 h. 23.95×16.91 i. 23.49×16.98

6. Estimate the following quotients:
   a. $2.5 \div 2$ b. $6.97 \div 1.7$ c. $49.9 \div 6.9$

   d. $15.96 \div 3.8$ e. $1025 \div 10.5$ f. $31.632 \div 8.45$

7. Andrea went to the show and spent the following:

Ticket	$2.75
Extreme Pinball	2 games @ $1.25
Food	$1.99 and $0.79

   a. Calculate the total cost.

   b. On the way home she found: a loonie, a quarter and a nickel.

   How much did her trip to the movies really cost?

8. Hannah and Rhys plan to go to a concert.
   They were able to buy a discounted ticket at the supermarket for $25.
   They bought the other one at a ticket agency and paid $34 for the ticket and $2.50 handling fee.
   They agree that each will pay half.

   How much should each pay?

9. Consider the number 6.174.
   The largest number that you can make by shifting the digits is 7.614.
   The smallest one is 1.467.
   Subtract 1.467 from 7.614.

TALLADEGA IN CONCERT

$$7.614$$
$$-\ 1.467$$

GRAPHS

10. This graph shows the television preferences of a group of students.

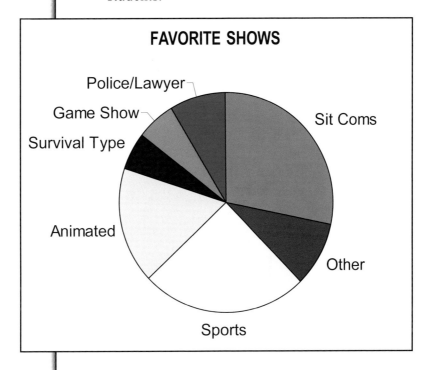

FAVORITE SHOWS

Police/Lawyer

Game Show

Survival Type

Sit Coms

Animated

Other

Sports

a. Which is the most popular kind of show?

b. Which is the least popular?

c. How do you think this would compare to the opinions of your friends?

d. Carry out a survey of the favourite types of television shows your friends watch.

e. Make a bar graph or a circle graph to show the results of your survey.

f. Explain why you chose the type of graph you did.

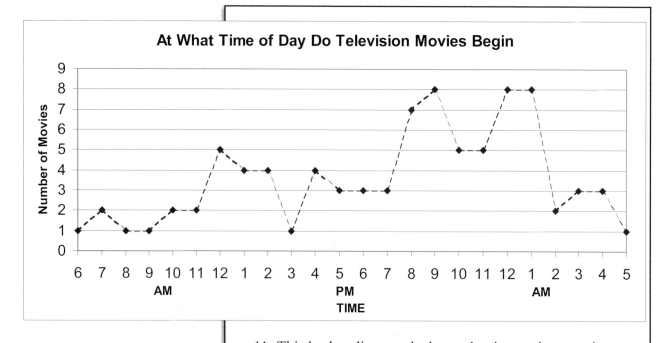

At What Time of Day Do Television Movies Begin

11. This broken-line graph shows the times when movies are shown on television in a 24-hour period

    a. What are the most popular start-times?

    b. If each movie is at least $2\frac{1}{2}$ hours long how many movies are on at 2:15 AM?

12. Make a broken-line graph showing when another kind of program is on.
    E.g. cartoons or sports.

Real World Project

Think about your presentation techniques for Step 4 of the project.

PROJECT

ENTERTAINMENT INDUSTRY

It is evident from this unit that aspects of the entertainment industry, including your own aspirations can be powerfully expressed by using your graphing skills. Graphs and charts are widely used to communicate popularity and opinions of stars and fans alike and to make predictions about the future of the industry.

The final project is to be a presentation about some aspect of the entertainment world as it is today or a detailed description of your plans for your future in the entertainment industry.

- You must have a minimum of three different graphs to communicate your ideas or findings.

- All graphs must be carefully constructed either by hand or with technology, with suitable labels and titles.

- Preliminary work with survey sheets must be available.

The band is GLENNS ORKESTER.
The guitarist on the right is a math teacher!

- There should be a conclusion for each graph which interprets the information and predicts what the information means for the future.

- Your project should include some information that involves fractions.

- You should find a part of your project that can illustrate an integer concept.

- Some suggestions for projects are the big ideas we discussed on day one:
    - How and why did my favourite superstar become so successful?
    - How has technology changed the entertainment world?
    - What is the future of movies? Or video games? Or live concerts?
    - Is the entertainment world fair to a particular minority group?

- How I will become a successful rock star, opera singer, set designer, movie director or disc jockey.

- What is the importance of the entertainment industry in Canada, your province, your town or your school?

- Career options in concerts and touring.

- Unique aspects of RAP in the marketplace.

- How the business of contemporary Christian music is a genre that is growing in popularity and economic viability.

STEP 1: INITIAL IDEAS

- Decide what you would like to research and carry out a preliminary investigation to make sure the information is available. For example the MEIEA (Music and Entertainment Industry Educators) is a professional association whose central goal is to educate the public about the music industry. Their website and newsletter offer many ideas on current entertainment issues.

- Make some notes about the different kinds of graphs you will include.

STEP 2: RESEARCH AND SURVEYS

After deciding on the subject of your presentation, it's time to do some research.
- Use websites with search engines such as Google, Ask Jeeves or Yahoo. Scan the websites quickly to see if the information might be useful and make notes to return to the most reliable and informative sites.

- Obtain information from books, brochures or magazines.

- Now survey teachers, students, relatives and people in the community for information and opinions.

- How will you word your questionnaire to ensure you get accurate information?

- Will you list the choices and ask the participants to rank them in descending order of importance?
  Will you include "None" or "Don't care" as options?

- Will you conduct interviews or give out questionnaires to be completed by the participants?

- Have you different ideas on how to collect the information you need?

STEP 3: CONSTRUCT GRAPHS

- Collect and tabulate all the data.

- Decide how you will analyze the data.

- Decide on what is the most important information you wish to show in your project to convince your audience about the truth of your information.

- Construct the graphs by hand or with technology so that they can be presented to the class.

- Make notes about how you will discuss the project with the class.

- Remember that your project can be presented using sophisticated technology such as hyperstudio if you wish.

- Your graphs should be attractively designed and presented.

STEP 4: THE PRESENTATION

Because you and your class have been immersed in the world of entertainment, try to make your project presentation as entertaining as possible. You should consider room arrangement, venue for the presentation, lighting, background music and sound effects, historical photographs, live presentations, video and audio tapes. All these techniques will help you communicate and visually represent your ideas for others to learn from.

HOME

GET THINKING

- ☐ What will I need to know about fractions to build, buy, renovate or redecorate my home?

- ☐ How could I determine the amount of sod to order for all the space around our new house?

- ☐ If we added a pool with an unusual shape, how could we estimate/calculate the amount of water required to fill it?

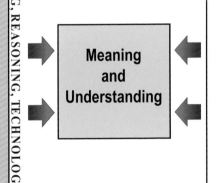

Content
AND MENTAL MATH, PROBLEM SOLVING, REASONING, TECHNOLOGY, VISUALIZATION, COMMUNICATION, CONNECTIONS, ESTIMATION

- *Identify and describe fractions*
- *Perform arithmetic operations on fractions*
- *Estimate, Measure, Calculate*
  - *length/perimeter*
  - *area*
  - *volume/capacity*
  - *mass/wieght*
- *Convert between metric and Imperial*

Meaning and Understanding

Intellectual Curiosity

Where is mathematics used in the home?
How can a ruler be used as an adding machine?
How do I develop benchmarks for simple measurements?

Real World Project

Room Design

Redesign a room; determine the material costs; make a budget.

FRACTIONS

Real World Project

Have you ever looked around a room and wished you could improve it? Whether it is a bedroom, a recreation room or another room you will need to do proper planning to do so.

Make a "wish list". Use your imagination and don't worry about the cost. In a paragraph, describe what you would like the room to look like.

WHAT IS A FRACTION?   TUTORIAL 1

INVESTIGATION

1. Jim runs a mail order business from home.
    He sells posters to students who want to use them to decorate their rooms.
    He has to mail the posters shown in the diagram using envelopes measuring 38 cm by 23 cm, or 24 cm by 12 cm.

    For each poster, he has to decide which envelope to use and how to fold the poster.

A

76 cm × 23 cm

B

69 cm × 38 cm

C

48 cm × 24 cm

Complete the table using the blackline master provided.
If possible, show more than one way of folding.

Poster	Which Envelope?	Sketch of Poster Showing Fold Lines	Folded Poster is What Fraction Of Original Size?
A			
B			
C			

2. a. In how many different ways can you fold a square
      paper into four equal parts?

   b. Compare your answers with your classmate.

   c. Draw your solutions in your notebook.

   d. How many quarters are there in one whole?

3. a. Take a rectangular piece of paper and fold it in
      eighths.
      Copy the rectangle in your notebook and show the
      folds as dotted lines.

   b. Shade three eighths of your rectangle.

   c. How many eighths are in one whole?

1. How many:

    a. halves in one whole?   b. thirds in one whole?

    c. quarters in one whole?   d. sixths in one whole?

    e. tenths in one whole?   f. fifths in one whole?

2. State the value of ?.

    a. $\dfrac{?}{6} = 1$ b. $\dfrac{?}{10} = 1$ c. $\dfrac{?}{5} = 1$

3. What fraction of:

    a. a loonie is 25¢?

    b. a week is one day?

    c. a hockey game is one period?

    d. the perimeter of a regular hexagon is one side?

    e. a toonie is a dime?

In the previous investigation you worked with fractions that are used in a number of real situations.

In this investigation you will use blocks and diagrams to develop a better understanding of fractions.

For this Tutorial you will need green triangles, blue rhombi, red trapezoids, yellow hexagons and pink double hexagons.

One whole

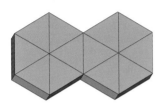

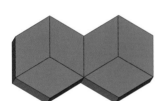

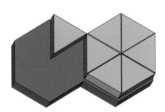

Find out how many of each shape are required to cover the pink double hexagon.

Complete a copy of the table below.

Shape Used To Cover Double Hexagon	Diagram	No. of Shapes Needed To Cover It	Fraction Represented By:	
Hexagon			One hexagon	2 hexagons
Trapezoid			One trapezoid	3 trapezoids
Rhombus			One rhombus	5 rhombi
Triangle			One triangle	7 triangles

When we write $\frac{5}{8}$ we mean that the whole is divided into 8 equal parts and that we are considering 5 of those equal parts.

5 is called the **numerator**.

8 is called the **denominator**.

4. What fraction of the pink double hexagon is represented by:

   a. 5 green triangles?   b. 3 red trapezoids?

   c. 5 blue rhombi?   d. 9 green triangles?

5. Draw a diagram to show:

   a. $\dfrac{3}{4}$ b. $\dfrac{1}{6}$ c. $\dfrac{5}{12}$

6. Which is greater?

   a. $\dfrac{1}{2}$ or $\dfrac{3}{4}$ b. $\dfrac{2}{3}$ or $\dfrac{5}{6}$ c. $\dfrac{1}{2}$ or $\dfrac{5}{12}$

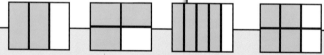

Most of the fractions in this Tutorial, such as $\dfrac{2}{3}, \dfrac{3}{4}, \dfrac{4}{5}, \dfrac{4}{6}$, are called **proper fractions** because they are less than one whole.

The number in the **numerator** is **smaller than** the number in the **denominator**.

A fraction, like $\dfrac{3}{2}$, that has the **numerator greater than** the **denominator** is called an **improper fraction.**

7. Here are examples of proper fractions:

   $$\frac{5}{8}, \frac{1}{4}, \frac{3}{5}, \frac{4}{7}$$

   Here are examples of improper fractions:

   $$\frac{11}{7}, \frac{4}{3}, \frac{7}{4}, \frac{17}{6}$$

   List the following under the headings
   Proper Fractions and **Improper Fractions**.

   a. $\dfrac{1}{7}$ b. $\dfrac{5}{3}$ c. $\dfrac{7}{9}$ d. $\dfrac{2}{11}$ e. $\dfrac{8}{7}$ f. $\dfrac{19}{17}$ g. $\dfrac{9}{2}$

INVESTIGATION

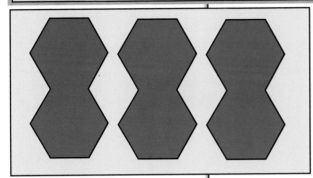

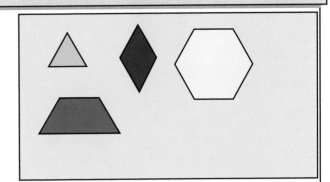

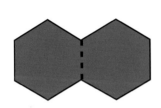

1. a. How many yellow hexagons are required to cover the three double hexagons?

   b. Draw the diagram.

   c. Copy and complete:

   Three wholes is the same as ☐ halves.

   $$3 = \frac{?}{2}$$

2. a. How many red trapezoids are required to cover three double hexagons?

   b. Draw the diagram.

   c. Copy and complete:

   Three wholes is the same as ☐ quarters.

   $$3 = \frac{?}{4}$$

3. How many green triangles are required to cover three double hexagons?

   Copy and complete:

   Three wholes is the same as ☐ twelfths.

   $$3 = \frac{?}{12}$$

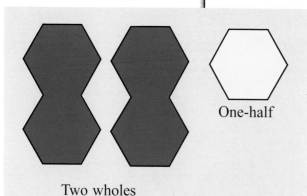

One-half

Two wholes

One-sixth

One-half

One-quarter

Example 1: How many halves in $2\frac{1}{2}$?

Solution: One yellow hexagon represents one half.

Five yellow hexagons are needed to cover $2\frac{1}{2}$.

There are 5 halves in $2\frac{1}{2}$.

$$2\frac{1}{2} = \frac{5}{2}$$

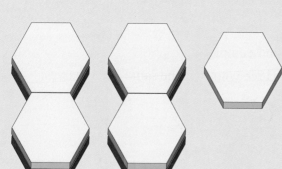

A number such as $3\frac{1}{2}$,

which is the sum of a whole number and a fraction, is called a **mixed number**

PUT INTO PRACTICE

1. a. How many quarters in $2\frac{1}{2}$?

   b. Draw the diagram.

   c. Copy and complete: $2\frac{1}{2} = \frac{?}{4}$

2. a. How many sixths in $2\frac{1}{2}$?

   b. Draw the diagram.

   c. Copy and complete: $2\frac{1}{2} = \frac{?}{6}$

Example 2:

One whole

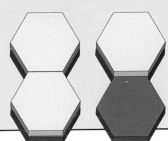

How many pink double hexagons can you cover with three yellow hexagons?
Draw a diagram.

Write $\frac{3}{2}$ as a mixed number.

Solution:
Three yellow hexagons can cover one and one half double hexagons.
One yellow hexagon represents one half.
Three yellow hexagons represent three halves.

$$\frac{3}{2} = 1\frac{1}{2}$$

3. a. How many wholes can seven red trapezoids cover?
        Copy and complete:

        One red trapezoid represents one □.

        So seven red trapezoids represent seven □.

        $$\frac{7}{4} = 1\frac{□}{□}$$

    b. Eight blue rhombi represent how many wholes?
        Copy and complete:

        One blue rhombus represents one □.

        So eight blues rhombi represent eight □.

        $$\frac{8}{6} = 1\frac{□}{□}$$

4. a. How many wholes can be represented by nine red trapezoids?
    b. How many wholes can be represented by 29 green triangles?

Example 3:

How many halves are in 3?

Solution:

One whole is two halves so three wholes is six halves.

$$\text{I.e., } 3 = \frac{(2 \times 3)}{2}$$

$$= \frac{6}{2}$$

Example 4:

Change each of the following mixed numbers to improper fractions.

a. $4\frac{1}{2}$

Solution:

$$4\frac{1}{2} = 4 + \frac{1}{2}$$

$$= \frac{(2 \times 4)}{2} + \frac{1}{2}$$

$$= \frac{8}{2} + \frac{1}{2}$$

$$= \frac{9}{2}$$

Change 4 wholes to halves.

b. $3\frac{1}{2}$

Solution:

$$3\frac{1}{2} = 3 + \frac{1}{2}$$

$$= \frac{(2 \times 3) + 1}{2}$$

$$= \frac{7}{2}$$

Change 3 wholes to halves.

6. Change each mixed number to an improper fraction.

   a. $2\frac{1}{4}$ b. $1\frac{1}{2}$ c. $3\frac{1}{5}$ d. $2\frac{1}{3}$ e. $2\frac{3}{8}$

7. a. How many quarters are in $2.50?

   b. How many quarters are in 3 football games?

   c. The school soccer team had shutouts for $2\frac{1}{2}$ games. How many halves was this?

8. a. Fold three identical square or rectangular pieces of paper into quarters.
   Keep two pieces and tear off one-quarter of the other piece.

   You now have $\frac{9}{4}$.

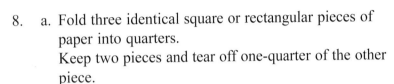

   b. How many wholes and how many quarters do you have?

   c. Write $\frac{9}{4}$ as a mixed number.

9. a. Fold two identical pieces of paper into eighths.
   Keep one piece and tear off five eighths of the other piece.

   You now have $\frac{13}{8}$.

   b. How many wholes do you have?

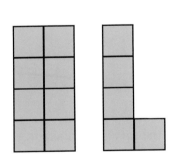

   c. How many extra eighths do you have?

   d. Write $\frac{13}{8}$ as a mixed number.

10. Change $\frac{5}{2}$ to a mixed number.

Here is another way to change improper fractions to whole or mixed numbers:

Example 5:

Change $\frac{8}{4}$ to a whole number.

Solution:

$\frac{8}{4}$ means $8 \div 4$.

$$4\overline{)8}^{2}$$

$$\frac{8}{4} = 2$$

Example 6:

Change $\frac{9}{4}$ to a mixed number.

Solution:

$\frac{9}{4}$ means $9 \div 4$.

2 times 4 with 1 left over

$$4\overline{)9}^{2}$$
$$\frac{8}{1}$$

$$\frac{9}{4} = 2\frac{1}{4}$$

11. Change the following improper fractions into mixed numbers:

    a. $\frac{7}{2}$ b. $\frac{4}{3}$ c. $\frac{8}{3}$ d. $\frac{11}{4}$ e. $\frac{23}{10}$

12. In the following examples change the mixed numbers to improper fractions and the improper fractions to mixed numbers:

    a. $1\frac{1}{2}$ b. $4\frac{2}{3}$ c. $2\frac{1}{4}$ d. $\frac{4}{3}$

    e. $\frac{9}{2}$ f. $\frac{11}{4}$ g. $2\frac{1}{8}$ h. $3\frac{7}{8}$

INTERACTIVE LESSONS

INVESTIGATION

WHICH FRACTIONS HAVE THE SAME VALUE?

1. Four friends are designing a poster for their rooms. They decide that each friend will be entitled to design one quarter of the poster.

   a. Fold a rectangular sheet of paper into four equal regions.
      Shade each quarter a different colour.
      Compare your strategy with your classmates.
      One friend suggests the posters could be made more interesting by dividing them in eighths or sixteenths with each member still being responsible for one quarter of the poster.

   b. Fold another rectangular sheet of paper into eighths.
      How will you allocate one quarter to each one of your friends?
      Colour each quarter a different colour.
      Compare your strategy with your partners.
      Are they the same or different?

      Compare $\frac{1}{4}$ with $\frac{2}{8}$. What do you notice?

   c. Fold another sheet of paper into sixteenths.
      How will you allocate one quarter to each of your friends?
      Colour each quarter a different colour
      Compare your strategy with your partners.

      Compare $\frac{1}{4}$ with $\frac{4}{16}$. What do you notice?

   d. What is the connection between $\frac{1}{4}$, $\frac{2}{8}$ and $\frac{4}{16}$?

   e. Write three more fractions with the same property.

Equivalent Fractions are two or more fractions that have different denominators but have the same value.

E.g., $\frac{1}{2} = \frac{25}{50}$

2. Let's see what happens when we fold a paper into thirds.

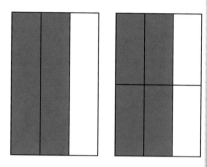

   a. Fold a piece of paper into thirds and shade two thirds.

   b. Fold the same piece into sixths by folding the other way.

   c. How many sixths are equal to $\dfrac{2}{3}$?

   d. Fold the paper into 12ths.

   e. How many twelfths are equal to $\dfrac{2}{3}$?

   f. What is the connection between $\dfrac{2}{3}$, $\dfrac{4}{6}$ and $\dfrac{8}{12}$?

   g. Write three more equivalent fractions.

In No.2 you changed from thirds to sixths by folding to double the total number of regions on the page.
This is the same as multiplying the denominator by 2.
But you can see that the number of shaded regions is also doubled.
This is the same as multiplying the numerator by 2.
If you multiply the denominator by 2 then you must also multiply the numerator by 2.

$$\text{I.e., } \frac{1}{3} = \frac{1 \times 2}{3 \times 2}$$

$$= \frac{2}{6}$$

To produce a fraction equivalent to a given fraction you can:

i) Multiply the numerator and the denominator by the same number.

$$\frac{12}{16}$$

$$=\frac{12\times2}{16\times2}$$

$$=\frac{24}{32}$$

ii) Divide the numerator and the denominator by the same number.

$$\frac{12}{16}$$

$$=\frac{12\div4}{16\div4}$$

$$=\frac{3}{4}$$

Get Thinking

What have the denominator and numerator been multiplied by to give the new fraction?

Example 1:
Ms Bell was looking at an old dress pattern which called for two thirds of a foot of ribbon for each cuff.
How many inches of ribbon will she need for each cuff?
(Ms Bell knows there are 12 inches in 1 foot).

Solution:

Change: $\frac{2}{3}$ to twelfths

To change 3 to 12 we can multiply by 4 because $3\overline{)12}^{\,4}$.

If we multiply 3 by 4 we must also multiply 2 by 4.

$$\frac{2}{3}=\frac{2\times4}{3\times4}$$

$$=\frac{8}{12}$$

Mrs Bell requires 8 inches of ribbon for each cuff.

PUT INTO PRACTICE

1. Write three equivalent fractions for each of the following:

   a. $\frac{3}{5}$ b. $\frac{5}{8}$ c. $\frac{5}{10}$

2. Calculate the value of ?.

   a. $\frac{4}{5}=\frac{?}{100}$ b. $\frac{5}{4}=\frac{?}{100}$ c. $\frac{2}{3}=\frac{?}{15}$

   d. $\frac{3}{8}=\frac{?}{16}$ e. $\frac{3}{4}=\frac{?}{16}$ f. $\frac{2}{3}=\frac{12}{?}$

When a fraction is in **simplest form** there is no natural number that will divide into both the numerator and denominator.

If we want to write $\dfrac{8}{12}$ in its **simplest form** we can divide the numerator and denominator by 4.

$$\text{I.e.} \quad \frac{8}{12} = \frac{8 \div 4}{12 \div 4}$$

$$= \frac{2}{3}$$

Get Thinking

What numbers will divide into 75 and 100?

Example 2:

Write each fraction in its simplest form.

a. $\dfrac{75}{100}$

Solution:

$$\frac{75}{100} = \frac{75 \div 25}{100 \div 25} \qquad 25\overline{)75}^{\,3}, \quad 25\overline{)100}^{\,4}$$

$$= \frac{3}{4} \qquad \textit{25 will divide evenly into both 75 and 100}$$

b. $\dfrac{10}{15}$

Solution:

$$\frac{10}{15} = \frac{10 \div 5}{15 \div 5} \quad \textit{Divide the numerator and denominator by 5.}$$

$$= \frac{2}{3}$$

c. $\dfrac{4}{8}$

Solution:

$$\dfrac{4}{8} = \dfrac{4 \div 4}{8 \div 4} \quad \textit{Divide the numerator and denominatr by 4.}$$

$$= \dfrac{1}{2}$$

3. a. Write the simplest form of each fraction.

i. $\dfrac{9}{72}$ ii. $\dfrac{3}{24}$ iii. $\dfrac{70}{100}$ iv. $\dfrac{14}{16}$ v. $\dfrac{12}{16}$ vi. $\dfrac{6}{8}$

b. Which pairs of fractions are equivalent?
Explain your answers.

4. Explain how to change a fraction into its simplest form.

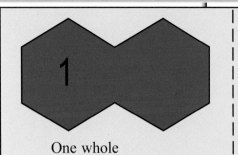

1

One whole

hexagon

rhombus

triangle

trapezoid

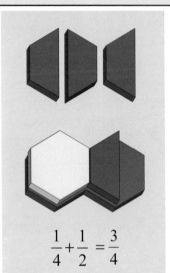

$$\frac{1}{4}+\frac{1}{2}=\frac{3}{4}$$

represents $\frac{1}{6}$

INVESTIGATION

1. a. Pick one block that represents $\frac{1}{4}$ of the whole.

    Pick two blocks that represent $\frac{2}{4}$ of the whole.

    Show $\frac{1}{4}+\frac{2}{4}$.

    b. What is the sum of $\frac{1}{4}+\frac{2}{4}$?

    c. What is the sum of $\frac{1}{4}+\frac{1}{2}$?

2. a. Model $\frac{4}{6}+\frac{1}{6}$.

    b. Calculate answers for:

    $\frac{4}{6}+\frac{1}{6}$ and

    $\frac{2}{3}+\frac{1}{6}$.

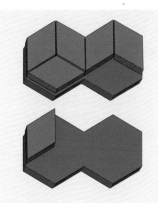

3. a. Show $\dfrac{5}{6}$. b. Take away $\dfrac{4}{6}$.

    How many rhombi would be left?

    c. Copy and complete:

    i. $\dfrac{5}{6} - \dfrac{4}{6} = \dfrac{\square}{6}$ ii. $\dfrac{5}{6} - \dfrac{2}{3} = \dfrac{\square}{\square}$

PUT INTO PRACTICE

Always give answers in simplest form

INTERACTIVE ⊙ **LESSONS**

1. Calculate:

    a. $\dfrac{8}{12} - \dfrac{5}{12}$ b. $\dfrac{2}{3} - \dfrac{5}{12}$

2. Evaluate:

    a. $\dfrac{1}{3} + \dfrac{1}{3}$ b. $\dfrac{1}{5} + \dfrac{2}{5}$

    c. $\dfrac{3}{10} + \dfrac{1}{10} + \dfrac{3}{10}$ d. $\dfrac{3}{100} + \dfrac{1}{100} + \dfrac{7}{100}$

    e. $\dfrac{4}{5} - \dfrac{1}{5}$ f. $\dfrac{14}{5} - \dfrac{10}{5}$

    g. $\dfrac{15}{5} - \dfrac{10}{5}$ h. $\dfrac{9}{10} + \dfrac{1}{10} - \dfrac{7}{10}$

3. Evaluate:

    a. $\dfrac{2}{3} + \dfrac{1}{6}$ b. $\dfrac{7}{10} - \dfrac{3}{5}$ c. $\dfrac{7}{12} - \dfrac{1}{3}$ d. $\dfrac{5}{6} + \dfrac{1}{2}$

4. Discuss the following with your partner then write a rule.
    a. When you **add** fractions with the **same denominator:**
        i. what happens to the numerators?
        ii. what happens to the denominators?

    b. When you **subtract** fractions with the **same denominator:**
        i. what happens to the numerators?
        ii. what happens to the denominators?

ADDING AND SUBTRACTING FRACTIONS WITH DIFFERENT DENOMINATORS

If you don't have a black chevron, you can use two blue rhombi instead.

$$\frac{1}{4} \quad + \quad \frac{1}{3}$$

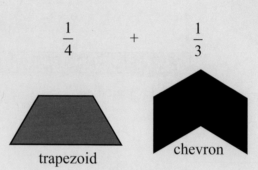

trapezoid   chevron

If we want to add these fractions it is easier if we represent both fractions using the same shape.

The red trapezoid can be replaced by __.   I.e., $\frac{1}{4} = \frac{\square}{12}$.

The black chevron can be replaced by __.   I.e., $\frac{1}{3} = \frac{4}{\square}$.

$$\frac{1}{4} + \frac{1}{3} = \frac{3}{12} + \frac{4}{12}$$

$$= \frac{\square}{12}$$

This is the same as writing $\frac{1}{4}$ and $\frac{1}{3}$ as equivalent fractions with denominator 12.

$$\frac{1}{4} + \frac{1}{3} = \frac{1\times3}{4\times3} + \frac{1\times4}{3\times4}$$

Change both fractions to twelfths.

$$= \frac{3}{12} + \frac{4}{12}$$

$$= \frac{7}{12}$$

Example 1:

Laly plans to bake muffins.

She decides to combine two favourite recipes to make a large batch of muffins.

One recipe calls for three quarters of a cup of nuts and the other for five sixths of a cup.

How many cups of nuts does Laly need for her recipe?

Solution:

Add $\dfrac{3}{4}$ and $\dfrac{5}{6}$

$\dfrac{3}{4} + \dfrac{5}{6}$ *Convert to the same denominator.*
Determine a common multiple of 4 and 6. It is 12.

$= \dfrac{3 \times 3}{4 \times 3} + \dfrac{5 \times 2}{6 \times 2}$ *Since 4 × 3 = 12, we multiply $\dfrac{3}{4}$ by $\dfrac{3}{3}$*

Since 6 × 2 = 12, we multiply $\dfrac{5}{6}$ by $\dfrac{2}{2}$

$= \dfrac{9}{12} + \dfrac{10}{12}$ *Add the fractions.*

$= \dfrac{19}{12}$ *Change to a mixed number.*

$= 1\dfrac{7}{12}$

Laly needs $1\dfrac{7}{12}$ cups of nuts.

Example 2: Subtract $\dfrac{5}{12} - \dfrac{1}{6}$

Solution:

$\dfrac{5}{12} - \dfrac{1}{6}$ *Convert to the same denominator.*
                 Determine a common multiple of 6 and 12. It is 12.

$= \dfrac{5}{12} - \dfrac{2}{12}$ *Since 6 × 2 = 12, we multiply $\dfrac{1}{6}$ by $\dfrac{2}{2}$*
                 Subtract the fractions.

$= \dfrac{3}{12}$

$= \dfrac{1}{4}$ *Change to simplest form by dividing numerator and denominator by 3.*

Example 3: Subtract $3\dfrac{1}{5} - 2\dfrac{1}{6}$

Solution: $3\dfrac{1}{5} - 2\dfrac{1}{6}$ *Change to improper fractions.*

$= \dfrac{(5\times3)+1}{5} - \dfrac{(6\times2)+1}{6}$

$= \dfrac{16}{5} - \dfrac{13}{6}$ *Convert to the same denominator, 30.*

$= \dfrac{16\times6}{5\times6} - \dfrac{13\times5}{6\times5}$ *Since 5 × 6 = 30, we multiply $\dfrac{16}{5}$ by $\dfrac{6}{6}$*
                 Since 5 × 6 = 30, we multiply $\dfrac{13}{6}$ by $\dfrac{5}{5}$

$= \dfrac{96}{30} - \dfrac{65}{30}$ *Subtract the fractions.*

$= \dfrac{31}{30}$ *Change to a mixed number.*

$= 1\dfrac{1}{30}$

5. Evaluate:

     a. $\dfrac{1}{3} + \dfrac{1}{6}$ b. $\dfrac{3}{8} + \dfrac{1}{2}$ c. $1\dfrac{3}{4} + 2\dfrac{1}{8}$ d. $\dfrac{3}{10} + \dfrac{7}{100}$

     e. $\dfrac{3}{10} - \dfrac{7}{100}$ f. $\dfrac{1}{3} - \dfrac{1}{6}$ g. $1\dfrac{5}{8} - \dfrac{1}{2}$ h. $2\dfrac{3}{4} - 1\dfrac{1}{8}$

     i. $\dfrac{5}{6} + \dfrac{5}{12}$ j. $\dfrac{5}{6} - \dfrac{5}{12}$ k. $2\dfrac{1}{3} - 1\dfrac{5}{6}$ l. $2\dfrac{1}{3} + 1\dfrac{5}{6}$

6. Evaluate:

     a. $\dfrac{2}{3} + \dfrac{1}{2}$ b. $1\dfrac{2}{5} + \dfrac{1}{2}$ c. $2\dfrac{2}{3} + 1\dfrac{1}{4}$

     d. $\dfrac{2}{3} - \dfrac{1}{2}$ e. $1\dfrac{2}{5} - \dfrac{1}{2}$ f. $2\dfrac{2}{3} - 1\dfrac{1}{4}$

7. Debra has three friends coming over to study for the exams.
   She estimates it will take her three quarters of an hour to shop for snacks and pop and three quarters of an hour to tidy her room.

   How long will it take her to prepare before her friends arrive?

8. Denver estimates it will take him one and three quarter hours to tune up his car, one third of an hour to wash it, and one and one quarter hours to polish it.

   How long will Denver spend working on his car?

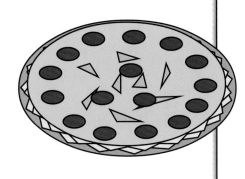

9. Darlene sold pizza to help raise money to buy a new TV for the local shelter.

   Dave asked for $\frac{1}{2}$ a pizza.

   Jeanette wanted $\frac{1}{6}$ of a pizza.

   Andrew asked for $\frac{1}{4}$ of a pizza.

   Suni ordered $\frac{5}{12}$ of a pizza.

   How many pizzas were needed for their orders?

10. The Somerville children are all learning to play the piano and have to take turns practicing on the family piano.

    Sara played for $\frac{1}{4}$ hour.

    Jacques practised for $\frac{1}{3}$ hour.

    Lily played for $\frac{1}{3}$ hour.

    Franklin played for half an hour.

    How many hours was the piano used in total?

11. Four students were hired to help decorate an apartment. Their fee was $230.
    Jean kept track of the number of hours worked by each person.

    Alan worked $7\frac{1}{2}$ hours, Karla worked $4\frac{1}{2}$ hours,

    Abie worked $1\frac{1}{2}$ hours and Jean worked for $9\frac{1}{2}$ hours.

    What was the total number of hours spent working on the apartment?

INVESTIGATION

HOW CAN YOU CALCULATE A FRACTION OF SOMETHING?

Jennifer decides to create a notice board for her bedroom. She decides that one quarter of the board will be used for pictures and three quarters for information.

Half of the information section will be for appointments and half for information on social activities.

1. Make an 8-square by 4-square poster on graph paper.

Shade $\dfrac{3}{4}$ of it to represent the area for information.

Shade $\dfrac{1}{2}$ of the shaded part in a second colour to represent the area for appointments.

What fraction of the board is shaded in two colours?

You have shaded $\dfrac{1}{2}$ of $\dfrac{3}{4}$.

$$\dfrac{1}{2} \text{ of } \dfrac{3}{4} = \boxed{}?$$

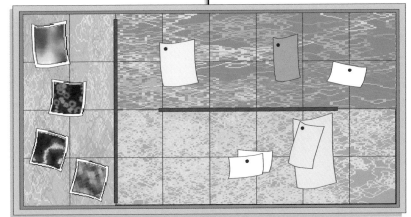

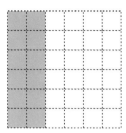

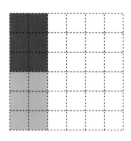

2. a. On graph paper draw a 6 by 6 square and shade

    $\dfrac{1}{2}$ of $\dfrac{1}{3}$.

    Copy and complete: $\dfrac{1}{2}$ of $\dfrac{1}{3} = \dfrac{\square}{\square}$

    b. i. What do you notice about the numerator of your answer?
        ii. What do you notice about the denominator of your answer?

    c. $\dfrac{1}{2}$ of $\dfrac{1}{3}$ means $\dfrac{1}{2} \times \dfrac{1}{3}$.

    $$\dfrac{1}{2} \times \dfrac{1}{3} = \dfrac{\square}{\square}$$

    d. $\dfrac{1 \times 1}{2 \times 3} = \dfrac{\square}{\square}$

3. a. On graph paper draw a 4 by 10 rectangle and shade

    $\dfrac{1}{2}$ of $\dfrac{3}{5}$.

    Copy and complete: $\dfrac{1}{2}$ of $\dfrac{3}{5} = \dfrac{\square}{\square}$

    b. i. What do you notice about the numerator of your answer?
        ii. What do you notice about the denominator of your answer?

    c. $\dfrac{1}{2}$ of $\dfrac{3}{5}$ means $\dfrac{\square}{\square} \times \dfrac{\square}{\square}$.

    $$\dfrac{1}{2} \times \dfrac{3}{5} = \dfrac{\square}{\square}$$

    d. $\dfrac{1 \times \square}{2 \times \square} = \dfrac{\square}{\square}$

4. a. On graph paper draw a 5 by 8 rectangle and shade $\frac{1}{3}$ of $\frac{3}{4}$.

   Copy and complete: $\frac{1}{3}$ of $\frac{3}{4} = \frac{\square}{\square}$

   b. $\frac{1}{3}$ of $\frac{3}{4}$ means $\frac{\square}{\square}$

   $\frac{1}{3} \times \frac{3}{4} = \frac{\square}{\square}$

   c. $\frac{1 \times \square}{3 \times \square} = \frac{\square}{\square}$

   d. Compare your answers to a, b and c.

5. Write a clear explanation of how to multiply fractions for a friend who was absent today.

To multiply fractions we multiply the numerators together and multiply the denominators together.

1. After decorating his room Peter was left with four fifths of a roll of wallpaper.
He decided to use half of it to line the shelves in his closet.
What fraction of the roll of paper was left?
Copy and complete the solution.

Calculate $\dfrac{1}{2}$ of $\dfrac{4}{5}$.

$$\frac{1}{2} \text{ of } \frac{4}{5} = \frac{1}{2} \times \frac{4}{5}$$

$$= \frac{1 \times 4}{2 \times 5}$$

$$= \frac{4}{10}$$

$$= \frac{4 \div \square}{10 \div \square}$$

$$= \frac{2}{5}$$

Peter is left with $\square$ of a roll of paper.

2. Evaluate: $\dfrac{5}{8} \times \dfrac{16}{25}$.

Copy and complete the solution.

$$\frac{5}{8} \times \frac{16}{25} = \frac{5 \times \square}{8 \times 25}$$

It is easier to reduce before multiplying.

$$= \frac{(5 \div 5) \times (16 \div \square)}{(8 \div \square) \times (25 \div 5)}$$

$$= \frac{1 \times 2}{1 \times 5}$$

$$= \frac{\square}{\square}.$$

Both 5 and 25 can be divided by 5.
Both 16 and 8 can be divided by $\square$.

3. Evaluate:

a. $\dfrac{1}{2} \times \dfrac{1}{8}$ b. $\dfrac{1}{4} \times \dfrac{1}{3}$ c. $\dfrac{1}{3} \times \dfrac{1}{4}$ d. $\dfrac{2}{3} \times \dfrac{1}{4}$ e. $\dfrac{2}{3} \times \dfrac{3}{4}$

4. a. Evaluate: $\dfrac{1}{2} \times \dfrac{2}{3} \times \dfrac{3}{4} \times \dfrac{4}{5} \times \dfrac{5}{6} \times \dfrac{6}{7}$

   b. Explain how you obtained your answer.

   c. Create a similar question with an answer of:

   i. $\dfrac{1}{9}$ ii. $\dfrac{2}{11}$

To multiply with **mixed numbers**, **change the mixed numbers to fractions** and then multiply.

Example 1:

Ms Quann estimates she needs two and one third yards of material to make a bedspread for her bed.
If the material is on sale at $2.25 per yard how much will the material cost (before tax)?

Solution:

Multiply $2\dfrac{1}{4}$ by $2\dfrac{1}{3}$

$2\dfrac{1}{4} \times 2\dfrac{1}{3}$ *Change to improper fractions.*

$= \dfrac{9}{4} \times \dfrac{7}{3}$ *Multiply numerators and denominators.*

$= \dfrac{\overset{3}{\cancel{9}} \times 7}{4 \times \underset{1}{\cancel{3}}}$ *Divide 9 by 3 and divide 3 by 3.*

$= \dfrac{3 \times 7}{4 \times 1}$

$= \dfrac{21}{4}$ *Change to a mixed number.*

$= 5\dfrac{1}{4}$

It will cost Ms Quann $5.25 plus tax for the material.

> $2.25 is $2\dfrac{1}{4}$

> $5\dfrac{1}{4} = \$5.25$

5. Evaluate:

   a. $1\frac{2}{5} \times 2\frac{1}{2}$ b. $1\frac{1}{3} \times 2\frac{1}{4}$ c. $2\frac{1}{10} \times 1\frac{2}{3}$

   d. 1.4×2.5 e. $2\frac{1}{3} \times 1\frac{1}{4}$ f. $1\frac{1}{10} \times 2\frac{1}{3}$

6. Felipe plans to make a large batch of chocolate chip cookies for his daughter's birthday party.
He estimates he has enough flour to make four and one half times the quantity given in the recipe.

If the original recipe requires one and one third cups of chocolate chips, how many cups of chocolate chips will Felipe require for his new recipe?

7. A town held a referendum to approve or reject a new subdivision.
Only one-half of the people voted.
Two-thirds of those who voted approved of the subdivision.

What fraction of the people voted for the subdivision?

8. Zachary used $10\frac{1}{2}$ bags of potting soil for his flowers.

Rachel has $1\frac{2}{3}$ times as many flowers.

How many bags of potting soil should she buy?

$\dfrac{4}{3}$ means there are four " $\dfrac{1}{3}$'s".

INTERACTIVE LESSONS

Remember that $1\dfrac{1}{3} = \dfrac{4}{3}$.

How many 3's in 12?

There are 4. $\qquad$ $12 \div 3 = 4$.

How many quarters are in \$5?

There are 20. $\qquad$ $5 \div \dfrac{1}{4} = 20$.

How many $\dfrac{1}{3}$'s are in $\dfrac{4}{3}$?

There are 4. $\qquad$ $\dfrac{4}{3} \div \dfrac{1}{3} = 4$.

How many $\dfrac{1}{3}$'s are in $1\dfrac{1}{3}$?

Since $\dfrac{4}{3} \div \dfrac{1}{3} = 4$ then $1\dfrac{1}{3} \div \dfrac{1}{3} = 4$.

PUT INTO PRACTICE

1. a. i. How many $\dfrac{1}{3}$'s are in $\dfrac{2}{3}$?

   ii. State the value of $\dfrac{2}{3} \div \dfrac{1}{3}$.

   b. i. How many $\dfrac{1}{2}$'s are in 3?

   ii. State the value of $3 \div \dfrac{1}{2}$.

   c. i. How many $\dfrac{1}{5}$'s are in $\dfrac{8}{5}$?

   ii. State the value of $\dfrac{8}{5} \div \dfrac{1}{5}$.

2. Ms Davis plans to make new tablemats for her dining table.
   She has two and a half yards of material and estimates she needs half a yard for each mat.

   How many mats can she make?

   Each mat requires $\frac{1}{2}$ yd of material.

   Think: $2\frac{1}{2} \div \frac{1}{2}$.

Hint:

15 min = $\frac{\square}{\square}$ hour

Hint:

"How many $\frac{1}{4}$ hours

are in $\frac{3}{2}$ hours?"

$\frac{3}{2} = \frac{3 \times 2}{2 \times 2}$

$\quad = \frac{6}{4}$

3. Isobel and her friends were watching a charity show on TV.
   The show lasted for an hour and a half and each act was on stage for 15 minutes.

   How many acts were there in the show?

   Think: $1\frac{1}{2} \div \frac{1}{4}$.

4. A TV commercial lasts for $\frac{1}{3}$ minute.

   How many commercials can be shown in a 3-minute commercial break?

   Think: $3 \div \frac{1}{3}$.

DIVISION WITH A NUMERATOR OF 1

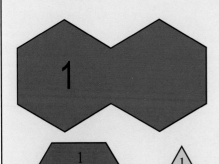

How many red trapezoids are required to cover the pink double hexagon?

How many $\frac{1}{4}$'s are in 1 whole?

$1 \div \square = \square$.

All three questions are equivalent.

The three answers are the same.

$1 \div \frac{1}{4} = \dfrac{\square}{\square}$

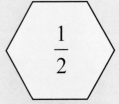

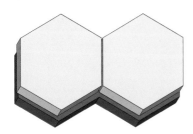

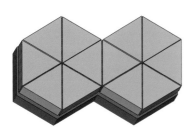

1. a. How many yellow hexagons are required to cover the pink double hexagon?

    How many $\frac{1}{2}$'s are in 1?

    Copy and complete: $1 \div \frac{1}{2} = \dfrac{\square}{\square}$

    b. How many blue rhombi are required to cover the pink double hexagon?

    How many $\frac{1}{6}$'s are in 1?

    Copy and complete: $1 \div \frac{1}{6} = \dfrac{\square}{\square}$

    c. How many green triangles are required to cover the pink double hexagon?

    How many $\frac{1}{12}$'s are in 1?

    Copy and complete: $1 \div \frac{1}{12} = \dfrac{\square}{\square}$

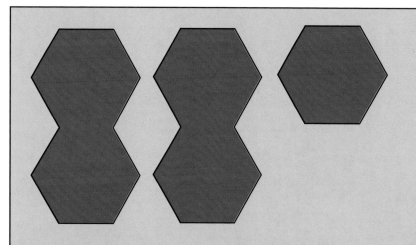

2. How many $\frac{1}{6}$'s are in $2\frac{1}{2}$?

   What shape represents $\frac{1}{6}$?

   How many of that shape do you need to cover one whole?

   How many do you need to cover $2\frac{1}{2}$?

   $2\frac{1}{2} \div \frac{1}{6} \qquad = \frac{5}{2} \div \frac{1}{6}$

   $\qquad\qquad\quad = \dfrac{\square}{\square}$

PUT INTO PRACTICE... continued

5. How many $\frac{1}{4}$'s are in $2\frac{1}{2}$?

6. How many $\frac{1}{2}$'s are in $2\frac{1}{2}$?

7. How many $\frac{1}{12}$'s are in $2\frac{1}{2}$?

DIVISORS WITH A NUMERATOR GREATER THAN 1

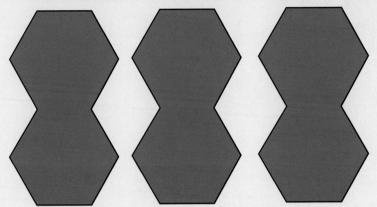

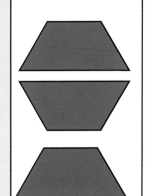

How many $\frac{3}{4}$'s are in 3?

What can you use to represent $\frac{3}{4}$?

How many sets of 3 red trapezoids will cover the 3 double hexagons?
Draw a diagram.

There are ☐ $\frac{3}{4}$'s in 3.

$3 \div \frac{3}{4} = \dfrac{\square}{\square}$

PUT INTO PRACTICE... continued

Hint:
How many blue rhombi in $\frac{5}{6}$?
How many blue rhombi in 5?

8. How many $\frac{5}{6}$'s are in 5?

9. How many $\frac{3}{4}$'s are in $1\frac{1}{2}$?

10. How many $\frac{5}{12}$'s are in $1\frac{1}{4}$?

DIVIDING FRACTIONS

Now let's look for patterns.

Here are some of the results of what you have done.

$$1 \div \frac{1}{6} = 6, \qquad 5 \div \frac{5}{6} = 6, \qquad 2\frac{1}{2} \div \frac{1}{6} = 15, \qquad 1\frac{1}{4} \div \frac{5}{12} = 3.$$

We know that division and multiplication are related to each other.

If we know that $4 \times 3 = 12$ then we know that $12 \div 4 = 3$.

In the table below you will see these four questions and a corresponding multiplication question that gives the same answer.

Division	Corresponding Multiplication	
$1 \div \dfrac{1}{6} = 6$	$1 \times \dfrac{6}{1} = \dfrac{6}{1} = 6$	
$5 \div \dfrac{5}{6} = 6$	$5 \times \dfrac{6}{5} = \dfrac{30}{5} = 6$	
$2\dfrac{1}{2} \div \dfrac{1}{6} = \dfrac{5}{2} \div \dfrac{1}{6} = 15$	$\dfrac{5}{2_1} \times \dfrac{6^3}{1} = \dfrac{15}{1} = 15$	*Divide both 6 and 2 by 2.*
$1\dfrac{1}{4} \div \dfrac{5}{12} = \dfrac{5}{4} \div \dfrac{5}{12} = 3$	$\dfrac{5^1}{4_1} \times \dfrac{12^3}{5_1} = \dfrac{3}{1} = 3$	*Divide both 5's by 5 and divide both 12 and 4 by 4.*

Develop a simple method for dividing by a fraction and discuss this with a partner.

Example 1: Evaluate: $\dfrac{1}{2} \div \dfrac{3}{8}$

Solution:

$\dfrac{1}{2} \div \dfrac{3}{8}$ *This is equivalent to $\dfrac{1}{2} \times \dfrac{8}{3}$.*

$= \dfrac{1}{2_1} \times \dfrac{8^4}{3}$ *Divide both 2 and 8 by 2.*

$= \dfrac{4}{3}$ *Change to a mixed number.*

$= 1\dfrac{1}{3}$

Example 2:

Evaluate: $1\frac{2}{3} \div 4\frac{1}{6}$.

Solution:

$1\frac{2}{3} \div 4\frac{1}{6}$ *Change the mixed numbers to fractions.*

$= \frac{5}{3} \div \frac{25}{6}$ *This is equivalent to $\frac{5}{3} \times \frac{6}{25}$.*

$= \frac{5^1}{3_1} \times \frac{6^2}{25_5}$ *Divide both 5 and 25 by 5.*
    Divide both 3 and 6 by 3.

$= \frac{1 \times 2}{1 \times 5}$

$= \frac{2}{5}$

PUT INTO PRACTICE... *continued*

11. Explain how you would divide $\frac{3}{4}$ by $\frac{1}{3}$.

    Draw a diagram to illustrate your strategy and solution.

12. Evaluate:

    a. $\frac{1}{3} \div \frac{1}{2}$ b. $\frac{1}{2} \div \frac{1}{3}$ c. $\frac{2}{3} \div \frac{1}{2}$ d. $1\frac{1}{5} \div 1\frac{1}{2}$

    e. $3\frac{1}{3} \div 1\frac{1}{4}$ f. $4\frac{2}{3} \div 1\frac{1}{6}$ g. $\frac{3}{4} \div \frac{1}{2}$ h. $\frac{5}{6} \div \frac{1}{4}$

    i. $3\frac{1}{2} \div 1\frac{2}{3}$ j. $\frac{1}{10} \div \frac{1}{100}$ k. $0.1 \div 0.01$

    l. $\frac{3}{10} \div \frac{5}{1000}$ m. $0.3 \div 0.005$ n. $0.75 \div 0.5$

13. Which questions have the same solutions?
    Explain why.

MEASUREMENT - LINEAR MEASURE

In this section you will:

Use Imperial and metric rulers, tapes, scales and containers.

Develop some useful references for everyday units of measure.

Convert between Imperial and metric units.

Use your measurement knowledge in perimeter, area and volume activities.

USING AN IMPERIAL RULER

INVESTIGATION

Here is a 6"ruler.

It is marked every $\frac{1}{4}$".

The first mark on the ruler is at the $\frac{1}{4}$" mark.

The second mark is at the $\frac{1}{2}$" mark and the third mark is at the $\frac{3}{4}$" mark.

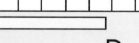

A is at the end of the ruler and B is at the $1\frac{1}{2}$" mark.

$AB = 1\frac{1}{2}$".

D is closer to the $\frac{3}{4}$" mark than it is to the $\frac{1}{2}$" mark.

CD is about $5\frac{3}{4}$".

1. Use the ruler above to measure, correct to the nearest $\frac{1}{4}$":
   a. the width of your calculator
   b. the width of your little finger
   c. the width of your thumb
   d. the width of two fingers together
   e. the length of your little finger
   Compare your results with those of your partner.

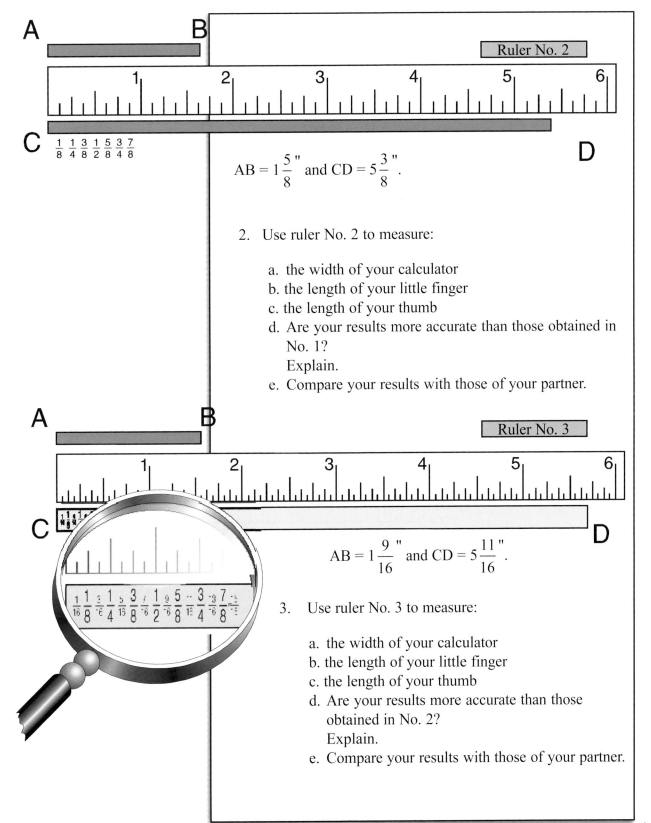

Ruler No. 2

$$AB = 1\frac{5}{8}" \text{ and } CD = 5\frac{3}{8}".$$

2. Use ruler No. 2 to measure:

   a. the width of your calculator
   b. the length of your little finger
   c. the length of your thumb
   d. Are your results more accurate than those obtained in No. 1?
      Explain.
   e. Compare your results with those of your partner.

Ruler No. 3

$$AB = 1\frac{9}{16}" \text{ and } CD = 5\frac{11}{16}".$$

3. Use ruler No. 3 to measure:

   a. the width of your calculator
   b. the length of your little finger
   c. the length of your thumb
   d. Are your results more accurate than those obtained in No. 2?
      Explain.
   e. Compare your results with those of your partner.

1. Estimate each of the following to the nearest inch:
   a. the length of your foot
   b. the width of your fist
   c. your handspan

2. Use a ruler or measuring tape to measure to the nearest inch:
   a. the length of your foot
   b. the width of your fist
   c. your handspan

3. Compare your answers for No. 1 and No. 2.
   Were your answers reasonably close?
   If they were not close can you explain how this happened?

4. What is the length of each line segment shown below?

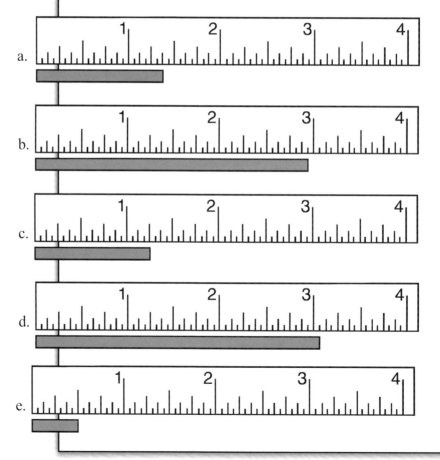

In the Imperial system we often measure length in feet and inches.
There are 12 inches in 1 foot.
This is normally written as: 12" = 1' or 12 in = 1 ft.

Example 1:

How would you write the width of this doorway in feet and inches?
What is the width in inches?

Solution:
The width is 6" past the 2' mark.
We can say that the width is 2' 6".
1' = 12",　　2' = 24"
2' 6" = 24" + 6"
　　　= 30"
The width is 30".

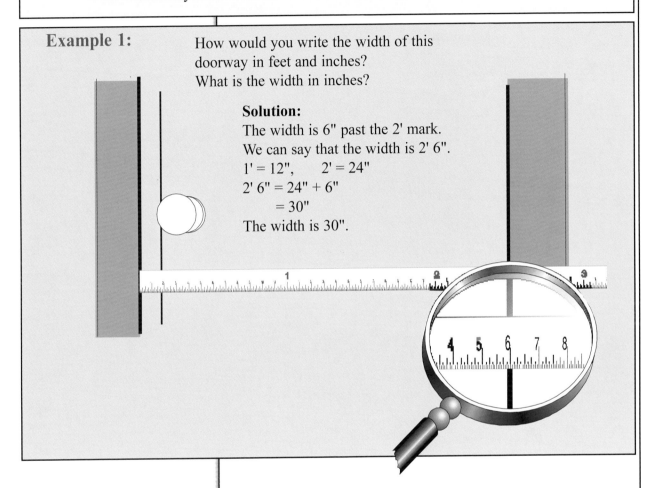

5. a. How many inches in 3 feet?

b. How many inches in 1' 8"?

c. How many inches in $2\frac{1}{4}$ ft?

6. a. How many feet in 60 inches?

    b. How many feet and inches in 80 inches?

    c. How many feet in 52"?

7. Estimate, in feet and inches:

    a. the height of the door

    b. the height of your partner

    c. the width of a window

    d. the width of your classroom

    e. the length of your stride

8. Use a tape to measure, in feet and inches:

    a. the height of the door

    b. the height of your partner

    c. the width of a window

    d. the width of your classroom

    e. the length of your stride

9. What businesses or services use Imperial measures?

    What businesses or services use metric measures?

Imperial measures can be added or subtracted using a number line or an Imperial ruler.

Example 1:

a. Evaluate $\dfrac{1}{4} + \dfrac{1}{2}$ using an Imperial ruler.

Solution:

Note that you can show $\dfrac{1}{2}$ on a ruler in many ways.

It can be the distance from 0 to $\dfrac{1}{2}$, or the distance from $2\dfrac{1}{2}$ to 3, or the distance

from $\dfrac{3}{4}$ to $1\dfrac{1}{4}$, etc.

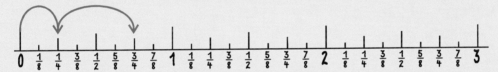

Start at 0 and move $\dfrac{1}{4}$ to the right. Then move $\dfrac{1}{2}$ to the **right**.

$$\dfrac{1}{4} + \dfrac{1}{2} = \dfrac{3}{4}.$$

b. Evaluate $\dfrac{3}{8} - \dfrac{1}{4}$ on an Imperial ruler.

Solution:

Start at 0 and move $\dfrac{3}{8}$ to the right. Then move $\dfrac{1}{4}$ to the **left**.

$$\dfrac{3}{8} - \dfrac{1}{4} = \dfrac{1}{8}$$ *Notice* $\dfrac{1}{4} = \dfrac{2}{8}$ *so we move 2 spaces to the left.*

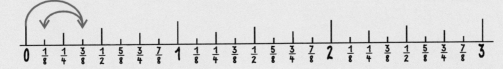

Example 2:

Justin is reorganizing the furniture in his room.
His bookcase measures 2'8" and his desk measures 3'6".
If he places them side by side how much space will they require?

Solution:

The bookcase measures $2'8" = 2\dfrac{8}{12}' = 2\dfrac{2}{3}'$.

The desk measures $3'6" = 3\dfrac{6}{12}' = 3\dfrac{1}{2}'$.

Together they require $(2\dfrac{2}{3} + 3\dfrac{1}{2})$ feet.

$$2\frac{2}{3} + 3\frac{1}{2} = \frac{(3\times 2)+2}{3} + \frac{(3\times 2)+1}{2} \qquad \textit{Change to improper fractions.}$$

$$= \frac{8}{3} + \frac{7}{2} \qquad \textit{Convert to the same denominator, 6.}$$

$$= \frac{8\times 2}{3\times 2} + \frac{7\times 3}{2\times 3} \qquad \textit{Multiply 8 and 3 by 2. Multiply 7 and 2 by 3.}$$

$$= \frac{16}{6} + \frac{21}{6} \qquad \textit{Add numerators.}$$

$$= \frac{37}{6} \qquad \textit{Change to a mixed number.}$$

$$= 6\frac{1}{6}$$

The bookcase and desk require $6\dfrac{1}{6}'$ or 6'2".

$$\frac{1}{6} = \frac{2}{12}$$

Example 3:

Justin's room is 10'4" long.
He would like to build a closet that is 4'10" wide.
How much space would be left on that wall?

Solution:

The room measures 10'4" which is $10\frac{4}{12}' = 10\frac{1}{3}'$

The closet measures 4'10" which is $4\frac{10}{12}' = 4\frac{5}{6}'$

$$10\frac{1}{3} - 4\frac{5}{6} = \frac{31}{3} - \frac{29}{6} \qquad \text{\textit{Convert to improper fractions.}}$$

$$= \frac{62}{6} - \frac{29}{6} \qquad \text{\textit{Convert to the same denominator, 6.}}$$

$$= \frac{33}{6} \qquad \text{\textit{Subtract numerators.}}$$

$$= \frac{11}{2} \qquad \text{\textit{Divide numerator and denominator by 3.}}$$

$$= 5\frac{1}{2} \qquad \text{\textit{Convert to a mixed number.}}$$

There is $5\frac{1}{2}$ ft or 5'6" of wall space left.

PUT INTO PRACTICE

1. Complete the following additions and subtractions using a number line or an Imperial ruler.

   a. $\frac{3}{8} + \frac{1}{2}$ b. $\frac{3}{4} + \frac{1}{8}$ c. $\frac{5}{8} - \frac{1}{2}$ d. $\frac{3}{4} - \frac{1}{8}$

2. Evaluate:

   a. $1\dfrac{1}{4}" + 2\dfrac{5}{8}"$ b. $2\dfrac{5}{8}" - 1\dfrac{11}{16}"$

   c. $2\dfrac{5}{6}' + 1\dfrac{3}{4}'$ d. $2\dfrac{5}{6}' - 1\dfrac{3}{4}'$

3. Estelle has a bookcase that is 2'6" long, a dressing table that is 3'4" long, and a desk that is 2'9" long.

   Can she place them side-by-side on a wall measuring 9'6"?

4. The closet in Shane's room is 5'10" wide.
   If the wall measures 10'4" how much wall space is there beside the closet?

5. In her training program Jen jogged for two and a quarter miles, walked for one and a third miles, then ran for one and a half miles.
   Derek, in his program jogged for one and two thirds miles, walked for one and a quarter miles and ran for one and a half miles.

   Who covered the greater distance in training?
   How much further?

Example 1:

What is the length of each line segment?

1 cm = 10 mm
The same ruler
could have been
marked 10 (mm),
20 (mm), 30 (mm),
… instead of 1 (cm),
2 (cm), 3 (cm),…
This means that
each mark between
the numbers
represents 1 mm.
The answer to
Example 1a can also
be written as
41 mm and the
answer for 1b can
be 63 mm.

a.

Solution:

This centimetre ruler has 10 spaces between each number.
This means that there are 9 marks between each number.
They can be considered as:
.1   .2   .3   .4   .5   .6   .7   .8   .9
The line is one mark past the 4-cm mark.
The line is 4.1 cm long.

b.

Solution:

The line is 3 marks past the 6-cm mark.
The line is 6.3 cm long.

Units and Symbols for Length:

METRIC	millimetre **mm**	centimetre **cm**	metre **m**	kilometre **km**
IMPERIAL	inches **in** or **"**	foot **ft** or **'**	yard **yd**	mile **mi**

1. Use the appropriate measurement tool to measure the following, in both SI and Imperial units.

   Complete a copy of the table below.

Item	Measurement Tool Used	Measure in SI Units	Measure in Imperial Units
a. Width of your small finger	Tape or ruler		
b. Width of two fingers			
c. Length of your foot			
d. Length of your large stride			
e. Length of your regular stride			
f. Length of a standard paper clip			
g. Thickness of a dime			

2. a. Design a set of personal benchmarks that will allow you to estimate a measurement in either SI or Imperial units.

   You should have benchmarks for each of the following units:
   1 cm, 1 m, 1 yd, 1 ft, 1 mm, 1 in
   E.g., The width of a thumb is approximately 2 cm.
   A handspan is approximately 9".

   b. Compare your benchmarks with others.

3. Complete a copy of the table below.

To estimate the measure, use the benchmarks that you established.

Item	SI Estimate	Imperial Estimate	Measurement Tool Used	Measure in SI Units	Measure in Imperial Units
a. Length of student desk					
b. Width of student desk					
c. Perimeter of (total distance around) student desk					
d. Thickness of 50 pieces of paper					
e. Height of a doorknob from the floor					
f. Length of classroom					
g. Distance between fingertips with your arms stretched out from side to side.					
h. Your height					
i. Distance around your wrist					
j. Distance around your neck					

4. Use the measure of the thickness of 50 pieces of paper from No. 3d, to determine the thickness of one piece.

5. George is building a room in the basement.
   It has an 8' ceiling.
   The framing is formed using "two by four" studs.
   The centres of the two by four's are 16" apart.
   One wall measures 9'.

   a. How many studs will be needed to frame the wall,
      counting the corner studs?
      Draw a sketch to help you.

   b. How many 4' × 8' sheets of drywall are needed for the
      wall?

6. State the length of each of the line segments shown below.
   State your answer correct to the nearest centimetre and to
   the nearest inch.

   a.
   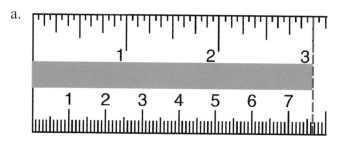

   b.
   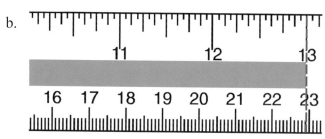

   c.
   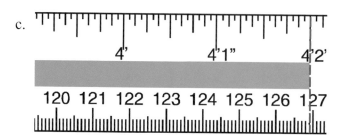

The Pattern to Calculate Conversions:

1. Identify the conversion factor of the given measure that changes it to the desired units.
2. Multiply the given measurement by the conversion factor.
   new measure = given measure × conversion factor

Linear Conversion Factors

1 in = 2.540 cm
1 cm = 0.394 in

1 ft = 0.305 m
1 m = 3.281 ft

1 yd = 0.914 m
1 m = 1.094 yd

1 mi = 1.609 km
1 km = 0.621 mi

Example 1:

a. Change 4" to centimetres.

Solution:

To change inches to centimetres, use the conversion factor 1 in = 2.540 cm.

1 in = 2.54 cm
4 in = 4 × 2.54 cm
4 in = 10.16 cm

b. Change 15 cm to inches.

Solution:

To change centimetres to inches, use 1 cm = 0.394 in.

1 cm = 0.394 in
15 cm = 15 × 0.394 in
15 cm = 5.91 in

PUT INTO PRACTICE

1. Write the conversion factor that you would use to change:

   a. 153 km to miles   b. 23.5 m to feet

   c. 7 yd to metres   d. 214 ft to metres

   e. 127 m to yards   f. 318 km to miles

2. You are driving at a speed of 100 km/h in Montana. The speed limit is 60 mph.
   Are you driving below the speed limit, above it or about at the speed limit?
   Explain your answer.

mph is the abbreviation for Miles Per Hour.

3. The Alaska Highway starts at Mile 0 in Dawson Creek, BC and ends in Fairbanks, Alaska at Mile 1568.
The Nguyen family plans to deliver a manufactured home from Edmonton to Fairbanks.
They plan to drive via Dawson Creek.
Edmonton is 586 km from Dawson Creek.

How far is it from Edmonton to Fairbanks, correct to the nearest kilometre?

4. The Hipwell family plans to build a new home on a plot of land measuring 65 feet by 150 feet.

What are the metric dimensions of the plot, rounded to the nearest metre?

5. A CFL field is 110 yd long.
A soccer pitch is 100 m long.

Which is longer and by how much?

6. The Calgary Tower is 190.8 m high.

a. How many yards high is it?

b. How many feet high is it?
How many inches high is it?

c. There are 802 steps to the top.
What is the approximate height, in inches, of each step?

Homeowners that have some knowledge of **perimeter** can carry out routine maintenance tasks.

A knowledge of **perimeter** helps when completing tasks such as: installing baseboards, putting an edge on a tablecloth, framing a picture, building a fence around your property or installing eaves-troughs.

Perimeter

is the **distance around** a figure.
Units used to measure perimeter are linear units such as:
centimetre (cm), metre (m),
kilometre (km), inch (in), foot (ft),
yard (yd) and mile (mi).

To calculate the **perimeter** you **add the lengths of all of the sides** of the figure.

Example 1:

Determine the perimeter of a triangle whose sides
are 5 cm, 12 cm and 13cm.

Solution: $P = a + b + c$
$= 5 + 12 + 13$
$= 30$
The perimeter is 30 cm.

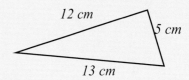

Example 2:

You want to fence a pentagonal dog run at the back of your house.
The measurements are shown on the diagram.
You estimate the cost will be $10/m.

How much should you budget for the fence?

Solution: $P = 9 + 10 + 8 + 10 + 9$
$= 46$
The perimeter is 46 m.
Cost: $46 \times 10 = 460$
The cost will be about $460.

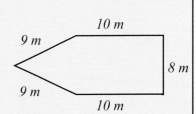

Perimeter is the **distance around** a figure.

1. Determine the perimeter of the following polygons.

a. A square whose sides are 6 cm long.

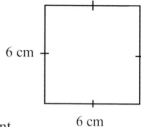

6 cm

6 cm

b. A parallelogram whose adjacent sides are 9 cm and 15 cm.

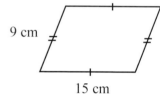

9 cm

15 cm

c. A rhombus whose sides are 8 cm.

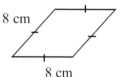

8 cm

8 cm

d. A trapezoid whose bases are 12 cm and 18 cm and whose non parallel sides are 8 cm and 8.5 cm.

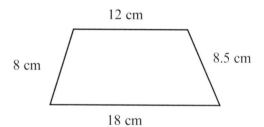

12 cm

8 cm

8.5 cm

18 cm

e. A hexagon with two sides $5\frac{1}{4}$ " long and four sides $7\frac{1}{2}$ " long.

2. Look at No.1 a, b, c.
Create a shortcut way to calculate the perimeter of these shapes.
Discuss your strategy with your partner.

Example 3: Calculate the perimeter of the rectangle shown.

Solution: $P = 4 + 7 + 4 + 7$
$= 22$

OR
$P = (4 + 7) + (4 + 7)$
$= 2(4 + 7)$
$= 2 \times 11$
$= 22$

The perimeter of the rectangle is 22 cm.

4 cm

7 cm

---

1 ft = 12"

3. Khadija is planning to put a single row of ceramic tiles behind the kitchen counter of her home.

   The tiles are $4\frac{1}{2}$ " by $4\frac{1}{2}$ ".

   How many tiles will she need to buy if the length of the counter is 5'9"?

4. A window measures 1.25 m by 1.9 m.
   Mr. Kassam wants to put a decorative border around the window.
   The border is sold in 8-ft lengths.
   He doesn't want any joints except at the corners.

   a. What is the perimeter in feet?

   b. How many 8-ft lengths does he need?

   c. If the border is sold in 12-ft lengths, how many would be needed?

1 m = 3.281 ft

5. Jose wants to purchase ceiling moulding for a room that is L-shaped.
   The dimensions of the room are shown in the diagram.
   Unfortunately for Jose, moulding is sold by the foot.

   What length of moulding should he purchase?

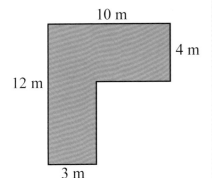

10 m

4 m

12 m

3 m

Area is the space covered by a shape. Many shapes can be divided into rectangles or triangles in order to determine their areas. The units used are square units such as: square centimetre (cm^2), square metre (m^2), hectare (ha), square inch (in^2), square foot (ft^2), square yard (yd^2), acre, square mile (mi^2) and section.

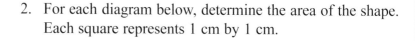

INVESTIGATION 1:

COUNT SQUARES OR CALCULATE?

What pairs of numbers will multiply to give 12?

1. On centimetre graph paper, draw three different rectangles that each have an area of 12 cm^2.
   Compare your rectangles with those of a classmate.

2. For each diagram below, determine the area of the shape. Each square represents 1 cm by 1 cm.

a.

b.
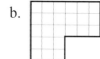

c.

d.

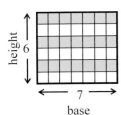

height 6

← 7 →

base

3. The diagram for No. 2a is shown on the left.
   You may have counted squares to determine the area of
   the rectangle. Copy and complete the following sentences.

   A shorter way is to realize that there are ☐ rows of
   ☐ squares so that the number of squares is ☐ × ☐ = ☐.

   To determine the area of a **rectangle**, **multiply** the ☐ by
   the ☐.

   Copy and complete the formula for the area of a
   rectangle.

   $A = ☐ × ☐$

PUT INTO PRACTICE

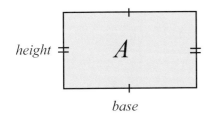

height

A

base

1. Pick one of the rectangles with area 12 cm^2 from
   Investigation No. 1.
   Use $A = bh$ to calculate the area of the rectangle.

2. Determine the following areas by measuring the
   necessary dimensions.
   Measure in units that will lead to an answer in the units
   indicated.
   E.g., in the first one, measure in centimetres.

   a. cover of this book (square centimetres),

   b. teacher's desk top (square feet),

   c. classroom door (square metres),

   d. student desk top (square inches),

   e. classroom (square yards).

$$10' \, 6" = 10\frac{1}{2}'$$

$$\text{because } 6" = \frac{6}{12}' = \frac{1}{2}'$$

3. A bedroom measures 10' 6" by 11'.

   What is the area of the bedroom floor?

Linear Conversion Factors

1 in = 2.540 cm
1 cm = 0.394 in

1 ft = 0.305 m
1 m = 3.281 ft

1 yd = 0.914 m
1 m = 1.094 yd

1 mi = 1.609 km
1 km = 0.621 mi

4. A patio measures 9.6 m by 6.1 m.
   The tiles used to cover the floor measure 1' by 1'.

   a. Change the dimensions of the patio to feet.

   b. Calculate the area of the room in square feet.

   c. How many tiles will be needed to cover the floor?

   d. Check your answer by drawing the tile layout.
      Use graph paper and let one square represent 1 ft^2.

5. For each of the following situations state whether you will use:
   perimeter (P), area (A), both perimeter and area (B) or neither perimeter nor area (N).

   a. varnishing a hardwood floor

   b. putting baseboards in a room

   c. filling a sandbox

   d. building a fence

   e. painting a fence

   f. applying wallpaper

   g. framing a picture

   h. installing a new counter top and border

The area of a rectangle is given by:

$$A = b \times h$$
$$= bh.$$

Example 1:

Keaton wanted to determine the area of a parallelogram so he drew the parallelogram (P) shown below.

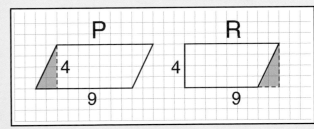

Solution:

He removed the coloured triangle from the left side of the parallelogram and slid it across to the right side to form a rectangle (R) whose area he could calculate.

Area of Parallelogram = Area of Rectangle

$$A = b \times h$$
$$= 9 \times 4$$
$$= 36$$

1. Copy each parallelogram on graph paper.
   Colour the triangle you would move from one side to the other.
   Draw the triangle in its new position.
   Calculate the area of each parallelogram.

   a.
   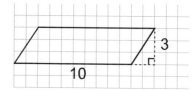

   b.
   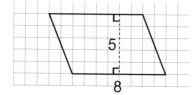

   c.
   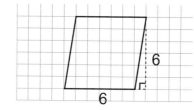

   d.
   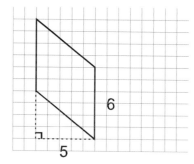

   Describe a method for calculating the area of a parallelogram without having to rearrange it into a rectangle.
   Discuss your ideas with your partner.

2. Calculate the areas of the following rectangles and parallelograms.

   Complete a copy of the table below.

Rectangle			Parallelogram		
Base (ft)	Height (ft)	Area (ft^2)	Area (ft^2)	Base (ft)	Height (ft)
9	4	36	36	9	4
5	2			5	2
$2\frac{1}{2}$	6			$2\frac{1}{2}$	6
10	5				
3	$6\frac{1}{2}$				

Example 2: You want to make a stained glass parallelogram to hang in your front window.
You would like it to have a base of 30 cm and a height of 20 cm.
The other side will be 25 cm long.
The stained glass will cost about 15¢/cm^2.

How much should you budget for the stained
glass hanging?

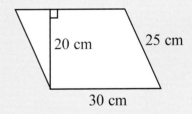

Solution:
$A = bh$
$A = 30 \times 20$
$\quad = 600$
The area is 600 cm^2.
The cost is $600 \times 15¢ = 9000¢$ or $90.

The area of a parallelogram is given by:

$$A = b \times h$$
$$ = bh.$$

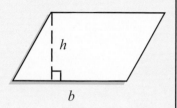

3. Calculate the area of each of the following parallelograms.

a.

8 ft

5 ft

b.
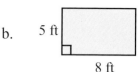
5 ft

8 ft

c.
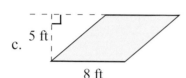
5 ft

8 ft

d.
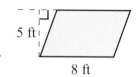
5 ft

8 ft

e.
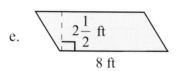
$2\frac{1}{2}$ ft

8 ft

f.
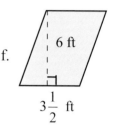
6 ft

$3\frac{1}{2}$ ft

INVESTIGATION

ARE THE AREAS OF TRIANGLES AND PARALLELOGRAMS RELATED?

Having created the formula for the area of a parallelogram Keaton now wondered about the area of a triangle.
He started by drawing a triangle.

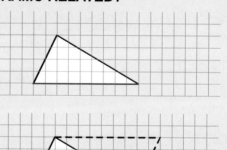

He then cut out another triangle that was the same size.

When he put them together what figure did he see?

How is the area of the triangle related to the area of the parallelogram?

What formula do you think that Keaton created for determining the area of a triangle?

Use the formula to determine the area of the figure shown.

Check your answer by counting squares.

4. Calculate the area of the following triangles.

a.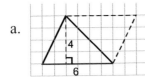

b.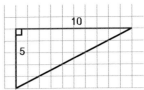

c.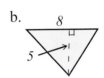

d.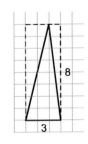

5. Calculate the area of the following triangles.

a.   b.   c.

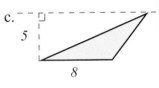

The area of a triangle is given by:

$$A = \frac{1}{2} \times b \times h$$

OR

$$A = 0.5 \times b \times h.$$

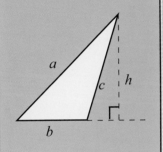

Example 3: Your budget will not allow you to spend the amount that you estimated for the stained glass parallelogram in Example 2.

Calculate the cost for a triangular shape with base 30 cm and height 20 cm with the other two sides of length 25 cm.

Solution:

$A = 0.5\ bh$
$A = 0.5 \times 30 \times 20$
$\quad = 300$
The area is 300 cm².
The cost is $300 \times 15¢ = 4500¢ = \$45$.

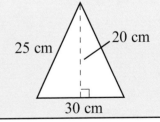

6. Mr Rosenberg has a small garden that measures 8' by 6'.
He has asked you to design a triangular flowerbed with base 8' and height 6'.
On graph paper, draw two 8 by 6 rectangles to represent Mr Rosenberg's garden.
Draw two different triangles to represent the flowerbeds.
Calculate the area of each triangle.
What do you notice about the areas?

7. Which of the gardens listed below has the largest area?

a. A square garden whose sides are 10.2 m.

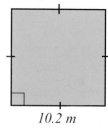

10.2 m

b. A rectangular garden whose adjacent sides are 15.3 m and 6.9 m.

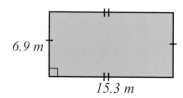

6.9 m

15.3 m

c. A garden in the shape of a parallelogram whose base is 12.4 m, the adjacent side 7.8 m and height 6.7 m.

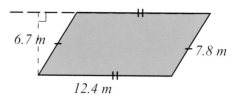

6.7 m

7.8 m

12.4 m

d. A triangular garden whose base is 16.8 m and whose length (height) is 12.5 m.

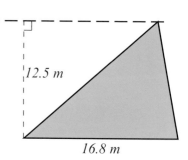

12.5 m

16.8 m

e. A garden in the shape of a trapezoid whose bases are 10.1 m and 18.4 m. The distance between the bases is 7.4 m.

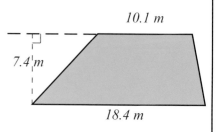

10.1 m

7.4 m

18.4 m

You can divide the trapezoid into two triangles (ΔACD and ΔABC).
ΔACD has a base that is 18.4 m and a height of 7.4 m.
ΔABC has a base that is 10.1 m and a height of 7.4 m.
Trap ACDB
= ΔACD + ΔABC

$$= \frac{1}{2} \times 18.4 \times 7.4$$

$$+ \frac{1}{2} \times 10.1 \times 7.4$$

= ...

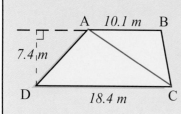

A   10.1 m   B

7.4 m

D   18.4 m   C

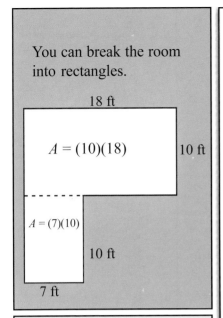

You can break the room into rectangles.

18 ft

$A = (10)(18)$ 10 ft

$A = (7)(10)$

10 ft

7 ft

You can multiply the number of square feet by 0.1 and then add this waste allowance to the original area.

You can divide the number of square feet—including waste allowance—by 15.
You will have to round up because you can not buy a part box.

8. A homeowner wants a hardwood floor in the L-shaped living room (sketched below).

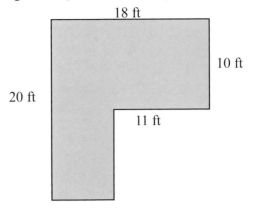

18 ft

10 ft

20 ft

11 ft

a. What is the area of the floor?

b. The installer knows that she needs to allow for waste. She knows that she should add 0.1 times the number of square feet in the room to account for waste. Calculate the number of square feet that she will likely need.

c. Pre-finished flooring is sold in packages that contain 15 ft².
What is the minimum number of packages that she should buy?

d. Each package costs $45.
How much will the flooring cost?

e. At the end of the job the installer discovered that she did not need the extra flooring that she had allowed for waste.
How many square feet of flooring were left over?

f. How many complete boxes can she return?

g. The installer charges for labour one of two ways: $12.50/h or $1.30/ft².
If she estimates that the whole job will take three 8-h days, what would the installation charge be at the:
i. hourly rate,   ii. rate per square foot?

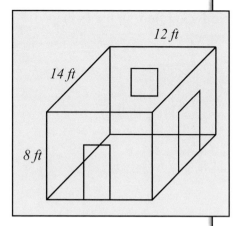

14 ft

12 ft

8 ft

Calculate the area of each wall separately. You can calculate the area of the plain wall by multiplying the base and the height.

For each of the other areas, calculate the area of the whole wall and then subtract the area of the space.

E.g., for the wall with the door, multiply 8 by 12 and multiply 2.5 and 6 and subtract the two answers.

$(8 \times 12) - (2.5 \times 6)$

1 L covers about 65 ft². Divide the total area by 65.

Add the labour cost and the paint cost.

9. Julia and Harry decided that the dining room walls should be painted.

The room is rectangular, 14 ft long by 12 ft wide and is 8ft high.

In one of the 12 ft long walls is a doorway 2.5 ft wide by 6 ft high.

Opposite that wall is a window 4 ft wide by 2 ft tall.

In one of the 14 ft walls is a rectangular opening 6 ft wide by $6\frac{1}{2}$ ft tall.

Paint is sold in 1-L cans for $13.95/can and 4L cans for $39.95/can.

1 L of paint should cover 65 ft².

They estimated that it would take at least 4 h for one of them to do it.

This would take time away from their business and they charge $35/hour for their time.

A professional painter charges $40/h and estimates that it can be done in about 3 h.

a. How large an area is to be painted?

b. How much paint is needed?

c. What is the total cost for the paint?

They need 6 L.
Consider the options that they have.
They can buy two 4 L cans and either save the leftover paint for touchups or bring it to the paint recyclers or the Habitat for Humanity store.
They can buy six 1 L cans and have very little left.
They can buy one 4 L can and two 1 L cans.
Try the three and see which is least expensive.

d. Should they hire the professional painter?

e. What are the savings if Julia and Harry use the least expensive way?

f. What is the cost for paint and labour?

10. Draw a simple floor plan of a house.
Include room dimensions, correct to the nearest foot, and the perimeter and area of each room.
Exchange your drawings with a classmate and evaluate each other's work using the following criteria:

   a. Is the drawing neat and easy to read?

   b. Are the measurements realistic?

   c. Are the perimeters and areas correct according to the given dimensions?

11. You have 144 m² of sod available and you want to sod a rectangular field that is 16 m long.

   a. How wide can the field be?

16 m

? m $A = 144$ m²

   b. What is the perimeter of the field?

   c. Fence panels cost $15.49 for each 3-m length. How much will it cost for enough panels to enclose the field?

The area of a rectangle can be calculated by multiplying base and height.
$16 \times ? = 144$.

Calculate how many panels you need by dividing by 3. You will need to round to the nearest whole because you cannot buy a partial panel. Now you can calculate the total cost because you know what each panel costs.

12. A stop sign is in the shape of a regular octagon.
   An octagon has 8 sides.
   Each edge is 30 cm long.
   The distance between parallel edges is 72.43 cm.

   a. What is the approximate length, in metres, of the
      white stripe around the outside?
      I.e., what is the perimeter of the sign?

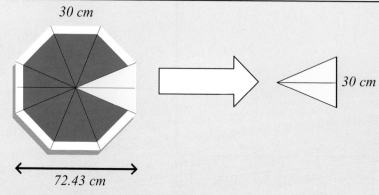

30 cm

72.43 cm

30 cm

The octagon has 8 equal sides and each side is 30 cm long.

Once you calculate the perimeter in centimetres you can divide
by 100 to change the answer to metres.

We can divide the regular
octagon into 8 congruent
triangles.
See the diagram at right.

The base of each triangle
is 30 cm.
The height of each
triangle is 36.215 cm
(half of 72.43 cm).

For one triangle
$A = 0.5bh$
$= 0.5 \times (30 \times 36.215)$
$= ...$

Therefore, the area of the
whole octagon is:
$8 \times 543.225 = ...$

   b. What is the area of the stop sign?
      Round your answer to the nearest square centimetre.

The outside dimensions of the picture and frame can be calculated by adding: the width of the frame, the picture length or width and the width of the frame again.

The height is
8 cm + 60 cm + 8 cm.

One way to calculate the area of the frame is to use the total area of the picture and frame and the area of the picture only.

The difference is the area of the frame.

The area is
4636 cm^2 – ... =

13. A painting is 60 cm long and 45 cm wide.
It has a wooden frame.
The width of the
frame is 8 cm.

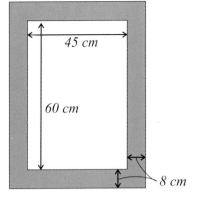

45 cm

60 cm

8 cm

a. Calculate the area of
the painting (only).

b. Calculate the area that
the painting covers on the wall
where it hangs.

c. Calculate the area of the frame (only).

d. Calculate the outside perimeter of the frame.

The outside dimensions
are 76 cm by 61 cm.

14. Beth wants to replace the countertop in her kitchen.

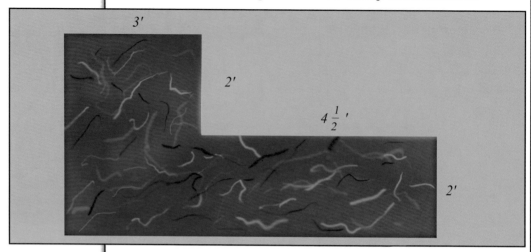

a. Calculate the area to be replaced.

b. The material costs $8.75/ft².
   How much will the countertop cost?

c. The company charges $35/hour and estimates it will
   take 3 hours to complete the job.
   How much is the installation charge?

d. What is the total cost of the new countertop?

15. Jody has to replace the shingles on his roof.
    The total area of the roof is 268 m².
    Each bundle of shingles costs $185.50.
    Each bundle of shingles can cover 10 m².

   a. How many bundles will Jody need?

   b. How much will the shingles cost?

   c. Jody also wants to replace the eavestrough.
      Two parallel edges at the base of the roof are each
      25.75 m long.
      The other two parallel edges are each 12.85 m.
      The cost to replace the eaves trough is $12.50/m.
      How much will it cost to replace the eavestrough ?

16. A fish pond in Irene's yard looks like the one sketched below.
The pond is surrounded by a border.

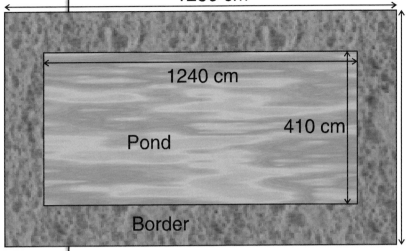

1280 cm

1240 cm

Pond

410 cm

450 cm

Border

It is easier to change to metres before you start.

a. What is the area of the pond?
Write your answer in square metres.

b. What area of the yard is taken up by the pond and border?

c. What is the area of the border?

17. Veronica owns a home in the suburbs.
Her yard is 40 m long by 30 m wide.
She wants to fertilize it and finds that one bag of fertilizer can cover 480 m^2.
Fertilizer costs $24.75/bag.

a. How many bags of fertilizer will she need to buy?

b. What is the cost per square metre?

18. A book has 266 pages of print (assume there is print on both sides of each page).
    The pages are 16 cm wide and 30 cm long.

    If the pages were removed from the book and placed on the floor (so there are no gaps and no pages overlapping), what area of the floor would they cover?
    Write your answer in square metres.

19. Five volumes of the encyclopedia numbered 1 to 5 are sitting on a shelf (in order from 1 to 5).

    The volumes are each $2\frac{1}{2}$" thick.

    A bookworm was on the outside of the front cover of book 1 and ate his way straight through the books until he was on the outside of the back cover of book 5.

    How far did he travel?

20. a. Which has the larger area:
        a rectangle 60 m by 100 m
        or
        a square with the same perimeter?

     b. What is the difference in their areas?

Real World Project

VOLUME		CAPACITY	
Imperial	**SI**	**SI**	**Imperial**
Cubic inch $\quad$ in^3	Cubic centimetre $\quad$ cm^3	Millilitre $\quad$ mL	Fluid ounce $\quad$ fl oz
Cubic foot $\quad$ ft^3	Cubic decimetre $\quad$ dm^3	Litre $\quad$ L	Pint $\quad$ pt
Cubic yard $\quad$ yd^3	Cubic metres $\quad$ m^3	Kilolitre $\quad$ kL	Quart $\quad$ qt
			Gallon $\quad$ gal

Volume
of a solid or liquid is the **amount of space it occupies**.

Use the appropriate measurement tool to measure the following, in both SI and Imperial units.

Complete a copy of the table below.

Item	Measurement Tool Used	Measure in SI Units	Measure in Imperial Units
a. Pop can contents			
b. Volume of a large milk jug			

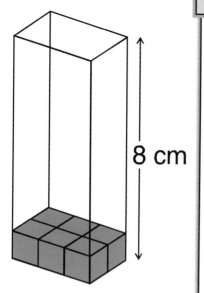

8 cm

1 cm
1 cm 1 cm

one cubic centimetre
(1 cm³)

COUNTING CUBES TO DETERMINE VOLUME

1. Josephine was asked to determine the volume of the box shown and was given a set of cubes measuring 1 cm by 1 cm by 1 cm (1 cm³).
    She began by filling the bottom of the box with the cubes.

    a. How many cubes fill the bottom of the box?

    b. How many cubes were needed to make 2 layers?

    c. How many cubes were needed to make 3 layers?

    d. How many cubes were needed to make 6 layers?

    e. Josephine did not have enough cubes to fill the box.

        Since each layer of the cubes is 1 cm high, she measured the height of the box.

        It was 8 cm.
        How many cubes would it take to fill the box?
        Explain how you arrived at your answer.

    f. Volume is the number of unit cubes that are needed to fill an object.
        The units for volume are cubic units.
        What is the volume of Josephine's box, in cubic centimetres?

2. Zara was asked to determine the volume of the box shown, and was given a set of cubes measuring 1" by 1" by 1".
    She began by filling the bottom of the box with cubes.

    a. How many cubes fill the bottom of the box?

    b. She measured the height of the box and found it was 5 in.
        How many layers of cubes will be needed to fill the box?

    c. How many cubes will it take to fill the box?

    d. What is the volume of the box?

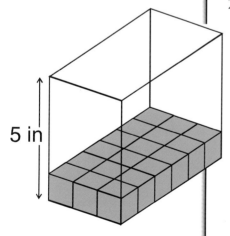

5 in

To calculate the **volume** of a rectangular solid, we can **multiply** the **area of the base** by the **height**.

$$\text{Volume} = \text{Area of Base} \times \text{Height}$$

Example:

Calculate the volume of a room that has a floor area of 9 ft by 11 ft and a height of 8 ft.

Solution:

$$\begin{aligned}
\text{Volume} &= \text{Area of Base} \times \text{Height} \\
V &= Ah \\
V &= (11 \times 9) \times 8 \\
&= 99 \times 8 \\
&= 792
\end{aligned}$$

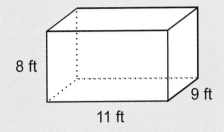

8 ft   9 ft   11 ft

The volume of the room is 792 ft^3.

Do you need the brackets in $(11 \times 9) \times 8$?
Explain.

PUT INTO PRACTICE

The **volume** of the box was calculated in **cubic centimetres** and the **capacity** of the box was measured in **millilitres**.

Volume is usually considered to be the amount of space occupied by a solid or a liquid.

Capacity is usually considered to be the volume of liquid that can be poured into a space.

1. If you were given a box and a tape measure, how would you determine the volume of the box?

2. Collect 5 rectangular boxes of different sizes.
   a. Measure and record the inside dimensions of each box, in both SI and Imperial units.

   b. Calculate the volume of each box, in SI and Imperial Units.

3. a. Obtain a small rectangular box. Measure the inside dimensions and calculate the volume in cubic centimetres.

   b. Fill the box with sand or salt. Measure the amount of sand or salt, in millilitres, using a graduated cylinder.

   c. Compare the value in No. a. to the value in No. b. What did you discover?

1. Change inches to centimetres.
   1" = 2.54 cm
   1 cm = 0.394"
2. Change cubic centimetres to millilitres.
3. Change millilitres to litres
   1L = 1000 mL = 1 000 cm³
   1 cm³ = 1 mL = 0.001 L

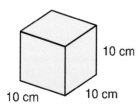

10 cm
10 cm
10 cm

1000 cm³ holds 1 L

4. George needs to put potting soil in three flower boxes. He wants to leave 1" of room at the top of the planter. The inside dimensions of the base of each box are 34" by 7".
   They each have a height of 8".

   a. What will the depth of the potting soil be?

   b. What volume of soil is needed for one flower box?

   c. How much soil does George need for the 3 flower boxes?

   d. How many litres of soil will George need? Round your answer to the nearest litre.

   e. The soil is sold in 25 L bags. How many bags should George buy?

   f. Each bag costs $1.98. What is the cost of the soil that George needs?

5. a. When inflated an air mattress measures 180 cm by 120 cm by 10 cm. How much air does it hold?

   b. A small air compressor delivers air at the rate of approximately 18 000 cm³/min. How long would it take to fill the air mattress?

Capacity and Volume Conversion Factors

1 in³	= 16.387 cm³	1 cm³	= 0.061 in³
1 yd³	= 0.765 m³	1 m³	= 1.308 yd³
1 gal	= 4.546 L	1 mL	= 1 cm³
		1 L	= 0.220 gal

For calculations, measurements must be in the same units.

Change centimetres to metres.
  100 cm = 1 m
    1 cm = 0.01 m

You are ready to start Step 2 of your project.

6. A sandbox measures 2 m by 1.5 m and is to be filled to a depth of 25 cm.

   a. What volume of sand, in cubic metres, is needed for the sandbox?

   b. Sand is usually sold by the cubic yard.
      You cannot buy part of a cubic yard.
      What amount of sand needs to be ordered?

7. For each of the following situations state whether you will use: area, volume or capacity, both or neither.

   a. Calculating the amount of concrete needed to make a patio.

   b. Calculating the amount of paint needed to paint a room.

   c. Calculating the number of boards needed to build a fence.

   d. Filling a sandbox with sand.

   e. Carpeting a floor.

PUT INTO PRACTICE

Mass and weight are terms generally used to describe the quantity of a substance.

The most common metric unit of mass is the kilogram.

The most common Imperial unit of weight is the pound.

We often convert between mass and weight as they are widely used throughout the world.

1. Complete and copy the table below.

Item	Measurement Tool Used	Measure in SI Units	Measure in Imperial Units
a. Mass of a standard single cheese slice			
b. Mass of a standard paper clip			Too small!
c. Mass of 500 mL of water			
d. Mass of 1L of water			

Conversion Factors

1 oz = 28.350 g
1 g = 0.035 oz

1 lb = 0.454 kg
1 kg = 2.205 lb

1 lb = 454 g
1 g = 0.002 lb.

2. Design a set of personal benchmarks that will allow you to estimate a measurement in either system.

You should have benchmarks for each of the following units:

1 lb, 1 kg, 1 g.

3. For each of the following masses, name two examples of objects that are approximately that mass.

a. about 1 kg

b. less than 1 kg

c. between 10 kg and 20 kg

d. about 1 lb

e. less than 1 lb

f. between 10 lb and 20 lb

4. Parin's cookbook recommends that you cook a turkey 20 min/lb.
   The turkey she plans to cook has a mass of 14 kg.
   a. How many pounds is the turkey?

   b. How long does Parin need to cook the turkey?
      Round your answer to the nearest half-hour.

5. Pottery clay is sold in boxes that weigh 10 lb.
   Ms Cross is planning to make 25 decorations for the recreation room.
   She estimates that she will need about 1 kg of clay for each one.

   a. How many kilograms of clay does Ms Cross need to purchase?

   b. How many kilograms of clay are in one 10-lb box?

   c. How many boxes of clay does Ms Cross need?

6. Kyle has a mass of 65 kg.
   His friend James weighs 118 lb.

   Who is heavier?
   By how much?

7. The ceiling of a room measures 19 ft by 12 ft.
   A 454 g pail of ceiling texture covers approximately 90 ft².

   a. What is the area of the ceiling?

   b. How many pails will be needed to cover the ceiling?

   c. What is the area (in square feet) of a ceiling measuring 8 m by 10 m?
   Round your answer to the nearest square foot.

   d. How many pails of ceiling texture are needed for the ceiling in No. c?

8. A recipe calls for 3 lb of chicken wings.
   How many kilograms of wings need to be purchased?

9. Azwar needs to order 400 lb of cement for renovations.
   The supplier sells the cement in 20 kg bags.

   a. How many kilograms of cement does Azwar need?

   b. How many bags of cement does Azwar need to order?

10. Agnes sells the apples from her garden at $1.22/lb.
    Calculate the price per kilogram.

11. The Marchand family runs a butcher shop on their farm.
    They have decided to convert their prices to SI units.

    Convert the following old prices to the new prices.
    a. bacon $3.13/lb to price per kilogram,

    b. lean ground beef at $3.42/lb to price per kilogram,

    c. sirloin roast at $4.56/lb to price per kilogram,

    d. bologna at $3.85/lb to price per kilogram.

Real World Project

You are now ready to start Step 3 of your project.

1 lb = 0.454 kg
1 kg = 2.205 lb

REVIEW

These questions will help you check whether or not you have mastered the concepts in this unit.
Look back in this book if you need help doing these questions.
As you do the questions be sure to think of how you can use fractions and graphing in your project.
Feel free to use any materials that will help you.

FRACTIONS

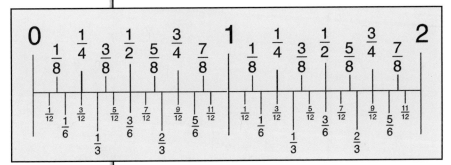

1. Which is greater?

   a. $\dfrac{1}{2}$ or $\dfrac{1}{3}$ b. $\dfrac{2}{3}$ or $\dfrac{3}{4}$ c. $\dfrac{3}{5}$ or $\dfrac{1}{2}$ d. $\dfrac{4}{8}$ or $\dfrac{6}{10}$

   e. $\dfrac{3}{5}$ or $\dfrac{3}{4}$ f. $\dfrac{1}{4}$ or $\dfrac{3}{8}$ g. $\dfrac{1}{4}$ or $\dfrac{3}{16}$ h. $\dfrac{1}{8}$ or $\dfrac{3}{16}$

This is one whole

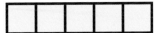

2. What fraction is represented by:
   a. 2 squares   b. 3 squares   c. 5 squares   d. 7 squares

3. Name three fractions equivalent to each of the following:

   a. $\dfrac{1}{2}$ b. $\dfrac{1}{3}$ c. $\dfrac{2}{8}$ d. $\dfrac{3}{4}$ e. $\dfrac{4}{6}$

4. Change each fraction to a mixed number:

   a. $\dfrac{5}{4}$ b. $\dfrac{10}{8}$ c. $\dfrac{5}{3}$ d. $\dfrac{51}{2}$ e. $\dfrac{51}{10}$

   f. $\dfrac{501}{100}$ g. $\dfrac{18}{8}$ h. $\dfrac{8}{3}$ i. $\dfrac{53}{2}$ j. $\dfrac{61}{10}$

5. Change each mixed number to an improper fraction:

   a. $1\dfrac{3}{4}$ b. $2\dfrac{1}{2}$ c. $2\dfrac{3}{6}$ d. $3\dfrac{3}{8}$

   e. $4\dfrac{3}{10}$ f. $5\dfrac{91}{100}$ g. $2\dfrac{5}{6}$ h. $3\dfrac{5}{6}$

6. Evaluate:

   a. $\dfrac{1}{2}+\dfrac{1}{4}$ b. $\dfrac{2}{8}+\dfrac{5}{10}$ c. $\dfrac{1}{4}+\dfrac{1}{8}$

   d. $\dfrac{3}{8}+\dfrac{1}{4}$ e. $\dfrac{5}{8}+\dfrac{1}{2}$ f. $\dfrac{3}{4}+\dfrac{7}{8}$

   g. $\dfrac{3}{10}+\dfrac{7}{100}$ h. $\dfrac{1}{3}-\dfrac{1}{4}$ i. $\dfrac{5}{6}-\dfrac{2}{5}$

   j. $\dfrac{7}{8}-\dfrac{7}{16}$ k. $\dfrac{7}{10}-\dfrac{69}{100}$ l. $6\dfrac{3}{4}+7\dfrac{3}{16}$

7. Evaluate:

   a. $\dfrac{1}{3}\times\dfrac{1}{3}$ b. $\dfrac{1}{2}\times\dfrac{1}{4}$ c. $\dfrac{2}{3}\times\dfrac{4}{5}$

   d. $\dfrac{3}{8}\times\dfrac{6}{5}$ e. $\dfrac{5}{8}\times 1\dfrac{1}{5}$ f. $2\dfrac{1}{3}\times 1\dfrac{5}{7}$

8. Evaluate:

   a. $\dfrac{1}{3} \div \dfrac{1}{3}$ b. $\dfrac{1}{2} \div \dfrac{1}{4}$ c. $\dfrac{2}{3} \div \dfrac{4}{5}$

   d. $\dfrac{3}{8} \div \dfrac{6}{5}$ e. $\dfrac{3}{8} \div 1\dfrac{1}{5}$ f. $2\dfrac{3}{8} \div 3\dfrac{4}{5}$

9. Marion was making some clothes for her sister's doll and needed to do the following calculations:

   a. Calculate the total length of two pieces with lengths $\dfrac{7}{8}''$ and $\dfrac{5}{16}''$.

   b. Calculate the total length of 8 pieces each $\dfrac{3}{4}''$ long.

   c. Calculate the length of one half of a piece that is $10\dfrac{3}{4}''$ long.

   d. You need to divide a piece that is $10\dfrac{3}{4}''$ long into two equal pieces.

   How long is each piece?

   e. How many pieces, each 2" long, can you get from a piece that is $10\dfrac{3}{4}''$ long?

   f. How many pieces, each $\dfrac{3}{4}''$ long, can you get from a piece that is $10\dfrac{3}{4}''$ long?

   g. How many pieces, each $2\dfrac{3}{4}''$ long, can you get from a piece that is $10\dfrac{3}{4}''$ long?

How to use Conversion Factors:

1. Identify the conversion factor that changes the given measure to the desired units.
2. Multiply the given measurement by the conversion factor.

Conversion Factors			
Linear		**Area**	
1 in = 2.540 cm	1 cm = 0.394 in	$1\ in^2 = 6.452\ cm^2$	$1\ cm^2 = 0.155\ in^2$
1 ft = 0.305 m	1 m = 3.281 ft	$1\ ft^2 = 0.093\ m^2$	$1\ m^2 = 10.764\ ft^2$
1 yd = 0.914 m	1 m = 1.094 yd	$1\ yd^2 = 0.836\ m^2$	$1\ m^2 = 1.176\ yd^2$
1 mi = 1.609 km	1 km = 0.621 mi	1 ac = 0.405 ha	1 ha = 2.471 ac
Capacity and Volume		**Mass / Weight**	
$1\ in^3 = 16.387\ cm^3$	$1\ cm^3 = 0.061\ in^3$	1 oz = 28.350 g	1 g = 0.035 oz
$1\ yd^3 = 0.765\ m^3$	$1\ m^3 = 1.308\ yd^3$	1 lb = 0.454 kg	1 kg = 2.205 lb
1 fl. oz. = 29.573 mL	1 mL = 0.034 fl oz	1 lb = 454 g	1 g = 0.002 lb.
1 gal = 4.546 L	1 L = 0.220 gal		
1 qt = 1.137 L	1 L = 0.880 qt		

10. What conversion factor would you use to change:
    a. centimetres to inches?
    b. metres to yards?
    c. metres to feet?
    d. cubic metres to cubic yards?
    e. grams to pounds?
    f. kilograms to pounds?
    g. feet to metres?
    h. yards to metres?
    i. inches to centimetres?
    j. pounds to kilograms?
    k. pounds to grams?
    l. feet to inches?

11. The buffalo jump at Head-Smashed-In Buffalo Jump Provincial Historic Site in Alberta has an accumulated depth of more than 11 m of archaeological deposits.

    Re-write this measure in Imperial units.

12. Estimate your mass in kilograms.
    Use your estimate to determine the following:

    a. Human bones are about 0.181 of your body mass.
       What is the mass of your bones?

    b. The brain is about 0.0299 of your body mass.
       What is the mass of your brain?

    c. The amount of water in your body is about 0.579 of
       your body mass.
       What is the mass of water in your body?

13. The tornado that hit Pine Lake, AB in July of 2000 cut a
    swath 800 m to 1500 m wide and 15 km to 20 km long.
    The wind speed was recorded at 300 km/h.

    Express these measurements in Imperial units.

14. Calculate the perimeter of each shape below.

Perimeter = the sum of
the measures of the
sides.

a. 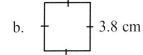 2 cm
   12 cm

b. 3.8 cm

c. 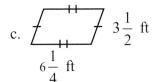 $3\frac{1}{2}$ ft
   $6\frac{1}{4}$ ft

d. 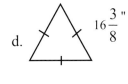 $16\frac{3}{8}$ "

e.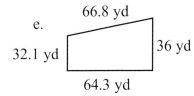
   66.8 yd
   32.1 yd   36 yd
   64.3 yd

f.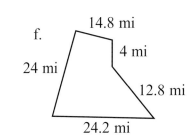
   14.8 mi
   4 mi
   24 mi
   12.8 mi
   24.2 mi

15. A rectangular garden in the Magee yard measures 5.5 m by 7.3 m.

   a. What is the perimeter of the garden?

   b. What is the perimeter of the garden in feet?

   c. Mrs. Magee wants to fence the garden using pre-built panels measuring 6 ft in width.

   How many panels will she need?
   (Assume that one of the panels will be a gate panel.)

16. Calculate the area of the following parallelograms.

   a.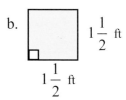
      5 cm
      30 cm

   b.
      $1\frac{1}{2}$ ft
      $1\frac{1}{2}$ ft

   c.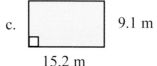
      9.1 m
      15.2 m

   d.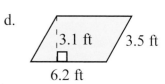
      3.1 ft   3.5 ft
      6.2 ft

17. Calculate the area of the following shapes.

   a.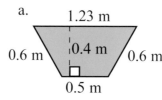
      1.23 m
      0.6 m   0.4 m   0.6 m
      0.5 m

   b.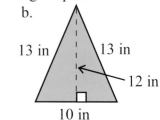
      13 in   13 in
      12 in
      10 in

18. Georgina plans to put new carpet in her bedroom that measures 10 ft by 11.5 ft.
The carpet is only available in a 12 ft width.

   a. What is the area of carpet that she will need to cover the floor?

   b. If the carpet costs $3.29/ft², what is the cost of the carpet required?

19. Calculate the shaded area of the following shapes.
   a.

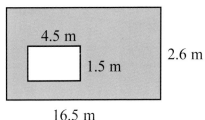

   b.

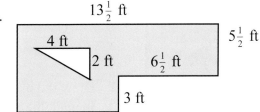

For a rectangular container,
Volume =
Area of the base × **h**eight

$V = Ah$

20. A feature wall in the Mackay residence is to be covered with a textured wall covering.
   Mrs. Mackay found that the wall measured 6 m by 3 m.
   A 0.6 kg container of texture contains approximately 3.9 m².
   a. What is the area of the wall?

   b. How many containers does Mrs. Mackay need?

21. Thuy wants to fill a sandbox with sand.
   The box measures 2.5 m by 0.9 m by 0.3 m.

   What is the volume of the sandbox?

PROJECT

ROOM DESIGN

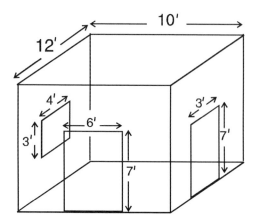

Real World Project

You may use metric or Imperial units.	

Use a simple scale: represent 1' by 1" (i.e. divide by 12) or represent 1 cm by 1 mm (divide by 10).	

This is a sample ideal room in a house designed for basketball players and for wheelchair access.

STEP 1: THE PLAN

In the introduction to this unit you made a wish list.
Review it and follow the steps below to plan your ideal room.

1. a. What room are you going to redesign?

   b. Measure and record the dimensions of the room. Justify your choice of units.
   Include ceiling height, doors, windows, closets, and other features you consider part of the plan.

   c. If you are planning to enlarge the room, what are the new dimensions?

   d. If your plan includes new windows, doors or decks, where will these features be placed, and what are the dimensions?

2. Draw the plans for the room to scale on grid paper. Include the measurements on your diagrams.
   a. Draw the floor plan.

   b. Draw each wall, including windows and doors.

Here are some formulas that may be useful for area and perimeter.

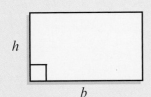

$A = bh$
$P = 2b + 2h$

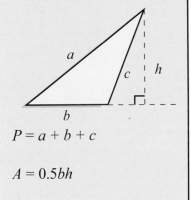

$P = a + b + c$

$A = 0.5bh$

Total cost:
the number of units to be purchased times the cost per unit.

STEP 2: THE MATERIAL COSTS

Use flyers from hardware and building suppliers to help determine the cost of materials.
List the items you will require and their price.

Organize your data in a table similar to the one below.

Item	Price for one

STEP 3: THE BUDGET

Complete a copy of the table below, or use a spreadsheet.

For each item, it is helpful to determine if you need to consider perimeter, area, or both in order to determine the number of units needed.

When calculating quantities show your calculations.
These may include the perimeter and/or area for sections of your room.
They may also include the calculations to find how many units of each item are required.

Total cost will be the total cost before tax.

Organize your data in a table similar to the one below.
You may wish to use a spreadsheet.

Item	Unit Price	Perimeter and/or Area	Number of Units	Total Cost

FOOD FARE

GET THINKING

- What can I do if I have more people coming over for dinner than the main course recipe allows for?

- How do I make sure I have enough food for the party, and still keep food waste to a minimum?

- When is the combo meal not the best value for me?

- When I take someone out for a nice dinner, how will I know if I can afford to look at the dessert menu?

Content

- Represent and apply fractions as percents, and percents as fractions and decimals.
- Apply the concepts of rate, ratio, percentage and proportion to solve problems in meaningful contexts.
- Demonstrate and explain the meaning of ratio concretely, pictorially and symbolically.
- Estimate and calculate percentages.
- Derive and apply unit rates.
- Express rates and ratios in equivalent forms to solve problems.
- Solving one and two step equations.
- Translate a written expression into an equivalent algebraic expression.
- Use equations as problem solving tools.

AND MENTAL MATH, PROBLEM SOLVING, REASONING, TECHNOLOGY, VISUALIZATION, COMMUNICATION, CONNECTIONS, ESTIMATION

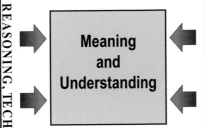

Meaning and Understanding

Intellectual Curiosity

Only one out of two restaurants succeed in the food industry.
If I were an owner, how could I use mathematics to ensure that my restaurant makes a profit and at the same time make sure that the quality of food and the service is still excellent?

Real World Project

Running a Successful Restaurant

Research the history of a restaurant; track information over a 4 hour shift on a spreadsheet; consider other expenses; conclude with ideas for catering to the customer while limiting expenses.

EQUATIONS

The following example is one of the simplest forms of algebraic equations:

Example 1:

$$x - 3 = 12$$

Several methods can be used to solve these type of equations.

Solve by Inspection:

You may immediately see that $x = 15$ simply by asking yourself
"what number minus 3 is equal to 12?" or
"3 less than what number is 12?"

$x = 15$

Solve by Representation:

Another method you may have used would be to visualize the numbers as actual items.
For example, the numbers could represent friends at a party.
If three people went home, and there are twelve people left, there must have been fifteen friends in total at the party.

$x = 15$

Solve by using Algebra Tiles:

You may also have represented the equation with algebra tiles,

$$x \quad - \quad 3 \quad = \quad 12$$

then adding three positive tiles to each side to eliminate the negative ones on the left side (since $-3 + 3 = 0$).

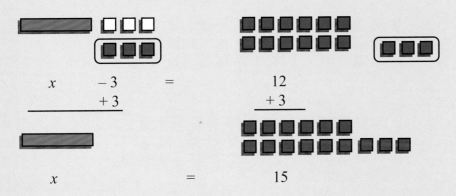

$$x \qquad -3 \qquad = \qquad 12$$
$$+3 \qquad\qquad +3$$

$$x \qquad\qquad = \qquad 15$$

To summarize:
$$x - 3 = 12$$
$$x - 3 + 3 = 12 + 3 \qquad \text{Add 3 to both sides of the equation.}$$
$$x = 15$$

Solve by using Reverse Operation:

Perhaps you solved the equation by adding 3 to 12.
The original equation involved subtraction of 3, and the reverse operation of subtraction of 3 is addition of 3.

$x = 15$

All of these methods are equally acceptable for solving one-step equations.

Example 2:

Solve: $x + 9 = 16$

Solve by Inspection: $\qquad\qquad x = 7$ $\qquad$ because $7 + 9 = 16$

Solve by Representation: $\qquad$ There are 16 people on student council.
$\qquad\qquad\qquad\qquad\qquad\qquad$ If 9 of them are boys, how many girls are there?

$\qquad\qquad$ *Answer:* 7 girls, or $x = 7$

Solve by using Algebra Tiles:

$\quad x \qquad\qquad\qquad +9 \qquad\qquad\qquad\qquad 16$

$\quad x \qquad\qquad\qquad\quad +9 \qquad = \qquad\qquad 16$
$\qquad\qquad\qquad\qquad\quad\underline{-9} \qquad = \qquad\qquad \underline{-9}$

$\qquad\qquad\qquad x \qquad\qquad = \qquad\qquad 7$

Solve by using the Reverse Operation: $\qquad x + 9 = 16$
$\qquad\qquad\qquad\qquad\qquad\qquad\qquad x + 9 - 9 = 16 - 9$ $\qquad$ *Subtract 9 from both sides*
$\qquad\qquad\qquad\qquad\qquad\qquad\qquad\qquad x = 7$

Example 3:

Solve: $3x = 6$

Solve by Inspection: $x = 2$ because $(3) \times (2) = 6$

Solve by Representation: Six children are divided into three groups.
How many children are in each group?

Answer: 2 children, or $x = 2$

Solve by using Algebra Tiles:

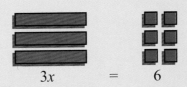

$$3x \qquad = \qquad 6$$

Match each x tile with an equal number of unit tiles.

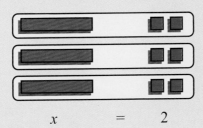

$$x \qquad = \qquad 2$$

Solve by using the Reverse Operation:

$$3x = 6$$

$$\frac{3x}{3} = \frac{6}{3} \qquad\qquad \textit{Divide both sides by 3.}$$

$$x = 2$$

Example 4:

Solve: $\dfrac{x}{3} = 4$

Solve by using Algebra Tiles: Since algebra tiles cannot be split into fractions, we will use a diagram to illustrate the solution.

$\dfrac{x}{3}$ can be written as $\dfrac{1}{3}x$

 Represent $\dfrac{1}{3}x$ by dividing an x-tile into three equal parts.

$$\dfrac{1}{3}x \quad = \quad 4$$

But since we can't really have $\dfrac{1}{3}x$ on the left side, we will lay out the arrangement 3 times.

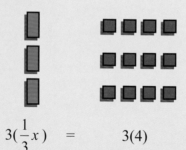

$$3\left(\dfrac{1}{3}x\right) \quad = \quad 3(4)$$

$$x \quad = \quad 12$$

Solve by Inspection: $x = 12$ because $12 \div 3 = 4$

Solve by Representation: Darren had a bag of cookies.
                                 He divided them equally on 3 plates.
                                 There are 4 cookies on each plate.
                                 How many cookies are there?

                   Answer: 12 cookies, or $x = 12$

Solve by using the Reverse Operation: $\dfrac{x}{3} = 4$

$$3\left(\frac{x}{3}\right) = 3(4) \qquad \textit{Multiply both sides by 3.}$$

$$x = 12$$

PUT INTO PRACTICE

1. Write a note to an absent friend explaining how they can solve an equation like $x + 2 = 3$ using each of the four methods (inspection, representation, algebra tiles, reverse operation).

2. Explain how to solve an equation like $2x = 6$ by each of the four methods.

3. Solve each of the following equations by using one of the four methods: inspection, reverse operation, algebra tiles, representation.
    You must use each method at least once.

    a. $x - 4 = 3$ b. $x + 1 = 5$ c. $x - 2 = -3$ d. $x + 2 = -1$

    e. $2x = 4$ f. $3x = -3$ g. $\dfrac{x}{2} = 4$ h. $\dfrac{x}{2} = -3$

In each of the previous equations we have used "*x*" as the variable. However you can use any letter to represent the variable (except *o*, which could be interpreted as 0).

4. Match each equation on the left with its correct answer from the right.
   For each equation, state which method you used.

a. $2x = 16$	7
b. $y - 7 = 3$	–3
c. $6 + a = 13$	–8
d. $\dfrac{x}{4} = -3$	–12
e. $8k = -24$	10
f. $b + 9 = 3$	–6
g. $\dfrac{m}{2} = -5$	8
h. $j - 12 = -20$	–10

5. Match each equation on the left with its correct solution from the right.

a. $4n = 48$	–90
b. $a - 15 = -73$	12
c. $\dfrac{x}{16} = 5$	52
d. $y + 31 = 54$	23
e. $21k = -63$	80
f. $\dfrac{c}{5} = -18$	–3
g. $p - 24 = 28$	–42
h. $x + 16 = -26$	–58

6. Micaela shared a bag of Halloween candies with the other 14 starters on her rugby team.
   She noticed that everyone had 5 candies.
   This is how she planned to calculate the total number of candies.

   Let the number of candies be *c*.

   $$\frac{c}{15} = 5$$

   Solve the equation for Micaela.

Real World Project

You are ready to start Step 1 of your project.

Example 1:

Greg decided to stop at Slice-of-Pizza on his way home from school. He wanted to buy one slice of pepperoni pizza and a drink, but he only had $3.49, and the total cost was $3.99. He looked around the store and noticed his friend Devon.

"Hey, Devon!" he called. "Can you lend me fifty cents? I'll pay you back tomorrow."

When Greg determined the difference between the amount of money in his pocket and the amount he needed, he was really solving an algebraic equation. We could interpret the problem as follows:

What did Greg calculate?

> **Answer:** the amount of money he needs to borrow

Step 1: *Define the variable:*   Let the amount of money Greg needs to borrow be x.

Step 2: *Set up the equation:*   Amount Greg has + amount he needs to borrow   = $3.99
$$3.49 \quad + \quad x \qquad\qquad = 3.99$$

Step 3: *Solve for x:*
$$3.49 + x = 3.99$$
$$x + 3.49 - 3.49 = 3.99 - 3.49$$
$$x = 0.50$$

> Subtract 3.49 from both sides.

Step 4: *State the solution in a sentence:*
> Greg needs to borrow $0.50 or 50¢.

Ellen works at a popular fast food restaurant.

She makes $6.50 per hour, and usually works four hours per shift.

The snowboard she wants to buy will cost $304.95, and she has already saved $155 towards its cost.

How many more hours does she have to work until she can pay for the snowboard?

THE FOUR STEPS

Problem-solving using algebra should include these four steps:

1. Determine what you are trying to find and then decide what unknown quantity the variable should represent.

2. Set up the equation by translating the original question into algebra.

3. Solve for the variable.

4. State the answer in a sentence.

Get thinking.

Always ask yourself: "Does my answer make sense?"
If you put the answer in a sentence you can see whether or not it seems reasonable.
If it does not, then you may have made an error in setting up your equation or in your calculations.

Example 2:

Bob is having a Christmas tree cutting party. He has three dozen hamburger buns, and needs to buy the ground beef.

If each hamburger requires $\frac{1}{4}$ lb of meat, how much meat does he have to buy to have exactly enough for the hamburgers?
How much will the meat cost at $2.75/lb?

What is Bob trying to determine?

Answer: The amount of meat he needs for 3 dozen hamburgers

Bob carried out Steps 1, 2, 3 and 4 and decided that he needs 144 lb of meat for 3 dozen hamburgers.
The cost will be 144 × $2.75 = $396.

Get thinking.

Does this seem reasonable?
Something's definitely wrong here, because that's over ten dollars per hamburger!

PUT INTO PRACTICE

For each of the following, use the four steps.

Ask yourself: "Is the answer reasonable?"
The question being asked in the problem will help you to define the variable.
For example, if the question asked "How much did the meal cost?", you could define the variable by stating: "Let the cost of the meal be $c".

1. Bob's calculations in Example 2 were not correct.
    Copy and complete the following solution to help Bob.

    3 dozen = 3 × ☐.
    Let the amount of meat needed be m lb.
    $m = \frac{1}{4} \times$ ☐
    $m =$ ☐

    Bob needs ☐ lb of meat.
    The cost will be 9 × $☐ = $☐.

2. Alicia paid $4.85 for a sandwich and juice.
   If the price of the sandwich was $3.50, how much did the juice cost?

3 . Jonathan is paid $6.40 per hour.
   How much will he be paid if he works five and a half hours?

4. A can of chili costs $2.79.
   How many cans of chili can you buy for twenty dollars?

5. Sarah is a waitress at a popular local restaurant.
   She was offered a raise of $1.20 per hour, which increased her hourly pay to $8.25.
   How much was she making per hour before the raise?

6. Mark wants to buy his mother a microwave for her birthday.
   The cost of the microwave is $174.39.
   If Mark makes $8.75 per hour, how many hours does he have to work in order to afford the microwave?

7. A recipe for apple pie requires 4 cups of apples.
   If 2 cups of apples are in the mixing bowl, how many more cups of apples need to be added?

8. Loaves of bread are advertised at a price of three for $2.79.
   What is the price per loaf?

9. Laura's parents took her out for dinner on her sixteenth birthday.
   The amount of the bill was $102.85.
   Her parents left a total of $120.
   What was the amount of the tip that they left?

When you are solving problems you should always check to make sure that the answer is reasonable. (Then you won't be paying $10 for a hamburger!)

When you are solving equations it is helpful to verify your answer to ensure that it is correct.

Verifying a solution means that we check to make sure that our answer is correct.
To do this, we split the original equation into its two sides, left and right, and work with each side individually.
Replace the variable by your answer and calculate the value of the expression.
Make sure that the left side and the right side have the same value.

Example 1:

Solve $x - 3 = 7$ and verify your answer.

Solution: $x - 3 = 7$

$$\begin{array}{rcl} x - 3 & = & 7 \\ +3 & & +3 \\ \hline x & = & 10. \end{array}$$ *Add 3 to both sides.*

Check the solution.

Substitute $x = 10$.

Left Side	Right Side
$x - 3$	7
$= (10) - 3$	
$= 7$	

To make sure you work with each side individually in your check, draw a vertical line between the left side and the right side

Since the left side and the right side are equal, we know that our solution, $x = 10$, is correct.

Solve $\frac{x}{4} = 5$ and verify your answer.

PUT INTO PRACTICE

1. Jalil solved each of the following equations.
   His solution for x is given in parentheses beside each equation.
   Verify each of his solutions by using a left side / right side check.
   If you find any incorrect solutions, re-solve the equation and check your answer.

   a. $x + 5 = 7$ (2)   b. $x - 3 = -2$ (−1)

   c. $\frac{x}{4} = 2$ (4)   d. $x - 8 = -2$ (6)

   e. $5x = 5$ (0)   f. $2x = 12$ (6)

2. The answer for each equation in Column A is contained somewhere in Column B.
   Determine the correct answer for each equation.

Column A	Column B
a. $2x - 8 = 10$	−15
b. $\frac{b}{4} + 5 = 10$	2
c. $3h + 4 = 10$	9
d. $5y - 5 = 10$	−2
e. $\frac{n}{8} + 15 = 10$	20
f. $\frac{k}{5} + 13 = 10$	27
g. $6d + 22 = 10$	3
h. $\frac{x}{3} + 1 = 10$	−40

Solving one–step equations involved **one** of the arithmetic operations: addition, subtraction, multiplication or division.

Solving two-step equations requires the use of **two** operations.
Usually there will be one of addition or subtraction and one of multiplication or division.

Example 1:

Solve $3x - 8 = 13$.

The four methods used in solving one-step equations can be used to solve two-step equations.

Solve by Inspection:

You can see that $x = 7$ by thinking:
"I multiply a number by 3 and then subtract 8 to get 13.
Therefore before I subtracted 8 I must have had 21.
Three times a number is 21, so the number is 7."

$x = 7$

Solve by Representation:

Relate the equation to a real life situation.
For example: I know my young sister gets an allowance every week.
When I took her shopping last weekend she told me that she had three weeks allowance with her.
She spent $8 and had $13 left.
She must have started with $21, so I now know she gets $7 a week.

$$3x - 8 = 13$$
$$3x = 21$$
$$x = 7$$

Solve using Algebra Tiles:

$$3x \qquad -8 \qquad = \qquad 13$$

Add 8 positive tiles to each side to eliminate the 8 negative ones on the left side.

$$3x \qquad -8 \qquad +8 \qquad = \qquad 13 \qquad + \qquad 8$$

$$3x \qquad\qquad = \qquad\qquad 21$$

Match each x tile with the same number of unit tiles

$$\frac{3x}{3} \qquad\qquad\qquad \frac{21}{3}$$

$$x \qquad = \qquad 7$$

Solve by using the Reverse Operations

$$3x - 8 = 13$$
$$3x - 8 + 8 = 13 + 8 \qquad \textit{Add 8 to both sides.}$$
$$3x = 21$$

$$\frac{3x}{3} = \frac{21}{3} \qquad \textit{Divide both sides by 3.}$$

$$x = 7$$

Example 2: Solve $\dfrac{x}{7} + 15 = 32$.

Solution:

Since the arithmetic operations in the equation are division ($\div 7$) and addition ($+15$), you would usually use **multiplication** and **subtraction** in reverse order to solve for x.

Step 1: $\quad \dfrac{x}{7} + 15 - 15 = 32 - 15 \qquad$ ***Subtract*** 15 *from both sides.*

$$\dfrac{x}{7} = 17$$

Step 2: $\quad (7)\dfrac{x}{7} = (7)\,17 \qquad$ ***Multiply*** *both sides by 7.*

$$x = 119$$

Alternate Solution:

$$\dfrac{x}{7} + 15 = 32$$

$$7 \times \dfrac{x}{7} + 7(15) = 7(32) \qquad \textit{\textbf{Multiply}} \text{ both sides by 7.}$$

$$x + 105 = 224$$

$$x + 105 - 105 = 224 - 105 \qquad \textit{\textbf{Subtract}} \text{ 105 from both sides.}$$

$$x = 119$$

> In general, for the two–step equations in this unit:
>
> ***Step 1***
> is either addition or subtraction, and
>
> ***Step 2***
> is either multiplication or division.

INVESTIGATION

1. Use the four methods to solve $2x - 3 = 7$.

INSPECTION

Think: $\boxed{?} - 3$ is 7, so $2x = 10$

$2 \times \boxed{?}$ is 10

$x = \boxed{?}$

ALGEBRA TILES

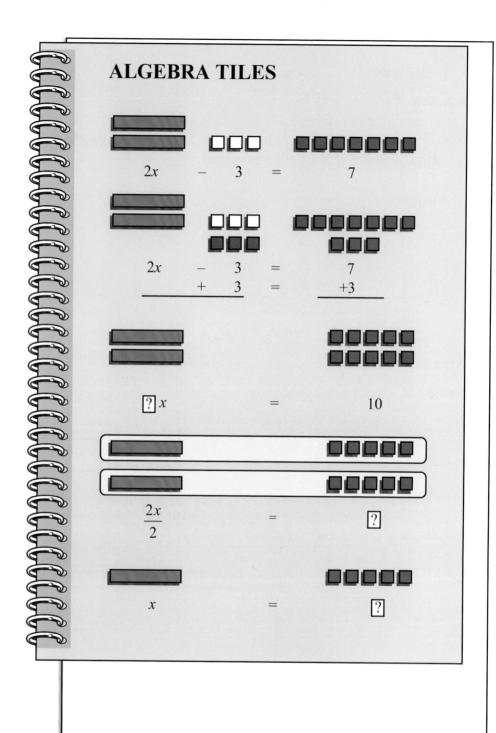

$$2x \quad - \quad 3 \quad = \quad 7$$

$$2x \quad - \quad 3 \quad = \quad 7$$
$$+ \quad 3 \quad = \quad +3$$

$$\boxed{?}\, x \quad = \quad 10$$

$$\frac{2x}{2} \quad = \quad \boxed{?}$$

$$x \quad = \quad \boxed{?}$$

REPRESENTATION

Janetta split each chocolate bar into two pieces.
She gave ? pieces away and had 7 pieces left.
She must have started with ? pieces.
If she started with 10 pieces then she had ? chocolate bars.

$$x = \boxed{?}$$

REVERSE OPERATIONS

$$2x - 3 = 7$$

$$2x - 3 + \underline{} = 7 + \boxed{?} \qquad \textit{Add } \boxed{?} \textit{ to both sides.}$$

$$2x = \boxed{?}$$

$$\frac{\boxed{?}}{2} = \frac{\boxed{?}}{2} \qquad \textit{Divide both sides by } \boxed{?}.$$

$$x = \boxed{?}$$

PUT INTO PRACTICE

1. Solve each of the following equations using one of the four methods (Inspection, Representation, Algebra Tiles, Reverse Operations).
   You must use each method at least once.

   a. $3x + 5 = 23$ b. $6x - 7 = -1$ c. $\dfrac{x}{3} + 5 = 7$

   d. $\dfrac{x}{2} - 3 = 6$ e. $4x - 9 = 11$ f. $11 - 2x = 5$

   g. $2x - 3 = 7$ h. $\dfrac{x}{4} + 1 = 0$ i. $\dfrac{x}{4} - 1 = 0$

COPYRIGHT © 2002   Rogue Media Inc.

2. Complete a copy of the table below.

–9	–8	–7	–6	–5	–4	–3	–2	–1	0	1	2	3	4	5	6	7	8	9
																		E

Solve the following two-step equations.

Write the letter that is to the right of each equation in the box that is under the solution to the equation.
E.g. The answer to No. a is 9 so put E in the box under 9.

You will find a popular dish for holiday meals.

a. $\dfrac{x}{3} - 5 = -2$ E   k. $\dfrac{x}{2} - 14 = -12$ T

b. $3x + 4 = -11$ T   l. $\dfrac{x}{3} + 7 = 4$ R

c. $\dfrac{x}{8} + 9 = 9$ E   m. $\dfrac{x}{3} + 8 = 6$ S

d. $\dfrac{x}{2} - 8 = -12$ O   n. $2x - 11 = -5$ I

e. $6x + 17 = -1$ U   o. $\dfrac{x}{3} + 16 = 18$ S

f. $9x - 2 = -20$ R   p. $2x + 13 = 5$ T

g. $\dfrac{x}{4} - 10 = -8$ G   q. $12x + 16 = 4$ K

h. $10x + 6 = 16$ Y   r. $\dfrac{x}{3} - 3 = -2$ W

i. $4x - 3 = 17$ H   s. $2x + 5 = 19$ A

j. $\dfrac{x}{7} - 5 = -6$ A

3. Complete a copy of the following table below.

15	2	18	23	10	3	12	▓	25	14	16	24	▓	▓	▓
							▓					▓	▓	▓
▓	▓	▓	▓	▓	▓	▓	▓	▓	▓	▓	▓	▓	▓	▓
17	20	9	6	11	8	21	13	4	▓	5	19	1	22	7
									▓			L		

Solve the two-step equations below.

Find your answer in the ANSWERS table, then write the matching letter beneath the *number* of the question in the box.

ANSWERS					
1	D	9	U	17	B
2	Y	10	C	18	O
3	P	11	N	19	E
4	L	12	J	20	W
5	M	13	H	21	I
6	F	14	T	22	Q
7	R	15	K	23	V
8	A	16	G	24	S

For example:
$$4y - 9 = 7$$
$$4y - 9 + 9 = 7 + 9$$
$$4y = 16$$
$$y = 4$$

Since the answer to No.1 is 4, the letter "L" is entered in the box beneath the number "1".

The final answer will spell a traditional aboriginal food.

1. $4y - 9 = 7$

2. $2a - 4 = 12$

3. $\dfrac{n}{2} + 13 = 18$

4. $3k - 7 = 26$

5. $\dfrac{d}{4} + 29 = 32$

6. $\dfrac{x}{5} - 11 = -8$

7. $8x - 9 = 7$

8. $\dfrac{b}{2} + 21 = 28$

9. $\dfrac{h}{2} + 43 = 55$

10. $3a - 16 = 38$

11. $7m + 9 = 65$

12. $2y - 7 = 23$

13. $\dfrac{v}{3} - 38 = -32$

14. $2t + 7 = 49$

15. $5n - 22 = 63$

16. $5w + 18 = 88$

17. $\dfrac{c}{6} - 27 = -23$

18. $4r + 42 = 86$

19. $3n - 38 = 19$

20. $\dfrac{p}{4} + 64 = 66$

21. $\dfrac{y}{9} - 31 = -29$

22. $10m - 21 = 19$

23. $4c - 26 = 18$

24. $4k + 15 = 67$

25. $\dfrac{q}{5} + 60 = 64$

Verifying a solution means that we check to make sure that our answer is correct.
To do this, we split the original equation into its two sides, left and right, and work with each side individually.
Replace the variable with your answer and calculate the value of the expression.
Make sure that the left side and the right side have the same value.

Example 1:

Solve $3x - 6 = 18$, and check the answer.

Equation: $3x - 6 = 18$

Step 1: *Add 6 to both sides.*

$$3x - 6 + 6 = 18 + 6$$
$$3x = 24$$

Step 2: *Divide both sides by 3.*

$$\frac{3x}{3} = \frac{24}{3}$$

$$x = 8$$

Check the solution.

Substitute $x = 8$.

Left Side	Right Side
$3x - 6$	18
$= 3(8) - 6$	
$= 18$	

To make sure you work with each side individually in your check, draw a vertical line between the left side and the right side

Since the left side and the right side are equal, we know that our solution, $x = 8$, is correct.
Note that we used the order of operations in the check.
We multiplied 3 by 8 before subtracting 6.

Example 2:

Solve $\dfrac{a}{5} + 4 = -2$

Step 1: *Subtract 4 from both sides.*

$$\dfrac{a}{5} + 4 - 4 = -2 - 4$$

$$\dfrac{a}{5} = -6$$

Step 2: *Multiply both sides by 5.*

$$(5)\dfrac{a}{5} = (5)(-6)$$

$$a = -30$$

Check the solution.

Substitute a = –30.

Left Side	Right Side
$\dfrac{a}{5} + 4$	-2
$= \dfrac{-30}{5} + 4$	
$= -6 + 4$	
$= -2$	

We divided –30 by 5 before adding 4 because division must be done before addition.

$a = -30$ is correct

PUT INTO PRACTICE

1. Jennifer solved each of the following equations.
   Her solution for x is given in parentheses beside each equation.
   Verify each of her solutions by using a left side / right side check.
   If you find any incorrect solutions, re-solve the equation and check your answer.

   a. $2x - 6 = -4$ (1)   b. $4x + 7 = -21$ (–6)

   c. $7x + 13 = 97$ (12)   d. $\dfrac{x}{11} + 38 = 42$ (44)

   e. $\dfrac{x}{6} + 10 = 1$ (–66)   f. $12x - 50 = 46$ (8)

Example 1

Elaine was in a hurry to do her grocery shopping, and wasn't paying attention to the pricing at the checkout counter. It wasn't until she was in her car that she thought about the cost of her purchases.

"The total bill for 8 cans of soup and a 4-litre jug of milk was \$13.18.

I know the milk was \$3.98, but I'm sure the soup was supposed to be on sale for 99¢ per can. Is that how much I paid for the soup?"

What does Elaine need to find?

   Answer: The price per can of soup

   Step 1:   *Define the variable:* Let the price she paid per can of soup be $\$p$.

   Step 2:   *Set up the equation:* 8 cans of soup plus milk = total bill
$$8p \quad + \ 3.98 \ = 13.18$$

   Step 3:   *Solve for p:*

$$8p + 3.98 = 13.18$$
$$8p - 3.98 = 13.18 - 3.98 \qquad \textit{Subtract 3.98 from each side.}$$
$$8p = 9.20$$
$$\frac{8p}{8} = \frac{9.20}{8} \qquad \textit{Divide each side by 8.}$$
$$p = 1.15$$

   Step 4:   *State the answer in a sentence:*

   Elaine paid \$1.15 per can, so she did not get the sale price.

You will find it helpful to follow the four steps when solving problems.

Each equation will follow one of these formats:

$$ax + b = c \qquad \frac{x}{a} + b = c \qquad ax - b = c \qquad \frac{x}{a} - b = c$$

where a, b and c are numbers, and x (or whatever letter you have chosen) represents the value you are trying to determine.

After a party, Jason was given all of the doughnuts that were left over.

He decided to share them with four of his friends.

When he delivered the doughnuts to Ariel she asked him "Why am I getting 14 doughnuts?"

He explained that he had shared them equally among 5 people and that she was getting her share plus one extra.

Ariel then said: "I know how many doughnuts were left over."

This is what Ariel did.

Hint: The answer is the number of doughnuts left over.

> *Step 1:* *Define the variable.*
>
> *Step 2:* *Set up the equation.*
>
> *Step 3:* *Solve for d.*
>
> *Step 4:* *State the answer in a sentence.*

PUT INTO PRACTICE

$$9m + 12 \times 2.10 = 42.21$$

1. The North Hills High School volleyball team stopped for lunch on their way to the tournament in Edmonton.

   They ordered nine milkshakes and twelve hamburgers.

   The manager paid the bill of $42.21.

   When the players were back in the van they were deciding how much each person owed.
   The manager remembered that the cost of one hamburger was $2.10.

   What was the price of one milkshake?

$$3 \times (\text{each share}) + 6 = 45$$

2. Carl, James and Rob decided to celebrate the end of the semester by going out for dinner.

   At the end of the meal, they each contributed an equal amount to the cost.

   Then they realized they forgot the tip, so they added an extra $6.00.

   If the entire cost of the dinner, including tip, was $45, how much did each boy pay before adding the tip?

3. On her last visit to the grocery store, Larrissa spent half the money she had on fruits and vegetables.

   She also bought a loaf of bread for $1.39.

   If she had $2.36 left after paying for her groceries, how much money did she have when she entered the store?

4. During a recent trip to the grocery store, Brian bought 2 dozen eggs and a litre of milk.
   His total bill came to $3.87.

   If a litre of milk cost $1.49, what was the price of one dozen eggs?

5. Tamara would like to buy a new pair of jeans which cost $74.90, tax included, and she has already saved $35 towards their cost.
Her job as a server pays $6.65/hour.

How many hours will Tamara have to work until she has enough money to buy the jeans?

$$\frac{tips}{6} \text{ and } 1.75 \text{ is } 11.25$$

6. Kevin works as a server at a busy family restaurant.
Last Saturday he spent one-sixth of his tips on dinner after his shift.
Bus fare home was $1.75, which Kevin also paid from his tips that day.
The total amount he spent was $11.25.

How much did he make in tips last Saturday?

7. Johann baked three kinds of cookies: chocolate chip, oatmeal raisin, and peanut butter.
He made equal numbers of chocolate chip and peanut butter cookies.
He also made thirty oatmeal raisin cookies.
He baked a total of 110 cookies.

How many peanut butter cookies did he make?

8. Tina works as a server Friday and Saturday evenings at a popular restaurant.
   On a recent Friday shift one-quarter of the tables in her section were reserved for groups celebrating birthday parties.
   Two of the groups did not show up.
   By the end of her shift, Tina had served three birthday parties.

   How many tables were in Tina's section that Friday evening?

9. After the divisional basketball championships, the winning team celebrated by ordering pizza.
   Pepperoni pizzas cost $10.00 each and a third of the bill was for Hawaiian pizzas.
   If the amount spent on pepperoni and hawaiian pizzas was $60.00

   How many pepperoni pizzas did the team buy?

Cost of pop ordered:
   $0.63p.

Credit for returns:
   $18 \times \$0.63$

10. For the final athletic awards night in June, the coaches of Westwood High School ordered submarine sandwiches and pop.
    Each can of pop cost the school 63¢, and any unopened cans could be returned for a full refund.
    The final amount paid for pop was $272.16 after 18 unopened cans were returned.

    How many cans of pop did the school order?

RATIOS, RATES AND PERCENTS

RATIO

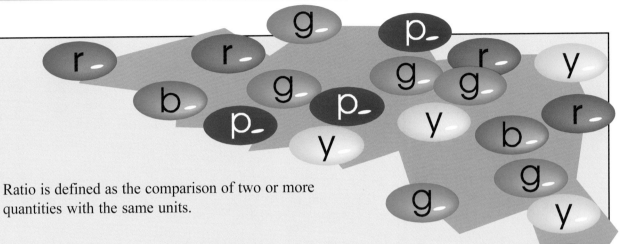

Ratio is defined as the comparison of two or more quantities with the same units.

NOTE

- Most ratios which have two terms can be written in fraction form.

- Ratios with more than two terms cannot be written in fraction form.

Example 1:

What is the ratio of purple to red?

What is the ratio of red to yellow to purple?

What is the ratio of purple to the total number of Smarties™?

Solution: The ratio of purple to red is $\dfrac{3}{5}$ or 3:5.

The ratio of red to yellow to purple is 5:4:3.

The ratio of purple to total is $\dfrac{3}{20}$ or 3:20.

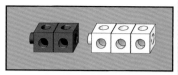

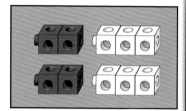

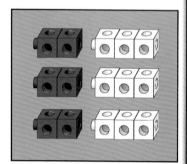

Raisin spice cake is made with molasses and sour milk in the ratio of 2:3. Model this using brown linking cubes to represent the molasses and white linking cubes to represent the sour milk.

By adding another identical length, we represent the amount of molasses and sour milk for double the recipe.

Now there are 4 measures of molasses and 6 measures of sour milk and the ratio is 4:6.

By continually including identical lengths, we can create many different but equivalent ratios:

The ratio is 6:9.

The ratio is now 8:12.
The sets of linking cubes indicate that 2:3 = 4:6 = 6:9 = 8:12.

Write these ratios as equivalent fractions.

If each term of a ratio is multiplied by the same number, then the new ratio is equivalent to the original one.

This is the same idea that you used with equivalent fractions. **(If the numerator and denominator of a fraction are multiplied by the same number, then the new fraction is equivalent to the original one.)**

1. Use coloured cubes to show the following ratios.
   Draw and colour the cubes and write the ratio beside each diagram.
   a. 3:5   b. 5:3   c. 4:7   d. 4:8

Example 2:

In a parking lot, there are 8 red cars and 12 blue ones.
Use coloured cubes, diagrams, computer graphics or other methods to display this situation.
What is the ratio of red cars to blue cars?

Solution:

The ratio can be written as:

$$R:B = 8:12 \quad \text{or} \quad \frac{R}{B} = \frac{8}{12}$$

These can be reduced to lowest terms in the same way that fractions are reduced to lowest terms.
Divide 8 by 4 and divide 12 by 4.

$$R:B = 2:3 \quad \text{or} \quad \frac{R}{B} = \frac{2}{3}$$

2. In a box of Smarties™ there were 7 green, 6 yellow, 2 blue, 8 red and 3 purple Smarties™.
   Using this information write the ratios of:
   a. red to yellow   b. green to purple
   c. blue to yellow   d. yellow to blue
   e. red to the total number   f. red to all the others

3. With a partner select twelve coloured cubes, making sure you have at least three different colours.
   Make up three different ratio questions for another student to answer.
   Make sure you include questions on colour to colour, and colour to total.
   In your notebook draw diagrams to represent the cubes and write the ratio, in lowest terms, beside each diagram.

Example 3:

A box of Smarties™ contains 12 green, 10 red, 6 yellow, 5 pink, 4 blue, and 3 purple Smarties.™
Write the following ratios of Smarties.™

    a. Green:pink:purple

    b. Red:yellow:blue

    c. Yellow:green;purple

    d. pink:yellow:blue:red:green

Solution:

Since each ratio contains three or more colours they cannot be written in fraction form.

    a. 12:5:3

    b. 10:6:4 = 5:3:2   *Divide each term by 2.*

    c. 6:12:3 = 2:4:1   *Divide each term by 3.*

    d. 5:6:4:10:12

4. Lay out 3 red cubes, 4 blue, 2 green, and 1 yellow cube.
   Draw diagrams to represent the following ratios.
   Write the ratio beside each diagram.

    a. Three red: one blue: two green

    b. Two red: three blue: one yellow

    c. Four blue:two red;two green

    d. One yellow: two green: three blue:one red

Example 4:

A 48 kg bag of fertilizer contains 2 parts nitrogen, 3 parts phosphorus, and 7 parts potash.

   a. Write this information in ratio form.

Solution:

   Nitrogen:Phosphorus:Potash = 2:3:7

   b. How many kilograms of each nutrient are in the bag?

Solution:

   There are 2 parts nitrogen, 3 parts phosphorus and 7 parts of potash.
   There are 12 parts altogether.

   Two of the 12 parts are nitrogen so $\frac{2}{12}$ or $\frac{1}{6}$ is nitrogen.

   $\frac{1}{6} \times 48$ kg = 8 kg of nitrogen.

   Three of the 12 parts are phosphorus so $\frac{3}{12}$ or $\frac{1}{4}$ is phosphorous.

   $\frac{1}{4} \times 48$ kg = 12 kg of phosphorus.

   Seven of the 12 parts are potash so $\frac{7}{12}$ is potash.

   $\frac{7}{12} \times 48$ kg = 28 kg of potash.

   There are 8 kg of nitrogen, 12 kg of phosphorous and 28 kg of potash.

5. A feed storeowner has to make up 60 kg of feed.
    The feed has to contain wheat, oats and corn in the ratio 5:3:4.

    How many kilograms of each cereal are required?

A recipe for a soft drink requires 80 parts of water, 8 parts colouring, 37 parts of flavoured sugar.

a. Write this in ratio form.

b. How many millitres of each ingredient are in a 750 mL bottle?

a. W:C:F = 80:□:37.

b. The total number of parts is □ + 8 + 37 = □.

$$\frac{80}{125} \text{ or } \frac{\Box}{25} \text{ of the contents is water.}$$

Divide numerator and denominator by □.

$$\frac{16}{25} \times 750 = \frac{16}{1} \times 30$$
$$= \Box$$

The bottle contains 480 mL of water.

$$\frac{\Box}{125} \text{ is colouring.}$$

$$\frac{8}{125} \times \Box = 48$$

The bottle contains □ mL of colour.

The rest of the soft drink is sugar and flavouring.

The total of water and colouring is (□ + □) mL.

The remaining amount is (750 − □) mL.

The bottle contains □ mL of flavoured sugar.

Example 5:

The ratio of oil to vinegar in a secret salad dressing was 7:3.
The chef put 357 mL of oil into a decanter.
How much vinegar did she have to add to maintain the ratio?

Solution:

$$\frac{\text{Oil}}{\text{Vinegar}} = \frac{7}{3}$$

$$\frac{357 \text{ mL}}{V} = \frac{7}{3}$$

When written this way, the variable (V) is in the denominator.
The equation will be easier to solve if you re-write the ratios so that V is in the numerator.
Since the ratio of oil to vinegar was 7:3, then the ratio of vinegar to oil was 3:7.

$$\frac{\text{Vinegar}}{\text{Oil}} = \frac{3}{7}$$

$$\frac{V}{357} = \frac{3}{7}$$

$$\frac{\text{Vinegar}}{\text{Oil}} = \frac{3}{7}$$

$$\frac{V}{357} = \frac{3}{7}$$

Use equivalent fractions.
(What do I have to multiply
by 7 to get 357?)

OR

Multiply both sides by 357.

$$357 \times \frac{V}{357} = 357 \times \frac{3}{7}$$

$$\frac{V}{357} = \frac{3 \times 51}{7 \times 51}$$

On the right side,
divide 357 and 7 by 7.

$$\frac{V}{357} = \frac{153}{357}$$

$$V = 51 \times \frac{3}{1}$$

Since the denominators are the same,
then the numerators are equal.

$$V = 153$$

$$V = 153$$

She added 153 mL of vinegar

In a survey done by the students it was noted that: "Five out of six smokers who quit smoking enjoyed their food more."

Use this ratio to calculate:

  a. How many people out of 42 ex-smokers enjoy their food more?

  b. How many ex-smokers were polled, if 200 of them reported that they enjoyed their food more?

a. The ratio of "enjoyed" to the total number is
    E:T = $\square$: $\square$

$$\frac{\text{enjoy}}{\text{total}} = \frac{5}{6}$$

$$\frac{e}{42} = \frac{\square}{6}$$

$$42 \times \frac{e}{42} = \square \times \frac{5}{6} \quad \text{Multiply both sides by } \square.$$

$$1 \times \frac{e}{1} = 7 \times \frac{\square}{1}$$

$$e = \square$$

$\square$ people enjoyed their food more.

b. $\dfrac{\text{enjoy}}{\text{total}} = \dfrac{5}{6}$

$\dfrac{200}{t} = \dfrac{5}{6}$

$\dfrac{t}{200} = \dfrac{6}{5}$

$\square \times \dfrac{t}{200} = \square \times \dfrac{6}{5}$ Multiply both sides by 200.

$1 \times \dfrac{t}{1} = \square \times \dfrac{6}{1}$

$t = 240$

$\square$ ex-smokers were polled.

PUT INTO PRACTICE

6. The chef in Example 5 made a mistake and reversed the ratios.
   I.e. the ratio of oil to vinegar was 3:7.

   If she still used 357 mL of oil, how much vinegar did she require?

7. A recipe recommends adding 3 cans of water to 1 can of concentrate.
   This means there is three times as much water as there is concentrate in the final solution.

   a. What is the ratio of concentrate to water?

   b. What is the ratio of concentrate to final solution?

   c. If the final mixture contains 304 mL of liquid, how much concentrate was used?

Example 1:

A metal alloy has 1 part gold, 5 parts copper and 12 parts nickel.

    a. Write this information as a ratio.

Solution:

   G:C:N = 1:5:12

    b. If a sample of the alloy contains 60 g of nickel, how many grams of copper does it contain?

Solution:

Since we are only dealing with copper and nickel, the ratio of copper to nickel is 5:12.

Write the ratio as a fraction.
We need to calculate the mass of copper, so write the fraction with the copper mass in the numerator.

$$\frac{\text{Copper}}{\text{Nickel}} = \frac{5}{12}$$

There are 60 g of nickel.

$$\frac{C}{60} = \frac{5}{12}$$

Multiply both sides by 60.

$$60 \times \frac{C}{60} = 60 \times \frac{5}{12}$$

Divide 60 by 12 and divide 12 by 12.

$$C = 5 \times \frac{5}{1}$$

$$C = 25$$

OR

$$\frac{C}{60} = \frac{5}{12}$$

Use equivalent fractions to make the denominators the same. (Multiply 12 by 5 and 5 by 5.)

$$\frac{C}{60} = \frac{5 \times 5}{12 \times 5}$$

$$\frac{C}{60} = \frac{25}{60}$$

Since the denominators are the same, the numerators are equal.

$$C = 25$$

Therefore, the alloy contains 25 g of copper.

Copy and complete the solution for this question.

In their last game, the Icemen had 23 shots-on-goal and scored 3 goals.
They had not kept track of the number of shots-on-goal but knew that they had scored 39 goals in the season.
Predict how many shots-on-goal they had.

Assume that the ratio for the season was the same as the ratio for the last game.

$$\frac{\text{goals}}{\text{shots}} = \frac{3}{23}$$

$$\frac{39}{s} = \frac{3}{23}$$

$$\frac{\square}{39} = \frac{\square}{3}$$

$$\square \times \frac{s}{39} = \square \times \frac{23}{3} \quad \text{Multiply both sides by 39.}$$

$$1 \times \frac{s}{1} = 13 \times \frac{23}{1}$$

$$s = \square$$

The Iceman probably had $\square$ shots-on-goal.

1. Headache tablets contain 6 mg of active ingredients, 2 mg of buffers and 1 mg of filler.
   The tablets in a full bottle have a mass of 810 mg.

   a. Write these ingredients as a ratio.

   b. How much of each ingredient is in the bottle?

2. Write each of the following ratios in their lowest terms:
   a. 6:4
   b. 12:18:24
   c. 6:9:3:12
   d. 140:70:280:210
   e. 8:2
   f. 10:24:16
   g. 27:30:60
   h. 40:30:15:10:5

3. Choose three of the ratios in No. 2 and state a possible situation that the ratio could represent.
   E.g., 6:4 could represent the ratio of males to females on the ice in a hockey game.

4. Determine which ratio is larger.
       5:6 or 7:9

$5:6 = \dfrac{5}{6}, \quad 7:9 = \dfrac{\square}{9}$

A common denominator for 6 and 9 is $\square$.

We multiply 6 by $\square$ to obtain the common denominator (18).

We multiply 9 by $\square$ to obtain the common denominator ($\square$).

$\dfrac{5}{6} = \dfrac{5 \times \square}{6 \times 3}$

$\dfrac{7}{9} = \dfrac{\square \times 2}{9 \times \square}$

$= \dfrac{\square}{18}$

$= \square$

$\dfrac{5}{6} > \dfrac{7}{9}$

5. Determine which ratio is larger.

$$\frac{3}{4} \text{ or } \frac{7}{8}$$

Divide 3 by 4.   Divide 7 by 8.

$$\frac{3}{4} = 0.\square$$ $$\frac{7}{8} = 0.\square$$

$$\frac{7}{8} > \frac{3}{4}$$

6. Determine which ratio is larger:

a. 1:3 or 3:5   b. $\frac{5}{12}$ or $\frac{10}{23}$

c. 8:11 or 7:10   d. $\frac{4}{5}$ or $\frac{2}{3}$

e. $\frac{11}{32}$ or $\frac{5}{16}$ f. 1:4 or 3:8

g. $\frac{6}{10}$ or $\frac{2}{5}$ h. $\frac{14}{20}$ or $\frac{7}{8}$

Example 2:

The recipe for a fruit punch specifies 1 part pineapple juice, 2 parts orange juice, 3 parts strawberry juice and 6 parts tonic water.

    a. Write this information in ratio notation and include the total number of parts in the punch.

Solution:

The total number of parts is $1 + 2 + 3 + 6$, or 12.

The ratio of pineapple to orange to strawberry to tonic water to total is 1:2:3:6:12. I.e., $P:O:S:W:T = 1:2:3:6:12$.

    b. You need to make 36 L of punch for a wedding reception. How much of each ingredient do you need?

Solution:

We know that 12 parts will be 36 L.
One part will be 36 L ÷ 12 = 3 L.
Two parts will be 3 L × 2 = 6 L, etc.

The information can be shown in a table.

Pineapple	Orange	Strawberry	Tonic	Punch
1 part	2 parts	3 parts	6 parts	12 parts
3 L	6 L	9 L	18 L	36 L

$$\frac{gold}{75} = \frac{9}{3}$$

$$\frac{copper}{total} = \frac{3}{24}$$

7. A gold goblet was made from an alloy that contained 3 parts copper, 8 parts nickel, 4 parts silver and 9 parts gold.

   a. Write this in ratio notation.
      (Include the total number of parts.)

   b. If the goblet contained 75 g of copper, how much gold did it contain?

   c. If the goblet had a total mass of 600 g, what was the mass of each of the metals?

   d. A wine decanter, made from the same alloy, contained 250 g of nickel.
      What was the mass of the decanter?

8. The gas used in a whipped cream dispenser is 3 parts carbon dioxide and 1 part nitrogen.
   In one such whipped cream dispenser, there were 380 g of gas.

   a. Write this information, including the total number of parts, in ratio form.

   b. How many grams of carbon dioxide did the dispenser contain?

   c. How many grams of nitrogen did the dispenser contain?

9. A restaurant employed two receptionists, four chefs and six servers.

    a. Write this information and the total number of people in ratio notation.

    b. A larger restaurant had the same positions of responsibility and employed 96 people in the same ratio as the smaller one.

        i. How many chefs were there in the larger restaurant?

        ii. How many servers were there?

10. A textile mill produced material that was a blend of 9 parts cotton, 4 parts rayon, and 2 parts nylon (by mass). The mill produced 75 000 kg of this cloth.

    a. Write this information and the total number of parts in ratio notation.

    b. How much rayon did they use?

11. An ingenious mother devised a way to get her son to eat a nutritious dinner most nights of the year.
She divided a dartboard into 73 identical sectors.
Seventy-two of them were labeled "F", for family dinner, and one was labeled "B", for a meal the boy could choose for himself.
The boy was asked to throw a dart at the board to determine whether he would eat the family dinner or not.
In one year, the boy threw the dart 365 times.

    a. What would be the most likely ratio of F:B?
(Assume that the dart would strike the target at a random point.)

    b. Predict how many times in the year the boy likely ate a family dinner.

Rate:

A comparison of two quantities measured in different units.

Unit Rate:

A comparison of two different quantities in which the second term (quantity) has a value of 1.

50 km/h is a unit rate because the unit of time is one hour.

INTERACTIVE LESSONS

Examples of rates:

a. Speed is the distance traveled in each hour.

b. Typing speed is the number of words typed per minute.

c. Density is the mass of one cubic centimetre.

d. Fuel consumption is the amount of fuel used in one hour.

e. Rate of pay is the amount you are paid for each hour of work.

f. Production rate is the number of items produced in one hour (or one day).

INVESTIGATION

What does it mean when we say:

a. The typist is typing at 80 words per minute?

b. The water is flowing at 50 L/min?

c. The car is traveling at 80 km/h?

d. The heart is beating at 78 beats per minute?

e. The gold has a density of 19.3 g/cm^3?

With your partner make a list of ten different examples of rates.

Example 1:

John took two hours to type his assignment.
He produced nine pages with an average of 800 words on each page.
What is John's rate of keyboarding?

Solution:

Total number of words	$= 9 \times 800$ words
	$= 7200$ words
Time	$= 2$ h
	$= 120$ min

$$\text{Rate of keyboarding} = \frac{7200 \text{ words}}{120 \text{ min}}$$
$$= 60 \text{ words/min.}$$

Example 2:

On average a cow can produce 20 L of milk per day.

   a. At this rate, how much milk can she produce in 1 year?

Solution:

20 L of milk/day for 365 days of the year.

Total production	$= (20)(365)$ L
	$= 7300$ L in one year

If each litre of milk contains 12% cream, how many litres of cream does this cow produce in 1 week?

Solution:

One week = 7 days

Weekly production	$= 20$ L/day for 7 days
	$= 20 \times 7$ L
	$= 140$ L

Each litre contains 12% cream	$(140 \text{ L}) \times 0.12$	$(12\% = 0.12)$
	$= 16.8$ L	

In one week, she produces 16.8 L of cream.

Example 3:

a. In a town of 5000 people there are four coffee shops. What is the rate of coffee shops to population?

Solution:

$$\text{Rate} = \frac{\text{Number of coffee shops}}{\text{Population}}$$

$$= \frac{4}{5000}$$

$$= \frac{4 \div 4}{5000 \div 4}$$

$$= \frac{1}{1250}$$

The rate is one coffee shop for 1250 people.

b. How many coffee shops would you expect in a city of 60 000 if the town's rate applies to the city.

Solution:

$$\frac{\text{Number of coffee shops}}{\text{Population}} = \frac{1}{1250}$$

$$\frac{c}{60000} = \frac{1}{1250}$$

$$60000 \times \frac{c}{60000} = 60000 \times \frac{1}{1250}$$

$$c = 48$$

You would expect 48 coffee shops to serve the town of 60 000 people.

1. Express each of the following as a rate:
   a. 105 km in 1.75 h

   b. 20 recipes among 5 people

   c. 960 people sitting at 120 banquet tables

   d. 1260 pages in 9 cookbooks

   e. 144 bags of potato chips in 12 boxes

   f. 312 eggs in 39 cartons

   g. 111 students in 3 cooking classrooms

   h. 52 L of cream in 4 identical containers

2. Calculate the missing values in the following tables:
   a.

Words typed	a	250	375	c
Minutes	1	2	b	8

   b.

Fuel used (L)	12.2	36.6	e	61
Time (h)	1	d	20	f

   c.

Tables	g	2	5	i
Chairs	8	16	h	264

   d.

Glasses	j	2	5	m
Volume (mL)	180	360	k	2700

3. A chef makes 35 pizzas in 175 minutes.

At what rate does she make pizzas?

How many complete pizzas can she make in 4 hours?

4. David is a caterer and last week he worked 32.5 hours. His rate of pay is $45/hour.

   a. How much did he earn last week?

   b. What would his rate of pay be if he earned $2209.88 for 41.5 hours?

5. Janush walked 35 blocks to her job at a snack bar in 14 minutes.

   a. How many blocks did she walk per minute?

   b. At that rate how many blocks could she walk in 2.5 hours?

6. Write each of the following as a unit rate:

   a. $14.96 for 4 mini meals

   b. $3.92 for 8 soft drinks

   c. Fruit pickers paid $426.00 for 40 hours work

   d. $2.88 for two-dozen cookies

   e. 400 words written on 80 birthday cakes

   f. 48 burgers for 16 players

   g. A total of 512 cookies on 32 trays

7. Stefan baked 28 pies in 14 hours.

   a. What was his baking rate in pies/hour?

   b. At this rate, how many pies would he bake in 74 hours?

Example 4:

A 250-mL cup of drip-brewed coffee has about 147 mg of caffeine.
A 170-mL cup of percolated coffee has about 120 mg of caffeine.

Which kind of coffee has the lower rate of caffeine?

Solution:

Calculate the unit rate for each.

Drip:

$$\frac{r \text{ mg}}{1 \text{ mL}} = \frac{147 \text{ mg}}{250 \text{ mL}} \qquad \text{Divide 147 by 250.}$$
$$r = 0.588$$

The rate of caffeine in drip coffee is about 0.588 mg/mL.

Percolator:

$$\frac{r \text{ mg}}{1 \text{ mL}} = \frac{120 \text{ mg}}{170 \text{ mL}} \qquad \text{Divide 12 by 17.}$$
$$r = 0.70588\ldots$$

The rate of caffeine in percolator coffee is about 0.706 mg/mL.

Drip coffee has the lower rate of caffeine.

Use cents instead of dollars.

$$\frac{c\cancel{c}}{1 \text{ g}} = \frac{1247\cancel{c}}{450 \text{ g}}$$

8. A chocolate rabbit has a mass of 450 g and costs $12.47 while a chocolate bar has a mass of 35 g and sells for $1.25.

   Which is the better buy? Why?

Get Thinking

If you are a server, you should be able to estimate the amount of a bill. Customers do not appreciate being overcharged, and undercharging customers may result in the loss of wages to you the server. Tips are calculated using percent. A useful skill is the ability to estimate a 15% tip. A customer may become irritated if you inquire as to whether they would like any change from a $20 bill if the cost of the meal was only $13.95. You would be giving the impression of expecting a $6 tip, which would be almost half the cost of the meal!

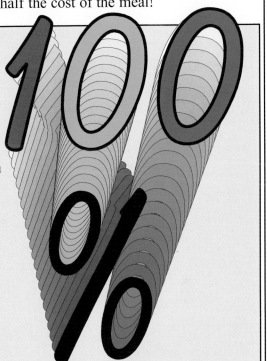

"What does % (per cent) mean?

Per cent comes from Latin.
It means *per* one hundred or out of 100.

Cent in Latin means **100**.
Per cent is a two term ratio in which the second term is 100.
I.e., it defines a fraction whose denominator is 100.

Percent is a useful number because it converts all fractions to the same denominator (100). It is then easy to compare different ratios.

INTERACTIVE LESSONS

INVESTIGATION

1. Percent has many applications in our daily lives. What do the following mean?
   a. There is a 20% chance of rain today.
   b. The bank rate is $8\frac{1}{2}$ %.
   c. The shopkeeper marked up the price by 15%.
   d. One serving of breakfast cereal contains 28% of your daily requirement of iron.
   e. 9.86% of the population of Canada live in Alberta.

Example 1:

a. In Joe's restaurant, Joe estimates that, on average, 85% of the tables are occupied. Express this as a fraction in lowest terms.

Solution

$$85\% = \frac{85}{100} \qquad \text{Simplify using equivalent fractions.}$$

$$= \frac{85 \div 5}{100 \div 5} \qquad \text{Divide numerator and denominator by 5.}$$

$$= \frac{17}{20}$$

b. If Joe has 40 tables how many are usually occupied?

Solution: $\dfrac{t}{40} = \dfrac{85}{100}$

$$\frac{t}{40} = \frac{17}{20}$$

$$40 \times \frac{t}{40} = 40 \times \frac{17}{20} \qquad \textbf{OR} \qquad \frac{t}{40} = \frac{17 \times 2}{20 \times 2}$$

$$t = 40 \times 17 \div 20 \qquad\qquad\qquad \frac{t}{40} = \frac{34}{40}$$

$$t = 34 \qquad\qquad\qquad\qquad\qquad t = 34$$

34 tables are usually occupied.

PUT INTO PRACTICE

Remember: Percent is a fraction with a denominator of 100

1. Convert the following to fractions in simplest form.
   a. 57%   b. 80%   c. 25%   d. 39%

Example 2:

Gerry bought a broken microwave for $40. He bought $10 worth of parts and repaired it. He sold it for $60.

Express his profit as:

a. a fraction of his total cost.

Solution: Profit $= \$60 - \$50$
                              $= \$10$

$$\frac{\text{Profit}}{\text{Total Cost}} = \frac{10}{50} \quad \text{Reduce using equivalent fractions.}$$

$$= \frac{1}{5}$$

b. a percentage of his total cost.

Solution:

$$\frac{\text{Profit}}{\text{Total Cost}} = \frac{\text{Percent}}{100}$$

$$\frac{10}{50} = \frac{x}{100} \qquad \text{Multiply both sides by 100.}$$

$$100 \times \frac{10}{50} = 100 \times \frac{x}{100}$$

$$2 \times 10 = x$$

$$x = 20$$

His profit was 20% of his cost.

---

2. Convert the following to percents.

a. 47:100

b. $\dfrac{23}{100}$

c. $\dfrac{225}{100}$

d. 43:50

e. 7:10

f. $\dfrac{6}{5}$

Example 3:

Convert the following to fractions in simplest form.

    a. One brand of cream cheese contains 4.5% protein.

Solution:

$$4.5\% \quad = \frac{4.5}{100}$$ *Change numerator to a whole number by multiplying numerator and denominator by 10.*

$$= \frac{45}{1000}$$ *Reduce to simplest form by dividing numerator and denominator by 5.*

$$= \frac{9}{200}$$

    b. One brand of jam contains $32\frac{1}{2}$ % sugar.

Solution:

$$32\frac{1}{2}\% \quad = \frac{65}{2}\%$$ *Change to an improper fraction.*

$$= \frac{65}{2} \div 100$$

$$= \frac{65}{2} \times \frac{1}{100}$$

$$= \frac{65}{200}$$ *Simplify by dividing numerator and denominator by 5.*

$$= \frac{13}{40}$$

Example 4:

a. Tatiana knows that in her milk bar, the ratio of milk shakes sales to other drinks sales is 5:3.

   Calculate the consumption of milk shakes as a percent of the total.

Solution:

The ratio of milkshakes to other drinks to total drinks is 5:3:8.
The ratio of milk shakes to all drinks is 5:8.

$$\frac{m}{100} = \frac{5}{8}$$

$$100 \times \frac{m}{100} = 100 \times \frac{5}{8} \qquad \textit{Multiply by 100 to get m.}$$

$$m = 100 \times 5 \div 8$$

$$m = 62.5$$

62.5% of the drinks are milk shakes.

b. Two-thirds of her customers are students.

   Calculate this as a percent.

Solution:

$$\frac{s}{100} = \frac{2}{3}$$

$$100 \times \frac{s}{100} = 100 \times \frac{2}{3} \qquad \textit{Multiply by 100 to get s.}$$

$$s = 100 \times 2 \div 3$$

$$s \doteq 66.7$$

66.7% of the customers are students.

c. In order to cover spoilage, preparation and serving costs, Tatiana charges 3.2 times the cost of the ingredients for each of her menu items.

Calculate this as a percent.

Solution:

The ratio of selling price to cost price is 3.2:1.

$$\frac{m}{100} = \frac{3.2}{1}$$

$$100 \times \frac{m}{100} = 100 \times \frac{3.2}{1} \qquad \textit{Multiply by 100 to get m.}$$

$$m = 100 \times 3.2$$

$$m = 320$$

The selling price is 320% of the cost price.

Note: A ratio in which the first term is greater than the second term becomes a percent that is greater than 100%.

3. Convert each of the following to a ratio and to a fraction in simplest form:

a. 12%   b. 3.2%   c. 10%   d. 147%

e. $\frac{1}{2}$%   f. $\frac{3}{4}$%   g. 0.6%   h. 84%

i. 63.5%   j. 92.5%   k. $92\frac{1}{2}$%   l. 1%

4. Write each of the following as a per cent:

a. 57:100   b. 25:50   c. 75:200

d. 60:75   e. 9:12   f. 8:10

g. 650:1250   h. 19:19   i. 24.3:1

j. 8.45:13.0   k. 1.9:1.9   l. 0.12:0.12

Example 5:

When Guy re-opened his food stand he advertised that his hamburgers contained 25% more meat.

Write this as a decimal.

Solution:

$$25\% = \frac{25}{100}$$

$$= \frac{25 \div 25}{100 \div 25} \qquad \textit{Divide 25 and 100 by 25.}$$

$$= \frac{1}{4} \qquad 1 \div 4, \quad 4\overline{)1.00}$$

$$= 0.25$$

5. Complete a copy of the table below.

	Fraction	Decimal	Per cent
a.	$\frac{3}{5}$		
b.		0.125	
c.			345%
d.		6.25	

6. Convert each of the following to decimal form:

a. 63% b. $\frac{3}{5}$ c. $4\frac{1}{2}$

d. 93.2% e. 145% f. $\frac{7}{8}$

g. $\frac{6}{8}$ h. $\frac{3}{16}$ i. 45% j. 12.3%

Example 6:

   a. Calculate a tip of 15% on a bill of $21.67

Solution:

$$\frac{\text{Tip}}{\text{Bill}} = \frac{\text{Percent}}{100}$$

$$\frac{t}{21.67} = \frac{15}{100} \qquad \textit{Multiply both sides by 21.67.}$$

$$21.67 \times \frac{t}{21.67} = 21.67 \times \frac{15}{100}$$

$$t = 21.67 \times 15 \div 100$$

$$t = 3.2505$$

The tip is $3.25.

   b. Marlene left a tip of $3.35 when her bill was $22.34.
What percent is this?

Solution:

$$\frac{\text{Tip}}{\text{Bill}} = \frac{\text{Percent}}{100}$$

$$\frac{3.35}{22.34} = \frac{x}{100} \qquad \textit{Multiply both sides by 100.}$$

$$100 \times \frac{3.35}{22.34} = 100 \times \frac{x}{100}$$

$$100 \times 3.35 \div 22.34 = x$$

$$x = 14.9955\ldots$$

Her tip was about 15%.

c. Brad usually tips 15% of the bill.
His tip was $3.50.

What was the likely amount of the bill?

Solution:

$$\frac{\text{Tip}}{\text{Bill}} = \frac{\text{Percent}}{100}$$

$$\frac{3.50}{b} = \frac{15}{100}$$

$$\frac{b}{3.5} = \frac{100}{15} \qquad \textit{Multiply both sides by 3.5.}$$

$$3.5 \times \frac{b}{3.5} = 3.5 \times \frac{100}{15}$$

$$b = 3.5 \times 100 \div 15$$

$$b = 23.33\ldots$$

The bill was likely $23.33.

$$\frac{\text{Part}}{\text{Whole}} = \frac{\text{Percent}}{100}$$

7. Determine each of the following:

    a. What is 14% of 250?

    b. What is 19% of 20?

    c. What is 108% of 150?

    d. What is 6% of 18?

8. Calculate each of the following:

    a. 50 is what per cent of 100?

    b. 9 is what per cent of 15?

    c. 18 is what per cent of 25?

    d. 70 is what per cent of 35?

9. Calculate each of the following:

    a. 50% of what number is 25?

    b. 200% of what number is 6?

    c. 75% of what number is 9?

Example 1:

Sandy wanted to re-paint her juice bar and calculated that she would need 8 L of paint.
Each can of paint contains 4 L of paint.
At the paint store, she noticed that paint was on sale at 25% off the regular price.
If the regular price of the paint was $39.80 what was the sale price of the paint
and how much did Sandy pay for her paint?

Solution:

$$25\% \text{ of } \$39.80 \quad = \frac{25}{100} \times \$39.80$$

$$= \frac{1}{4} \times \$39.80$$

$$= \$9.95$$

Cost of one can of paint   = $39.80 − $9.95
                           = $29.85   Since she needed 2 cans, Sandy paid $59.70.

Example 2:

Joe wanted to refit the kitchen in his restaurant and estimated it would cost him $12 500.00.

When he went to the supplier he was told he could get the equipment for $\frac{3}{4}$ of that price.

    a. How much would Joe have to pay for his new equipment?

Solution:

$$\frac{3}{4} \times \$12500 \qquad = \$9375$$

Joe would have to pay $9375

    b. If he had to pay 7% tax what would be the total cost of the equipment?

Solution:

Sales tax $= \frac{7}{100} \times \$9375$

                         = $656.25

Total cost   = $9375 + $656.25
                        = $10 031.25

Example 3:

a. In Joe's restaurant 40% of the 60 restaurant employees are male.
    What is the ratio of males to females?

Solution:

Number of males $\quad = \dfrac{40}{100} \times 60$

$$= (40 \div 100) \times 60 \qquad \textbf{OR} \qquad = 0.40 \times 60$$
$$= 24 \qquad\qquad\qquad\qquad\quad = 24$$

There are 24 males, therefore there are
$$60 - 24$$
$$= 36 \text{ females}$$

The ratio of males to females is 24:36 or 2:3   *Divide both numbers by 12*

b. Joe observed there were 76 males and 55 females eating dinner in the restaurant.
    What percent of the dinner guests were female (to the nearest whole number)?

Solution:

Total number of diners is $\quad 76 + 55$
$$= 132$$

Fraction of females $\quad = \dfrac{55}{132}$

$$\dfrac{f}{100} = \dfrac{55}{132}$$

$$100 \times \dfrac{f}{100} = 100 \times \dfrac{55}{132} \qquad \textit{Multiply both sides by 100.}$$
$$f = 100 \times 55 \div 132$$
$$f = 41.666\ldots$$
$$f \doteq 42$$

About 42% of the guests were female.

c. Joe is catering a special dinner party and he observes that nine of the guests have arrived.
If this represents $\frac{1}{4}$ of the expected guests, how many guests are expected?

Solution: **OR** $\frac{1}{4} = \frac{9}{g}$

If 9 represents one quarter then
4×9 represents the entire group.

$\frac{4}{1} = \frac{g}{9}$

$9 \times \frac{4}{1} = 9 \times \frac{g}{9}$

36 guests are expected. $36 = g$

PUT INTO PRACTICE

1. What is:
   a. 12% of $50?
   b. 25% of 250 L of milk?
   c. 18% of 60 g of cheese?
   d. 10% of 70 frozen dinners?

2. Laurie exercises regularly.
   She tries to burn at least 2000 Calories every day.
   Express each of the following as a percent of 2000 Calories.
   a. Cycling: 300 Calories   b. Swimming: 250 Calories
   c. Running: 500 Calories   d. Tennis: 400 Calories

3. The air we breathe contains 4% pure oxygen and 27% nitrogen, as well as other gases.
   a. If a room contains 960 m³ of air, how much is:
      i. pure oxygen?   ii. nitrogen?

   b. Another room whose volume is 500 m³ contains 53 m³ of carbon dioxide.
      What percent of carbon dioxide does it contain?

Example 4:

On the menu meal No.1 is listed at $7.99.
Calculate the GST on this meal.

Solution:

The GST is 7%.   OR   Change $7.99 to 799¢.

$$\frac{t}{7.99} = \frac{7}{100}$$

Multiply by 7.99.

$$\frac{t}{799} = \frac{7}{100}$$

Multiply by 799.

$$7.99 \times \frac{t}{7.99} = 7.99 \times \frac{7}{100}$$

$$799 \times \frac{t}{799} = 799 \times \frac{7}{100}$$

$$t = 7.99 \times 7 \div 100$$

$$t = 799 \times 7 \div 100$$

$$t = 0.5593$$

$$t = 55.93$$

The GST is $0.56.   The GST is 56¢.

4. Nikki uses a simple method to calculate what she should charge for catering.
   She charges 350% of the cost of the food that she supplies.
   She is catering for a seniors meeting and knows that the food will cost her $45.
   She offers a 30% discount for seniors.

   a. What would the normal charge be?

   b. What is the amount of the discount?

   c. What will she charge the group?

5. In some provinces the tax is 15%.

   What is the tax on a meal that costs $44.99?

$$1m = 100 \text{ cm}$$

6. The organizers of a school fund-raising drive ordered a 4 metre long sub sandwich from the Supersub sandwich shop.
The people who attended the fund-raising event could buy as much of the sandwich as they wished provided it was in multiples of 5 cm.
Each 5 cm section sold for $1.25.

a. Judy bought one section, Dave bought three sections and Harold bought four sections.
What fraction of the sandwich did they buy?

b. One teacher bought 20 sections for her class.
What percent of the sandwich did she buy?
How much did she have to pay?

c. The principal bought 25 sections to send to the staff room.
What percent of the sandwich is left now?

d. What is the ratio of sold to unsold sections of the sandwich?

e. If the entire sandwich is sold, how much money will be collected?

7. In Tony's pizzeria, one of the pizza ovens broke down.
To repair it would cost $3825.
The cost of a new oven would be 20% more than the cost of repairing the old one.

a. What is the cost of a new oven?

b. If Tony repairs the oven he has to pay the full cost of repair.
If he buys a new one he can pay 60% of the cost and pay the rest in installments.

How much does he have to give as a down payment if he buys a new oven?

8. A farmer planted 1200 acres of corn but she only managed to harvest 1176 acres of her corn. Each acre yielded an average of 50 bushels of corn.

   a. What fraction of her corn could NOT be harvested?

   b. How many bushels of corn would the 1176 acres yield?

   c. In one day, she could harvest one eighth of the 1176 acres.
   How many acres was she able to harvest per day?

   d. If she sold 95% of her crop at $2.75/bushel, how much money did she receive?

9. Ben is a wholesaler who imports fruit and vegetables. On average, his mark-up is 60% of his cost.

   a. For a shipment of bananas, Ben paid $12 000.
   He sold 25% of the shipment to a food store chain.
   How much did he receive?

   b. A truckload of oranges cost Ben $15 000.
   He sold 12% of this load to a supermarket.
   How much did the supermarket pay for the oranges?

   c. A storeowner paid Ben $5000 for a shipment of lettuce.
   What did Ben pay for the lettuce?

   d. Ben gave 1.5% of his shipment of bananas and 1.5% of the load of oranges to his local food bank.
   What is the equivalent amount of money he could have donated?

10. Rhonda rents an industrial building for her catering business.
    The (rectangular) building has a floor space of 5000 ft².

    a. If the building is 100 ft long, how wide is it?

    b. The kitchen occupies 54% of the floor space.
        What is the floor area of the kitchen?

    c. The cold storage area occupies 32% of the floor space.
        What is the floor area of the storage area?

    d. Each of the two washrooms has the same area.
        The total area of both washrooms is 5% of the floor space.
        What is the floor area of each washroom?

    e. The remaining area is occupied by office space.

        i. What per cent of the building's floor space is occupied by the office?

        ii. What is the area occupied by office space?

11. During the depression a loaf of bread cost 5¢.
    Today, a similar loaf of bread costs $1.39.

    What is the increase in price?

    Express this increase as a percent of the original price.

$$\$1.39 = 139¢$$

Get Thinking

Rachel and Brian each made some orange juice.
Rachel used one cup of concentrate and added two cups of water.
Brian used one cup of concentrate but added five cups of water.

a. Who has the stronger solution?

b. What can Rachel do to make the ratio of concentrate to water in her container the same as Brian's?

Proportion:

A proportion is formed when two ratios are equal.

Two figures are similar if the corresponding angles are equal and the lengths of their corresponding sides are proportional or in the same ratio.
For example, in the figure, the sides of the larger figure are double the sizes of the sides of the smaller figure.

4:2 = 2:1
14:7 = 2:1
10:5 = 2:1
12:6 = 2:1

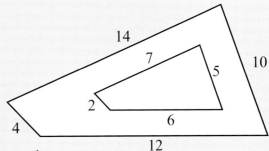

Think of a movie theatre as another example.
The image on the film is smaller than what you see on the screen.
However, one is proportional to the other.
For example if the screen image is 100 times the film image, then everything on the screen is 100 times larger than on the film.

- We know that the ratio of 5 to 8 is equivalent to a ratio of 10 to 16.

You can write this proportion in two different ways:

5:8 = 10:16

OR

$$\frac{5}{8} = \frac{10}{16}.$$

The second way is identical to the way that we write two equivalent fractions.

Example 1:

Trudy plans to make muffins and she knows the flour and sugar have to be mixed in the ratio of 5 to 1.
If she uses 6 cups of flour how much sugar should she use?

Solution:

The ratio of flour to sugar is $\dfrac{5}{1}$.

The amount of sugar is required, so rewrite this as the ratio of sugar to flour is $\dfrac{1}{5}$.

$$\frac{s}{6} = \frac{1}{5}$$

$$6 \times \frac{s}{6} = 6 \times \frac{1}{5} \qquad \textit{Multiply both sides by 6.}$$

$$s = 6 \times 1 \div 5 \quad \text{OR} \quad s = 6 \times 0.2$$

$$s = 1.2$$

Trudy needs 1.2 cups of sugar.

(This is a little less than 1.25 cups or, a little less than $1\dfrac{1}{4}$ cups.)

INVESTIGATION

A photographic negative has a height of 3.5 cm and a width of 2.5 cm.

When Harjit asked about an enlargement she was told that it could be made 17.5 cm high.

What would be the width of the print?

1. Calculate the missing term in each of the following proportions.
   Copy and complete the following solutions:
   a. $x:3 = 4:12$

$$\frac{x}{3} = \frac{\square}{12} \qquad\qquad \frac{x}{3} = \frac{\square}{12}$$

$$3 \times \frac{x}{3} = \square \times \frac{4}{12} \qquad \textbf{OR} \qquad \frac{x}{3} = \frac{1}{\square}$$

$$x = 3 \times \square \div \square \qquad\qquad x = \square$$
$$x = 1$$

b. $\dfrac{5}{y} = \dfrac{25}{30}$

$$\frac{y}{5} = \frac{\square}{25} \qquad \textbf{OR} \qquad \frac{y}{5} = \frac{\square}{25}$$

$$\square \times \frac{y}{5} = \square \times \frac{30}{25} \qquad\qquad \frac{y}{5} = \frac{\square}{5}$$

$$y = 5 \times \square \div \square \qquad\qquad y = 6$$

$$y = 6$$

$$\frac{11}{6} = \frac{k}{18}$$

2. Find the missing terms in the following proportions.
   a. $2:5 = w:20$ b. $6:11 = 18:k$
   c. $\dfrac{j}{3} = \dfrac{5}{16}$ d. $\dfrac{6}{9} = \dfrac{b}{3}$
   e. $7:c = 1:2$ f. $d:5 = 8:20$

3. Two ingredients of a special salad dressing are oil and vinegar and they have to be mixed in the proportion of five parts oil to two parts vinegar.
   Gail found she had only 9 mL of oil left.

   How much vinegar will she need to make the salad dressing?

Example 2:

A photograph of a hot dog is enlarged using a scale of 9:2.
In the original photograph, the hot dog is 7.6 cm long.
How long is it in the enlargement?

Solution:

$$\frac{h}{7.6} = \frac{9}{2}$$

$$7.6 \times \frac{h}{7.6} = 7.6 \times \frac{9}{2}$$

$$h = 7.6 \times 9 \div 2$$

$$h = 34.2$$

The hot dog is 34.2 cm long.

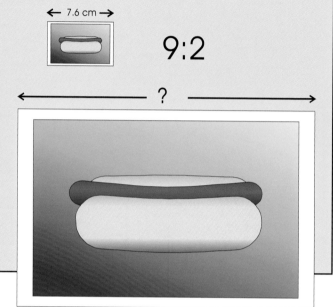

9:2

← 7.6 cm →

?

4. The front face of a restaurant is 12 m long.
   On its roof is an antenna which is 15 m tall.
   In an advertising photo the front face of the resturant
   is 3 cm long.
   What would be the height of the antenna in the photo?

5. The scale on the plans for a restaurant is 1:25.

   a. If the restaurant is 87 m long, what is the length of the
      restaurant on the plan?

   b. One room on the plan is 6 m wide.
      What is the width of the room in the actual restaurant?

The ratio of the length in
the plans to the real
length in the restaurant is
1:25.

$$\frac{l}{87} = \frac{1}{25}$$

6. Beside a picture of a lobster on a menu was a scale: picture: real = 1:6.
Juanita measured the lobster's tail in the picture and found it to be 1.75 cm.

   a. How long should the actual lobster's tail be?

   b. Juanita ordered the lobster and when it came she measured one of its claws.
   The claw was 8.4 cm long.
   How long would it be in the picture?

7. A health report stated that 5 out of 6 people who started an exercise program enjoyed their food more.
If this is true,

   a. out of 30 people in an exercise program how many enjoy their food more?

   b. how many people were polled, if 200 people claim to enjoy their food more?

8. In a special sauce, two major ingredients were honey and molasses in the ratio 13:9, respectively.
If 6 mL of honey were used to make the sauce, how much molasses was used?
(Answer to the nearest millilitre.)

9. In a high school health study it was reported that the ratio of females to males who exercised more than four times a week was 5:6.
If 80 female students exercised more than four times last week, how many males would you expect to have exercised more than four times last week?

Real World Project

You are now ready to start Steps 2 and 3 of your project.

In this unit you have used one and two-step equations, and rate, ratio and proportion, to solve for an unknown value.

Try using the skills you have developed to solve each of the following problems.

COOKING AT HOME

1. Laura is doubling a recipe that calls for $2\frac{1}{2}$ cups of flour.

   How much flour should she use?

2. The original recipe for a banana loaf calls for 2 cups of sugar and $3\frac{1}{4}$ cups of flour.

   Angel has used 13 cups of flour.

   a. How many loaves can he make?

   b. How much sugar does he need?

3. Margherita has her grandmother's favourite recipe for spaghetti sauce, but the recipe serves 12 people, and she would like to reduce the ingredients to serve two people only.

   If the recipe requires 3 tablespoons of oregano, how many tablespoons of the spice should Margherita use?

4. Anita is using a cookbook which was not written for the high altitude area in which she lives.

   At school she learned to adjust most cake recipes by raising the oven temperature 25°F and reducing the amount of baking powder by 25%.

   a. At what temperature should she bake a chocolate cake if the cookbook gives an oven temperature of 350°F?

   b. If the original recipe calls for 2 teaspoons of baking powder, how much baking powder should Anita use?

WORKING IN A RESTAURANT

5. Thomas is shredding cheese for tacos.

   He needs 3 cups of cheese, and he has already grated 1 cup.

   It has taken him 4 min.

   How much longer will it likely take?

6. A standard recipe for pita dough calls for $1\frac{1}{2}$ tbsp of oil per pita.

   Alex needs to prepare enough dough for 50 pitas.

   How many tablespoons of oil does he need?

   Alex would like to save time by using cups instead of tablespoons.
   A cup of oil is equal to 20 tbsp.
   How many cups of oil does he need?

7. Shannon is serving during a busy lunch hour.

   The regular price for a turkey sandwich is $3.95 and a bowl of soup is $2.95.

   The soup and sandwich combination is $5.95.

   A customer asks her how much he would save if he purchased the combination.

   What should she tell him?

8. Francis is interested in hosting at a local restaurant.

   He is offered two choices for pay: a salary of $7.20/h or 3% of the total restaurant receipts for the four-hour shift.

   a. Determine the total amount he would make per shift if he took the straight salary offer.

   b. What would the total receipts of the restaurant have to be for him to make the same amount as he would on straight salary?

   c. On a typical four-hour shift, the restaurant serves around 70 customers, with an average bill of $14.

      Based on this information, determine which method of payment you would recommend to Francis, and explain why.

$$\frac{\text{No. 8a Answer}}{t} = \frac{3}{100}$$

EATING OUT

9. At a popular fast food restaurant, the house special is priced at $3.45 and consists of a cheeseburger, fries and a medium drink.

   The prices per item are: $1.95 for a cheeseburger, $1.10 for an order of fries, and $1.25 for a medium drink.

   How much do you save by ordering the special?

10. Jason wants three buckets of wings.
    His neighbourhood store charges $12.95 for one bucket or $19.95 for two.

    a. How much should he pay for the three buckets?

    b. If he buys four buckets how much is he paying for the fourth bucket?

11. For his parent's wedding anniversary, Kevin took them to a trendy downtown restaurant.

    The bill, before taxes, was $93.35.

    a. How much should Kevin leave as a tip if he wants to tip 15%?

    b. The 7% GST was $6.53.

       Some people calculate the 15% tip by doubling the GST and adding 1% (divide by 100) of the original bill.
       Use this method to determine the amount of the tip.

    c. Explain any advantage there would be in using the second method.

12. Jonathan and Nikki have finished the main course at their favourite restaurant in Edmonton and would like to order dessert. They are not sure that they have enough money.

So far Jonathan's meal is $11.99 and Nikki's is $9.99. They each ordered a soft drink at $2.25.

Between the two of them, they have $35.00.

a. How much GST would they have to pay?

b. What is the total cost of the meal including GST?

c. Would they have enough money to order dessert if each dessert cost $3.95?

d. If they would like to leave a tip of 15% on the amount of the bill before GST, how much should they leave?

e. How much money would they have left after paying for the meals, including GST, and the 15% tip?

POINTS OF INTEREST

13. This statue of a Pyrogy on a Fork is located in Glendon, Alberta.

The width of the statue is 12 ft.
If its height is one foot greater than twice the width, how high is the statue?

14. Fahler, Alberta boasts this enormous statue of a honey bee.

The town is famous for its honey production, with 48 000 beehives producing 4.5 million kg of honey per year.

If the total number of bee hives in Canada is 600 000 what percent of Canadian beehives are in Fahler?

15. The town of Mundare, Alberta is home to this giant statue of a Kolbassa sausage ring.

This area of the province is renowned for its Ukrainian sausage.

If a local smokehouse produces 3300 kg of sausage in 3.5 hours, how many kilograms of sausages will be produced in 42 hours?

16. This giant cornstalk is located in Taber, Alberta.

A certain grain corn hybrid yielded 132 bushels/acre.

If a quarter section is 160 acres, how many bushels of this hybrid will a quarter section of land yield?

PROJECT

RUNNING A SUCCESSFUL RESTAURANT

Running a successful restaurant is the dream of many people, but unfortunately many restaurants fail within the first year. There are consulting businesses that specialize in helping create and maintain successful restaurants. Succesful restaurants are the products of hard work and determination by the individuals who start them.

Choose a successful restaurant in your neighbourhood. Select one that is especially popular with you and your friends.
It could also be one in which you have worked or are presently working as an employee.

STEP 1: RESEARCH THE HISTORY OF THE RESTAURANT OR RESTAURANT CHAIN.

Who first started the business, and where?
How many years has the business been in operation?
What factors led to the success of this restaurant?
Why does the restaurant continue to prosper?

STEP 2: COPY AND COMPLETE ONE OF THE FOLLOWING THREE TABLES FOR A 4-HOUR SHIFT.

Make sure you note the time of day of the shift, then answer the questions pertaining to the table that you chose.
You can adapt the tables to fit the information for the selected restaurant.
For example, the positions may have different names or an employee shift may be longer than four hours.
If possible, use a computer spreadsheet.

(A) STAFFING

Employee Position	Hourly salary ($)	Amount earned per 4-h shift ($)	Number of employees	Total Salary Paid ($)
Server				
Cook				
Manager				
Dishwasher				
Busboy				

Total Payroll Cost [   ]

1. Calculate the overall total payroll for the 4-hour shift.

2. What percentage of the total calculated in No.1 is paid to the server(s)?

3. Determine the new hourly salary of the dishwashers if they each receive a 10% raise.

(B) COST OF STOCKED ITEMS (DRY GOODS)

Item	Cost per Item	Number used per 4-hour shift	Total Cost ($)
Napkins			
Straws			
Plastic Forks			
Paper Cups			

Overall Total Cost [   ]

1. Calculate the total cost of all the dry goods for the 4-hour shift.

2. Write a ratio that compares the number of napkins to the number of paper cups.

3. How many napkins would be used when 1000 paper cups are used.

(C)   MENU ITEMS

1.   What is the overall total revenue from **all** of the menu items for the 4-hour shift?

2.   Many restaurants determine the price of the menu item as a percentage increase of the original cost of the ingredients. This percentage can be as low as 15% or as high as 35-40% depending on various factors such as supply and demand.

   Set the percent increase at 25% and use the overall total from No.1 to determine the original cost of the menu items sold during the 4-hour shift.

3.   The amount of profit made from the menu items is equal to the difference between the cost of the items to the restaurant and the total revenue made from their sale.

   Write an equation to calculate the profit (p) in terms of the cost (c) and the total revenue (r).

4.   Using your equation from No. 3, calculate the profit made on the menu items during the 4-hour shift.

	Cost ($)	Average number served per 4-hour shift	Total Revenue ($)
Appetizers			
1.			
2.			
3.			
Main Courses			
1.			
2.			
3.			
4.			
5.			
Salads			
1.			
2.			
3.			
Side Orders			
1.			
2.			
3.			
Beverages			
1.			
2.			
3.			
Desserts			
1.			
2.			
		Overall Total Revenue	

STEP 3: CONSIDER OTHER EXPENSES

1. The actual running of a restaurant is much more complicated than is outlined in this project.
   There are many other costs to the restaurant besides those given here.

   List three other general expenses that a restaurant owner has to consider.

2. How could a restaurant owner limit expenses and still run a restaurant that caters to the customer?

PERSPECTIVES: *ANGLES & CIRCLES*

GET THINKING

- ❑ How do pilots and air traffic controllers use angles to direct flights, arrivals and departures?

- ❑ What instruments could I design and build to help me follow the clues on a treasure map that uses angles and distance?

- ❑ What is the best combination of water heads to use in an underground sprinkler system to ensure even watering of a lawn?

- ❑ How do fabric designers such as quilters and kite builders use angles and circles to create vivid pictures using shapes?

AND MENTAL MATH, PROBLEM SOLVING, REASONING, TECHNOLOGY, VISUALIZATION, COMMUNICATION, CONNECTIONS, ESTIMATION

Content

- Estimate, measure and draw angles.
- Calculate the size of angles.
- Circles - diameters, radii, and circumference
- Calculate the Area of a circle.
- Circle patterns and relationships.

Meaning and Understanding

Intellectual Curiosity

What situations in the real world will I encounter that involve the knowledge and use of angles and circles?

Real World Project

Where's the Cache?

Make a transit and a trundle wheel;
design a map to scale;
create clues;
test the map and clues;
follow someone else's map;
report the results.

ANGLES

CONSTRUCTING & MEASURING ANGLES

In No. 1 and No. 2 you will be working with the basic directions (**North**, **South**, **East** and **West**).

INVESTIGATION

PAPER FOLDING

1. Fold a square sheet of paper in half as shown.
   Use a straight edge to draw the line made by the fold.

   Put a point on one end of the line and label it **N** for North.
   Put an **S** for South on the other end of the line.

   Fold the sheet of paper in half the opposite way and draw the line made by this fold.
   Put an **E** for East on a point at the right end of this new line.
   Put a **W** for West on a point at the left end of this line.
   Label the point where the two lines cross **M**.

   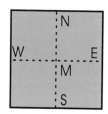

   a. What is the measure of $\angle$NMS made by the first fold?
      Use your protractor to measure it.

   b. The second fold made four angles on your sheet of paper. ($\angle$NMW, $\angle$NME, ...)
      What do you expect their measure to be?
      Use your protractor or a set square to check.

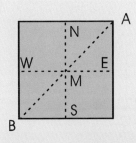

MA cuts the angle between **N**orth and **E**ast into two equal parts. We say that it is in the **N**orth**E**ast direction. MB is in the **S**outh**W**est direction.

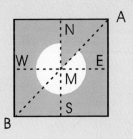

2. Fold the paper along a diagonal. (Fold so that the **N** is on the **E.)**

Draw the line made by this fold. The line will go from the page corner that is between **N** and **E** to the corner that is between **S** and **W**.

Label the first point **A** and the second point **B.**

a. What is the measure of ∠ NMA?

b. Measure and name another angle that is 45°.

c. What is the measure of ∠ AMS?

d. Measure and name another angle that is greater than 90° but less than 180°.

e. What is the measure of the ∠ NMA shown in yellow?

f. Measure and name another angle that is greater than 180°.

g. Create a 22.5° angle by folding. Explain your method.

h. Create a 67.5° angle by folding. Explain your method.

Example 1:
NAMING ANGLES

Look at the following triangles.

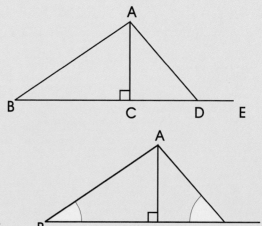

Angles ABC, BAC, CAD and ADC are **acute.**
An angle that is **less than 90⁰** is an **acute** angle.

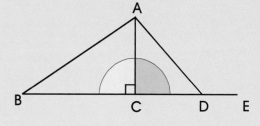

Angles ACD and ACB are **right** angles.
An angle that is **90⁰** is a **right** angle.

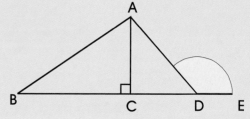

∠ADE is **obtuse.** An angle that is **greater than 90⁰ but less than 180⁰** is an **obtuse** angle.

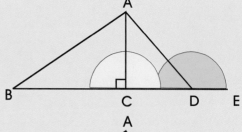

Angles BCD and CDE are **straight** angles. An angle that is **180⁰** is a **straight** angle.

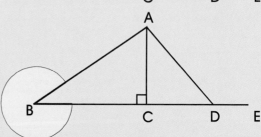

Reflex ∠ABC is the angle at B lying outside the triangle. An angle that is **greater than 180⁰ but less than 360⁰** is a **reflex** angle.

CONSTRUCTING A TRIANGLE

Use your protractor and a ruler to draw $\triangle AWX$ with $\angle W = 40°$ and $\angle X = 60°$.

Method:

Draw a horizontal line WX.

At W draw $\angle XWY = 40°$ so that $\angle XWY$ is above WX.

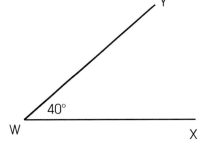

At X draw $\angle WXZ = 60°$
so that $\angle WXZ$ is above WX.

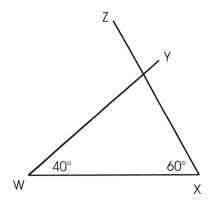

Name the point where they intersect A.

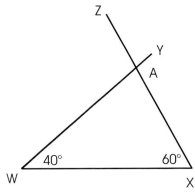

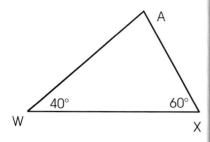

Draw WX.
At W draw ∠W = 40°.
At X draw ∠X = 100°.

1. a. Estimate the size of ∠ WAX.

    b. Measure the size of ∠ WAX.

    c. Calculate the value of:
        ∠ XWA + ∠ WXA + ∠ WAX.

2. Draw △ AWX with ∠ W = 40° and ∠ X = 100°.

    a. Estimate the size of ∠ WAX.

    b. Measure the size of ∠ WAX.

    c. Calculate the value of:
        ∠ XWY + ∠ WXZ + ∠ WAX.

3. a. Compare your answers from No.1c. and No. 2c.

    b. Draw another triangle and measure each of the angles inside the triangle.

    c. Calculate the sum of your measures from No. b.

    d. Compare your answer with others.

    e. Describe the pattern.

1. Use your protractor to draw the following angles.
   Describe each one (acute, obtuse, reflex, right or straight).

   a $\angle ABC = 35$ b. $\angle DEF = 160°$

   c. $\angle GHJ = 80°$ d. $\angle KLM = 15°$

   e. $\angle NOP = 340°$ f. $\angle QRS = 90°$

   g. $\angle TUV = 120°$

2. Identify two angles of each type in your classroom, your home or outdoors.

3. a. Draw a vertical line and label the top North and the bottom South.
      Pick a point M in the centre of NS.

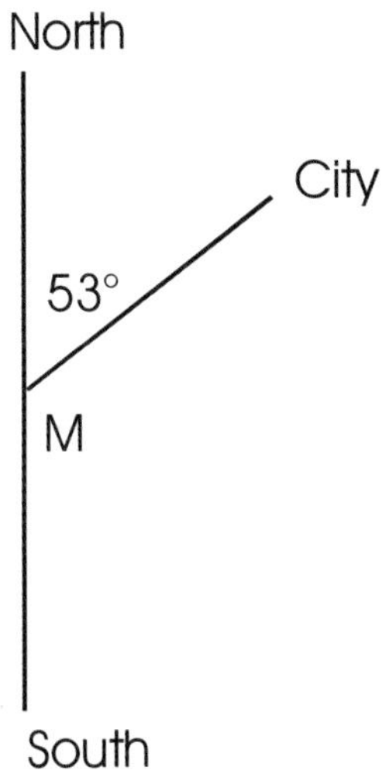

   b. Use your protractor to draw $\angle NMC$ for each of the following situations.
      A plane leaves M and flies along the line MC.
      $\angle NMC$ is :

      i. 53°   ii. 91°   iii. 182°   iv. 274°

   c. If M is where your school is, what city might the plane be flying to in each of the situations described in No. b?

North

City

53°

M

South

INVESTIGATION

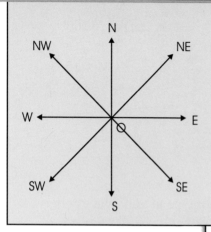

This diagram shows the four basic directions (**East**, **West**, **North**, **South**).

It also shows the directions **NW** (**NorthWest**), **NE** (**NorthEast**), **SE** (**SouthEast**) and **SW** (**SouthWest**).

1. What is the size of the angle between:
   a. North and East?

   b. West and East?

   c. NorthWest and West?

   d. NorthEast and North?

   e. NorthEast and West?

Bisect means to cut in half.

2. The line in the NorthWest direction divides the angle between North and West into two equal angles. It is called an **angle bisector**.

   What is the size of each of these two angles?

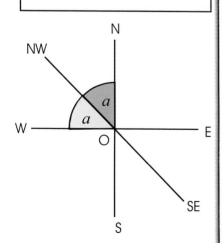

3. Use your protractor and ruler to accurately draw a diagram that shows North, South, East, West, NortWest and SouthEast.

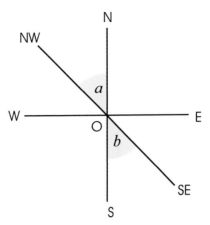

Measure the angle between North and NorthWest.
Measure the angle between South and SouthEast.
They are called **opposite angles**.

Compare the sizes of these two angles.
Name another pair of opposite angles.

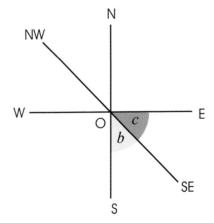

The angles marked *b* and *c* are beside each other.
Angles that share a **common arm** are called **adjacent angles**.

Name another pair of adjacent angles.

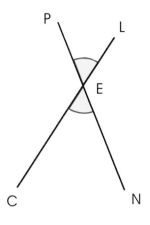

1. Cross two pencils as shown in the diagram.
    Keep your fingers at E and rotate the pencils about E.
    Notice what happens to the four angles:
    $\angle$ PEL, $\angle$ CEN, $\angle$ PEC and $\angle$ LEN.
    Copy and complete:
    As $\angle$ PEL gets larger, $\angle$ CEN gets _.
    As $\angle$ PEL gets smaller, $\angle$ CEN gets _.
    As $\angle$ PEC gets smaller, $\angle$ LEN gets _.
    As $\angle$ PEC gets larger, $\angle$ LEN gets _.

    What is true about $\angle$ PEL and $\angle$ CEN?
    What is true about $\angle$ PEC and $\angle$ LEN?

2. a. In the diagram $\angle$ PEL and $\angle$ CEN are called *opposite*
        angles.
        Name the other pair of opposite angles.

    b. Measure and record the size of each of the angles in
        the diagram.

    c. State the pairs of angles that are equal.

    d. Draw your own pair of intersecting lines.
        Measure each of the angles and mark the angles that
        are equal.

    e. Based on your measurements, what can you say about
        the sizes of opposite angles?

3. a. Calculate:
        i. $\angle$ PEL + $\angle$ LEN   ii. $\angle$ CEN + $\angle$ LEN
        iii. $\angle$ CEN + $\angle$ PEC   iv. $\angle$ PEL + $\angle$ PEC

    b. What did you notice about the answers for each pair of
        angles?

    c. For each pair of angles in No. a, name the angle
        formed by the two angles.
        E.g. $\angle$ PEL + $\angle$ LEN = $\angle$ PEN.

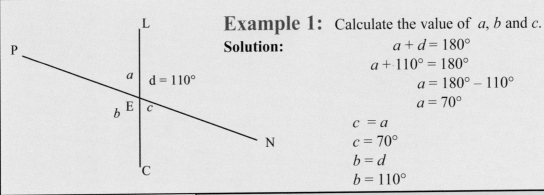

Example 1: Calculate the value of a, b and c.

Solution:

$$a + d = 180°$$
$$a + 110° = 180°$$
$$a = 180° - 110°$$
$$a = 70°$$

$$c = a$$
$$c = 70°$$
$$b = d$$
$$b = 110°$$

INVESTIGATION

An acute-angled triangle has three acute angles.

An obtuse-angled triangle has **one** obtuse angle.

1. a. Draw a right triangle JKL.
      Measure each of the three angles.
      Determine their sum.

   b. Draw an acute-angled triangle.
      Measure each of the three angles.
      Determine their sum.

   c. Draw an obtuse-angled triangle.
      Measure each of the three angles.
      Determine their sum.

The **sum of the interior angles** of any triangle is 180°.

$$a + b + c = 180°$$

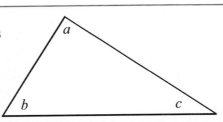

Example 2: Calculate the value of d.

Solution:

$$90° + 43° + d = 180°$$
$$133° + d = 180°$$
$$d = 180° - 133°$$
$$d = 47°$$

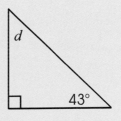

1.

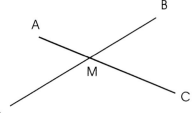

a. Name two pairs of equal opposite angles.

b. If $\angle AMB = 121°$, calculate the sizes of the other three angles.

2.

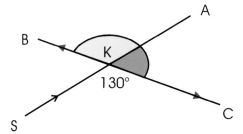

Boris and Cheriane are walking home from school along road SK.

At K they separate to go to their homes.

Boris turns to go along KB and Cheriane turns to go along KC.

What angle does each turn through in order to head for home?

3. Calculate the sizes of the angles indicated.
Explain the reasons for your calculations.

a.

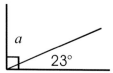

b.

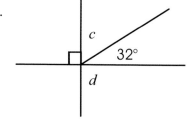

Do not use a protractor.

4. Calculate the sizes of the angles indicated.
   Explain the reasons for your calculations

   a.

   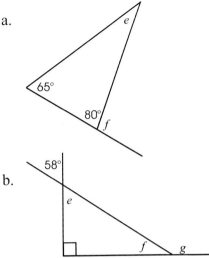

   b.

   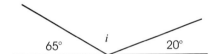

   c.

   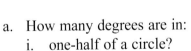

5. There are 360° in a complete rotation of a circle.

   ∠ QOR = 90°

   ∠ QOR is one-quarter
   of a circle.

   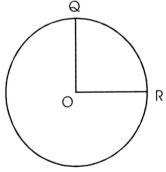

   a. How many degrees are in:
      i.   one-half of a circle?
      ii. three quarters of a
           circle?

   b. What is the size of reflex ∠ QOR?
      What fraction of the circle does it represent?

   c. Construct ∠ QOS which is one-eighth of the circle.
      What is the size of ∠ SOR?

$$\frac{90}{360} = \frac{1}{4}$$

Bearing is an angle measurement used for navigation in the air. The **bearing** of a course taken by a plane is the size of the angle **measured clockwise from the North line**.

Example 1:   State the bearing of: a. O b. OB.

Solution:

a. $\angle NOA = 60°$
The bearing is 60°.

b. $\angle BOW = 30°$ and
$\angle SOW = 90°$.
$\angle SOB = 60°$.
$\angle SON = 180°$.
Reflex $\angle NOB = \angle SON + \angle SOB$
$= 180° + 60°$
$= 240°$.
The bearing is 240°.

PUT INTO PRACTICE

1. a. Estimate the bearing of OA and OB to the nearest 10°.

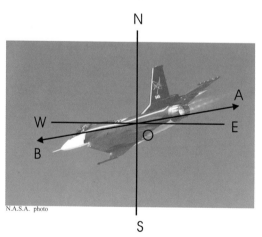

N.A.S.A. photo

b. Determine the bearings by measurement.
Round each bearing to the nearest 10°.

N.A.S.A. photo

2. a. Estimate the bearing of OC and OD to the nearest 10°.

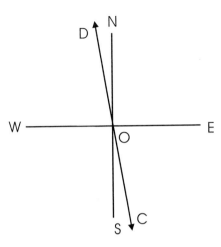

b. Determine the bearings by measurement.
Round each bearing to the nearest 10°.

3. a. Estimate the bearing of OF and OG to the nearest 10°.

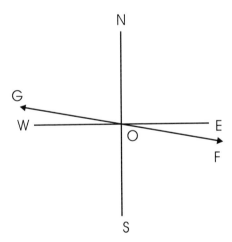

b. Determine the bearings by measurement.
Round each bearing to the nearest 10°.

Example 2:

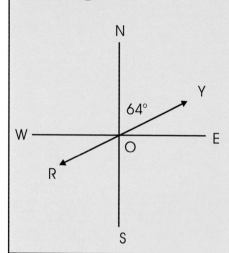

The diagram shows a runway RY.
If a plane departs or arrives in the direction OY, then the bearing is 64°.
If it departs or arrives in the direction OR, then what is the bearing?

Solution:

$$\angle NOY = 64°$$
$$\angle ROY = 180° \text{ (straight line)}$$
$$\angle NOR = 64° + 180°$$

The bearing of OR is 244°.

Example 3:

Each runway has two "names".
The names are determined by:
- Rounding each bearing to the nearest 10°
- Dividing the number by 10

A plane departs on runway RY in the direction OY.
What "name" does the runway have for this plane?

Solution: $\angle NOY = 64°$ This rounds to 60°.
$60 \div 10 = 6$.
The first plane is told to take off on Runway 6.

Another plane lands in the direction OR.
What "name" does the runway have for this plane?

Solution: $\angle NOR = 244°$ This rounds to 240°.
$240 \div 10 = 24$.
The second plane is told to land on Runway 24.

N.A.S.A. photo

PUT INTO PRACTICE

4. Determine the runway names using direction OY and direction OR when the bearing of OY is:

   a. 66°   b. 70°   c. 150°   d. 146°

Your diagram could look like this.

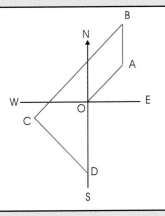

∠ABC = 45°.

1 cm represents 200 m.
5 cm represents 5 × 200 m.

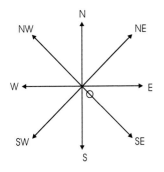

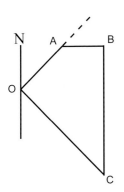

5. On a sheet of grid paper draw a vertical NorthSouth line down the centre of the page and mark it NS.
Draw a WestEast line perpendicular to NS at the centre of the page and mark it WE. Mark the intersection as O. Mark the following hiking trail on your map.

a. Draw OA = 5 cm in the direction NE.

b. Draw AB = 4 cm in the direction N.

c. Draw BC = 12 cm in the direction SW.

d. Draw CD = 7 cm in the direction SE.

e. Draw DO = 6 cm in the direction N.

f. If your diagram represents an afternoon's hike and the scale is 1 cm represents 200 m, how far did you hike?

6. On an orienteering course the competitors traveled:
700 m in a NorthEast direction
500 m due East
1500 m due South and
1400 m in a NorthWest direction to the finish.

a. Choose a suitable scale.

b. Draw a NorthSouth line and draw a line going NorthEast.

c. On this line mark A so that OA represents 700 m.

d. Then draw a horizontal line, AB, to the East that represents 500 m.

e. Then draw a vertical line, BC, to the South that represents 1500 m.

f. Finally, draw a line to the NorthWest that represents 1400 m.

CIRCLES

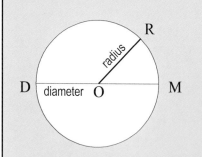

This is a circle with centre O.

A line that goes from **a point on the circle**, through the **centre** to a **point on the opposite side of the circle** is called a **diameter** (*d*).
DOM is a diameter.

A line that goes from the **centre to any point on the circle** is called a **radius** (*r*).
OR is a radius.

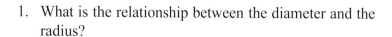

PUT INTO PRACTICE

1. What is the relationship between the diameter and the radius?

2. a. The diameter of the earth at the equator is about 12 680 km.
   What is the distance from the equator to the centre of the earth?

   b. The diameter of the earth reaching between the poles is about 12 640 km.
   How far is it from the North Pole to the centre of the earth?

   c. What does this tell you about the shape of the earth?

3. Bees will sometimes travel anywhere within a circle with a 1500 m radius.
   What is the diameter of the circle that shows their territory?

N.A.S.A. photo

ESTIMATING THE CIRCUMFERENCE

1. Take a twist tie and make it the length of a diameter of a circular lid.
    Bend the twist tie to fit the arc of the circle and place it on the circumference of the lid.

    a. How many of these identical twist ties do you need to fit around the circumference?

    b. Copy and complete:
        The **circumference** of a circle is **a little more than** __ times the length of the **diameter**.

2. Explain how you can calculate the approximate value of the circumference of a circle when you know the length of the diameter.

3. Calculate the approximate value of the circumference of a circle with a diameter of 6 cm.

> Diameter of the circle, d = 6 cm.
> $C = \_d$
> $C = \pi \ (\_)$
> $C = 18.8495559...$
> The circumference of the base is about __ cm.

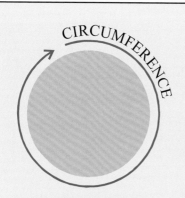

CIRCUMFERENCE

The **distance around** a figure is called the **perimeter.**

The **perimeter** of a circle is called the **circumference**.

The symbol π represents pi.

A decimal approximation of pi is 3.14 .

CALCULATING CIRCUMFERENCE

a. Complete a copy of the table below.

Object	Diameter (d)	Circumference (C)	Circumference ÷ diameter C ÷ d

b. Measure and record the circumferences and diameters of a variety of circular objects (cans, wheels, lids, …) in your table.

c. Complete the last column of the table. Round the answers to one decimal place.

d. What do you notice about the ratio $\dfrac{C}{d}$?

e. Compare your results with others.

You found that the value of $\dfrac{C}{d}$ was a little more than 3.

For any circle the value of $\dfrac{C}{d}$ is exactly π.

Pi is a number whose decimal value continues on forever.

$$\pi = 3.141\ 592\ 653\ 589\ 793\ 238\ 462\ 64\ldots$$

If you have a π button on your calculator, you can use that value in any calculations.

$$\frac{C}{d} = \pi$$

314

CIRCLES

Example 1:

Calculate the circumference, correct to one decimal place, of each of the following circles:

    a. a circle with diameter 5 cm

Solution:

$C = \pi d$ and $d = 5$.

$C = \pi \times 5$ *Use the π button on your calculator.*

$C = 15.707\ 963\ 27\ldots$

The circumference is about 15.7 cm.

    b. a circle with radius 5 cm

Solution:

The radius $r = 5$ and $d = 2 \times 5$.

$C = \pi d$ and $d = 10$.

$C = \pi \times 10$

$C = 31.415\ 926\ 54\ldots$

The circumference is about 31.4 cm.

Example 2:

A bicycle wheel has a circumference of 78 cm.
What is the length of one of its spokes?
Round your answer to the nearest millimetre.

Solution:

$C = \pi d$ and $C = 78$.

$78 = \pi d$

$$\frac{78}{\pi} = \frac{\pi d}{\pi}$$ *Divide both sides by π.*

$$d = \frac{78}{\pi}$$

$d = 24.828\ 171\ 12\ldots$

$r = 24.828\ 171\ 12\ldots \div 2$

$r = 12.414\ 085\ 56\ldots$

The spoke is about 12.4 cm long.

Example 3:   Solve $\dfrac{C}{d} = \pi$ for C.

Solution: $\dfrac{C}{d} = \pi$

$d \times \dfrac{C}{d} = \pi \times d$ *Multiply both sides by d.*

$C = \pi\, d.$

The **circumference (C)** of a circle with **diameter (d)** is given by: $C = \pi\, d$
($\pi = 3.141\,59\ldots$ but you can use the π button on your calculator).

PUT INTO PRACTICE

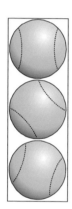

4. Here is a sketch of three tennis balls packed tightly in a cylindrical container.
   a. Predict which will be larger: the height of the container or the circumference of the base of the container.

   b. Discuss your prediction with another student.

   c. The diameter of a tennis ball is about 6 cm.
      i. Determine the height of the container.

      ii. Calculate the circumference of the base of the container.
         Round your answer to the nearest 0.1 cm.

      iii. Compare the height and the circumference.

5. The second hand on a clock is 4.1 cm long.

   a. How far will the tip of the second hand travel in 1 minute?
      Round your answer to the nearest centimetre.

   b. How far will it travel in 2 hours?
      Round your answer to the nearest metre.

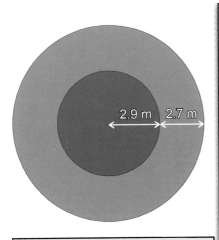

2.9 m   2.7 m

One rotation:
$C = \pi (5.8)$

The wheel will travel one circumference in one revolution.

1 km = 1000 m.

6. There is an antique carousel (merry-go-round) in Rome that you can still ride.
   It is 2.9 m from the centre of the carousel to the inside of the platform.
   The platform is 2.7 m wide.

   a. If you stand at the inside edge of the platform how far will you travel in 50 rotations of the carousel?
      Round your answer to the nearest metre.

   b. If you stand on the outside edge how far will you travel in 50 rotations of the carousel?
      Round your answer to the nearest metre.

   c. If the cost of a ride is 5000 lira then what is the cost per metre traveled when you stand on the outside edge?

7. A small trailer tire has a diameter of 36 cm.
   The diameter of the tires on the car that is pulling the trailer is 60 cm.

   a. If you roll the trailer tire in a straight line for 20 rotations how far will you travel?
      Round your answer to the nearest metre.

   b. If you travel 1 km how many rotations will the trailer tire make?

   c. How many rotations will the car tire make when the car travels 1 km?

   d. Compare the speed of rotation of the two tires.

$$T = 2 (l + w)$$
$$60 = 2(4r + 2r)$$

8.

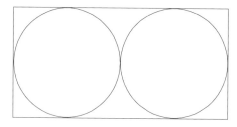

The perimeter of the rectangle is 60 cm.

a. What is the radius of each circle?

b. What is the circumference of each circle?

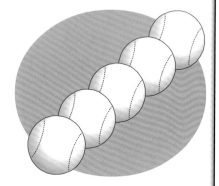

9. A school softball team is flying to a softball tournament.
They pack their softballs in a box for the plane.
Their softballs each have a diameter of 3.6 cm.
They are packed in a sleeve that is 5 softballs long.
There are two layers of three sleeves packed in each box.
a. What are the dimensions of a sleeve?

b. Draw the box showing the softballs inside.

c. What are the dimensions of the box?

10. The diameter of the earth at the equator is about
12 680 km.

a. How far does a stone, that is lying on the equator,
travel in one day?
Round your answer to the nearest kilometre.

b. At what speed is the stone travelling?

c. A bush at the equator is 1 m tall.
How far does the top of the bush travel in one day?

N.A.S.A. photo

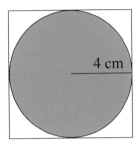

4 cm

INVESTIGATION

ESTIMATING THE AREA OF A CIRCLE

1. The radius of the circle is 4 cm.

   a. What is the length of each side of the square containing the circle?

   b. What is the area of the square?

   c. The area of the circle will be a little __ than __ cm².

2. Do this construction to get a better estimate of the area of the circle.

   a. On 1-cm grid paper draw a circle using the 4-cm radius.

   b. Count the squares to estimate the area of the circle.

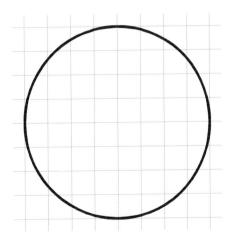

   The area is about __ cm².

Here are two different ways for you to deal with the part squares.

Count **every** square (no matter how large or small) as a half-square.

OR

Find pairs of part-squares that can combine to be about one square.

CALCULATING THE AREA OF A CIRCLE

The formula used to calculate the **area** of a circle with **radius** r is:

$$A = \pi r^2$$

($\pi = 3.141\ 59\ldots$ but you can use the π button on your calculator).

Example 1:

Calculate the area of a circle with radius 4 cm.
Round your answer to the nearest square centimetre.

Solution: $A = \pi r^2$

$A = \pi \times 4^2$ *(4^2 means 4×4)*

$A = \pi \times 16$

$A = 50.26548\ldots$

The area is about 50 cm².

Example 2:

If you travel to Carmanah Valley on Vancouver Island you will see some very large and old fir trees.

One of the trees has a diameter of 92 cm.
Calculate the area of the cross-section of the tree, correct to the nearest square centimetre.

Solution: The diameter is 92 cm, so the radius is 46 cm.

$A = \pi r^2$

$A = \pi \times 46^2$

$A = 6647.61\ldots$

The area is about 6648 cm².

The radius is one-half the diameter.
$r = d \div 2$.

1. An irrigation sprinkler system rotates about a central water source.
   The sprinkler pipes are 93 m long.

   Calculate the area that can be irrigated by the system. Round your answer to the nearest square metre.

   The radius, r, is 93 m.

   $$A = \_ r^2$$

   $$A = \pi (\_)^2$$

   $$A = \_$$

   The area that can be irrigated is about □.

2. You have been told that you can take a one-way trip up to a distance of 100 km.

   a. Calculate the area of a circle with radius 100 km.

   b. Check the scale on a map and calculate how many centimetres on the map are equivalent to 100 km.

   c. Check with your partner.

   d. Locate where you live. With that as the centre and the radius that you just calculated draw a circle.

   e. Name the largest town, city or landmark that lies within your circle.

   f. Are there any of these towns, cities or landmarks that lie outside your province?

   g. Compare the area of the 100 km circle with the area of Prince Edward Island.

3. Explain how you can calculate the area of a circle when you know the:

   a. radius   b. diameter.

4. A horse is tied to a post by a line that is 9 m long.

   What is the area in which the horse will be able to graze? Round your answer to the nearest square metre.

5. A washer has an outside diameter of 4.5 cm and an inside diameter of 2.5 cm.

   a. What area will the washer cover?
      Round your answer to the nearest square centimetre.

   b. You have a rectangular sheet of metal that measures 250 cm by 270 cm.
      How many washers can you stamp out of that sheet of metal?

   c. Every square centimetre of the metal has a mass of 2 g.
      You need to deliver 1800 washers to Salt Lake as soon as possible.
      One of the employees is scheduled to fly there today for a meeting concerning biathlon targets.
      If she brings the container of washers as luggage will she exceed the limit of 40 kg?

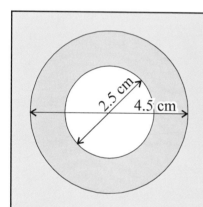

- First calculate the area of the large circle.
- Next calculate the area of the small circle.
- Then ___.

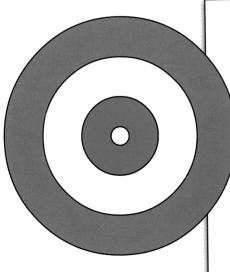

6. "The house" in curling has four circles with the same centre.
   The button is a circle with diameter 1'.
   The four-foot circle has a diameter 4'.
   The eight-foot and twelve-foot circles have diameters of 8' and 12'.

   a. Calculate the area of the button.

   b. Calculate the area of the red part of the four-foot.

   c. Calculate the area of the white part of the eight-foot.

   d. Calculate the area of the blue part of the twelve-foot.

Example 3: *CALCULATING RADIUS OR DIAMETER*

You have been asked to construct the circular targets for the biathlon at the Winter Olympics.
Since this will get you a free trip to the games you agree!
Each target has an area of 1963 mm².
You will need to know the radius.

Solution:

$$A = \pi r^2 \text{ and } A = 1963.$$
$$1963 = \pi r^2$$
$$\frac{1963}{\pi} = \frac{\pi r^2}{\pi}$$
$$\frac{1963}{\pi} = r^2$$
$$r^2 = \frac{1963}{\pi}$$
$$r^2 = 624.842...$$

$$r = \sqrt{624.842...}$$
$$r = 24.9968...$$

The radius must be 25 mm.

To solve $r^2 = 624.842...$ we needed to know what number we should square in order to get an answer of 624.842...

So we had to determine the square root of 624.842…

Make sure that you can do these calculations.

On most calculators, you will key in:

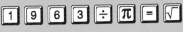

7. Complete and copy the table below.

Radius (nearest 0.1 cm)	Diameter (nearest 0.1 cm)	Area (nearest cm²)
2.9 cm		
	2.6 cm	
		78 cm²

8. A pizza pie plate has an area of 637.6 cm².

   a. What is its diameter correct to the nearest 0.1 cm?

   b. How many plates can be cut from a sheet of metal that is 200 cm by 180 cm?

9. Jenna made an ice skating rink in her back yard. She made a rectangle with a semi-circle on each end.

   What is the area of ice, correct to the nearest square metre?

Hint:
Break it up into two semi-circles and a rectangle.

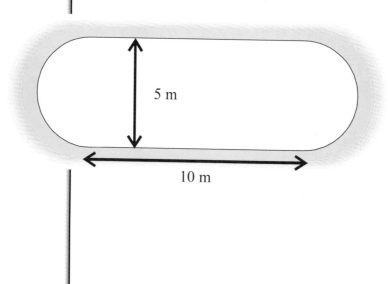

5 m

10 m

10. The national flag of Japan consists of a red circle on a white rectangle.
Here is the description.
The vertical-to-horizontal ratio of the flag is set at 2:3.
The disc is placed at the exact centre.
The diameter of the disc is equal to three-fifths of the vertical measurement.

Make a drawing of the flag as follows.

a. Choose a horizontal length for the base of the rectangle.
(If you make it a multiple of 3 then the calculation of the height will be easier.)

$$\frac{x}{\text{My Choice of Base Length}} = \frac{2}{3}$$

b. Calculate the corresponding height of the rectangle.

c. Locate the centre of the circle at the centre of the rectangle.
(Draw the two diagonals.)

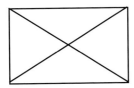

d. Calculate the diameter and radius of the circle.

$d = 0.6 \times \text{height of the rectangle}$

e. With a set of compasses, draw the circle.

f. Calculate the area of the circle and the area of the rectangle.

g. Write the ratio of the area of the circle to the area of the rectangle.

11. One Olympic ring on a flag has a diameter of 26 cm.
How much cloth is required for one ring?

12. You want to make the five Olympic circles using jewelers' wire.

Calculate the minimum number of centimetres of wire that you need if you want the diameter of each ring to be 2 cm.

13. The shape and design of the Olympic medals varies but at the Nagano Olympics the medals were circular and had a diameter of 8 cm.

They are 9 mm (0.9 cm) thick and have the following masses: Gold 256 g
Silver 250 g
Bronze 230 g.

a. Calculate:
i.   the circumference of a medal, correct to the nearest centimetre.

ii. the area of one side of a medal, correct to the nearest square centimetre.

b. The volume of each medal can be obtained by multiplying the area of one side by the thickness, in centimetres.

> Volume = Area of Top × Thickness

Calculate the volume of a medal.
Round your answer to the nearest cubic centimetre.

c. Calculate the cost of the material in each of the gold and silver medals.
Use a price of $15.75/g for gold and $0.25/g for silver or look up the prices on the Internet.

d. Up until 1996 the material in the one-cent piece was similar to the material in a bronze medal.
The diameter of a one-cent coin is about 1.9 cm.
Its thickness is about 0.145 cm.

Calculate the volume of the coin and compare it to the volume of the bronze medal.

ANGLES

1. Construct the following angles and name them (acute, obtuse, etc.).

   a. 47°   b. 231°   c. 125°   d. 82°

   e. 175°   f. 18°   g. 90°   h. 320°

   i. 180°   j. 140°   k. 270°   l. 100°

2. Determine the value of each variable.
   Explain how you calculated the values in the first two diagrams.

a.

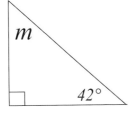

b.

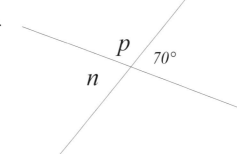

c.

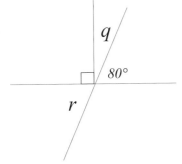

d.

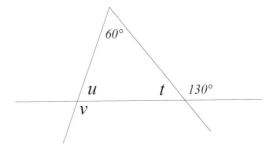

3. Sarah rode the cross-country bicycle course shown. She rode from A to B to C to D to E and back to A. At B she turned through an angle of $b°$, at C through an angle of $c°$, etc.

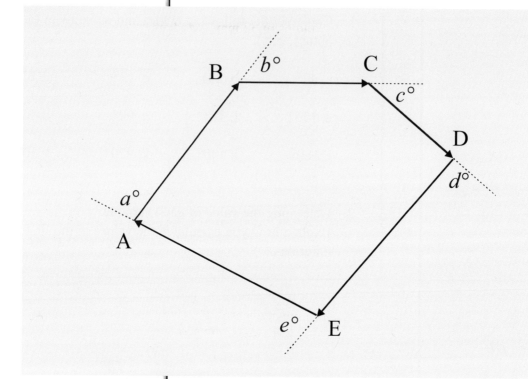

a. Draw a polygon ABCDE with the sides extended as in the diagram.

b. Measure each of the angles that she turned through and calculate their sum
$(b° + c° + d° + e°)$.

c. Measure $a°$ and add it to the sum of the other four angles from b.

d. Compare your answers to b and c with other students.

e. Explain the result in d.

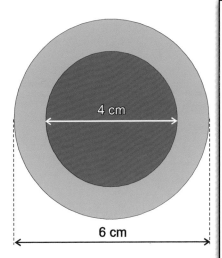

4 cm

6 cm

CIRCLES

4. Calculate the circumference and area of circles with the following dimensions.
   Round the answers to 2 decimal places.
   a. diameter of 6 cm   b. radius of 12 m
   c. radius of 32 mm   d. diameter of 15 cm

5. The circumference of a circle is 50.24 cm.
   Calculate the length of the diameter and radius.
   Round the answer to 1 decimal place.

6. The area of a circle is 153.86 m^2.
   Calculate the length of the diameter and radius.
   Round the answer to 1 decimal place.

7. A metal washer has an outside diameter of 6 cm and an inside diameter of 4 cm.
   What is the area of metal in the washer?
   Round the answer to 2 decimal places.

8. The outside wheel of a pivotal irrigation sprinkler (circular) travels 722.5 m in one rotation.
   What area is irrigated?
   Round the answer to the nearest square metre.

9. Many of the First Nations peoples of the prairies were hunters and gatherers.
   They often traveled where the buffalo roamed and so the tipi was an ideal portable shelter.
   The tipi consisted of tanned hides supported on long wooden poles.
   The number of poles varied from nation to nation. They varied from 11 poles to 21 poles.
   The base of a circular tipi has a radius of 6 m.

   Calculate the:
   a.   circumference, correct to the nearest metre.
   b.   area, correct to the nearest square metre.

First you should calculate the diameter or radius.

On the banks of the Bow River east of Calgary you can find many reminders of Blackfoot campsites.
You can see circles of stones known as Tipi Rings.

Discuss the origin and purpose of these rings.

PROJECT

STEP 1: MAKING THE TOOLS

- Using the instructions that will be provided to you, make a transit (a device to measure angles).

- Next make a trundle wheel (a circular tool that measures distance). It should be one or two metres in circumference.
  You will want to count by one's or two's each time the wheel goes around.

STEP 2: MAKING UP THE TREASURE HUNT

- Working in pairs (so that you can use the tools), create the clues (directions) that another group will use in order to find the "buried treasure".

- Make a map of the area to scale.

- Your directions must:
  Have a minimum of 5 turns
  Have a distance of at least 10 m between turns and
  Must make use of the *transit* and the *trundle wheel*.

STEP 3: FOLLOWING DIRECTIONS

- Alternate with another group.

- Follow their directions and use the tools to see if you can find the buried treasure.

- To use your transit, you will need to put stakes with coloured ties to mark points of change in direction.

- Let the other group try yours.

STEP 4:   SELF EVALUATION

Use a letter format, or a learning map to explain what you learned from this project experience.

- Comment on your experience of communicating and following directions in the treasure maps.

- Consider what you learned today about angles and circles.

- Make a connection about today's experience to the real world.

- Think of a question that are you are still wondering about.

- Evaluate your ability to learn in an environment that takes a 'discovery' approach to learning.

SPORTS

GET THINKING

☐ How can I use measures of central tendency to compare my test score with the rest of my classmates?

☐ When is mathematics used to interpret the meaning behind survey results?

☐ Where is the mathematics in the sports or recreational activities that I enjoy?

☐ Why is the Theorem of Pythagorean used on construction sites?

☐ How does a buyer for a shoe store use central tendency measurements to decide what size of shoes to order?

Content

- Evaluate and use measures of central tendency and variability (mean, median, mode, range).
- Investigate the Pythagorean relationship.
- Use the Pythagorean relationship to solve problems

AND MENTAL MATH, PROBLEM SOLVING, REASONING, TECHNOLOGY, VISUALIZATION, COMMUNICATION, CONNECTIONS, ESTIMATION

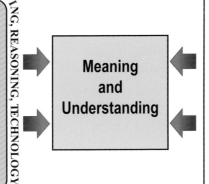

Meaning and Understanding

Intellectual Curiosity

How do communities use mathematics to determine the best sports services and amenities for their neighborhood?

Real World Project

Choosing a Community Sports Facility

Design a sports survey and interpret the results; decide on a facility you will build to meet the needs; make a model.

CENTRAL TENDENCIES

SPORTS STATISTICS

GET THINKING

What do you need to know in order to answer questions like:
Who is the best player?
What kind of salary does the average player get?

Every sport uses numbers in some form or another.
They are used to tell whether a team wins or loses, to indicate league standing and to provide information on players' salaries.

Teams keep statistics on games and players.
E.g.

Plus/Minus scores in hockey and basketball.
Scoring records
Penalties
Batting averages
Pitching statistics
Record Times

Mean: the **arithmetic average** of the numbers
Add the numbers in the data and then divide by the number of numbers in the data.

Median: the **middle** number after they are put in order
Arrange the data in order. Find the middle number.
If there is an odd number of items, then the middle number is the median.
If there is an even number of items, then add the two middle numbers and divide by two.

Mode: the **most frequent** number
Find the most frequently occurring number in the data.
If there is more than one number that appears the same number of times, then there is more than one mode.
If each number occurs only once then there is no mode.

Range: the **difference** between the **largest** and **smallest** numbers.

Example 1:

Tomson is one of the better players on the basketball team.
In the first seven games of the season he scored: 25, 20, 18, 20, 17, 13 and 20 points.
Calculate the: a. mean   b. median   c. mode   and   d. range
of these numbers.

Solution: a. $25 + 20 + 18 + 20 + 17 + 13 + 20 = 133$
$133 \div 7 = 19$
The mean is 19.

b. The scores, in order, are: 13, 17, 18, **20**, 20, 20, 25.
The median is 20.

c. The scores, in order, are: 13, 17, 18, **20, 20, 20**, 25.
The mode is 20.

d. The scores, in order, are: **13**, 17, 18, 20, 20, 20, **25**.
$25 - 13 = 12$
The range is 12.

1. In his first seven games Cameron scored the following numbers of points: 25, 20, 8, 20, 7, 5 and 20.
   a. Calculate the mean.   b. Find the median.
   c. Find the mode.   d. Calculate the range

   Copy and complete these solutions.

   a. $25 + 20 + 8 + 20 + 7 + 5 + 20 = \square$
      $105 \div \square = 15$
      The mean is $\square$.

   b. Arrange the numbers in order.
      $25, 20, \square, \square, 8, \square, 5$
      The middle number is $\square$.
      The median is 20.

   c. The most frequent number is 20.
      (There are three 20's.)
      The mode is $\square$.

   d. The range is $25 - \square = 20$.
      The range is $\square$.

2. Explain how to:

   a. calculate the mean of a set of numbers

   b. find the median of a set of numbers

   c. find the mode of a set of numbers

   d. calculate the range of a set of numbers.

3. In her first seven games, Buffey scored the following numbers of points: 18, 20, 8, 20, 7, 5 and 20.

    a. Calculate the mean.   b. Find the median.

    c. Find the mode.   d. Calculate the range.

4. Calculate and compare the means, medians, modes and ranges for Tomson, Cameron and Buffey.

    Complete a copy of the table below.

Player	Scores	Mean	Median	Mode	Range
Tomson	25, 20, 18, 20, 17, 13, 20				
Cameron	25, 20, 8, 20, 7, 5, 20				
Buffey	18, 20, 8, 20, 7, 5, 20				

5. For each of the following sets of data calculate, correct to one decimal place:
    i.   The mean
    ii. The median
    iii. The mode
    iv. The range.

    a Points scored in a basketball game: 8, 15, 7, 21 and 12

    b. Goals scored in a hockey game: 2, 6, 1, 4, 3, 6 and 8

    c. Goals scored in a ringette game: 7, 3, 5, 7, 2, 8, 4 and 9

6. Dan knew that the mean salary of the starting five on his team was $2000/game.
He knew that his salary was $2000/game.
He also knew that the salaries of three other starters were:
Keith—$2000
Mike—$3000
Sandy—$1000.
He was able to calculate Shannon's salary from this information.

a. Explain how he was able to do this.

b. Calculate Shannon's salary.

7. In her first seven games Randa scored:
   24, 20, 20, 18, 20, 12 and 19 points.

a. Determine the:
   i. mean   ii. median   iii. mode   iv. range.

b. In her next two games Randa scored 13 and 25 points.

Determine the effect on each of the mean, median, mode and range.

You are now ready
to do Steps 1 and 2
of your project.

INVESTIGATION

The table shows the numbers of points scored by Tomson, Cameron and Buffey in the last seven games of the season.

Player	Points Scored						
	Game 1	Game 2	Game 3	Game 4	Game 5	Game 6	Game 7
Tomson	20	19	20	22	19	20	18
Cameron	26	10	15	25	17	15	16
Buffey	21	10	21	12	14	11	15

a. For each player:
   i. calculate the mean, correct to one decimal place
   ii. find the median
   iii. find the mode
   iv. calculate the range.

b. Choose the most valuable player.

c. Compare your choice with others and discuss why you made your choice.

d. Make a list of the choice of each person in the class and find the mode of the choices.

PUT INTO PRACTICE

1. Use the set of numbers: 5, 3, 6, 5, 6, 16, 11, 9, 14 and 5.

    Determine the:
    a. mean   b. median   c. mode   d. range.

2. Determine the mean, median, mode and range of the following set of numbers:
    8.2, 3.4, 0.3, 2.7, 9.1, 5.6, 8.2, 6.2, 4.2 and 10.1

3. A player has the following monthly incomes from endorsements for the last six months of the year: $1256, $2900, $2595, $2475, $3680, $3372.

   What was the player's mean monthly income?

4. The 20 students "trying out" for the basketball team have the following heights:
   166 cm, 165 cm, 165 cm, 163 cm, 162 cm, 162 cm, 161 cm, 161 cm, 160 cm, 160 cm, 160 cm, 160 cm, 158 cm, 157 cm, 157 cm, 157 cm, 156 cm, 155 cm, 154 cm, 153 cm.

   a. What is the mean height, correct to the nearest centimetre?

   b. What is the median height?

   c. What is the mode height?

   d. What one number would best describe the heights?

5. a. State some examples of where you could use the ideas of mean, median, mode or range.

   b. Discuss your list with others.

   c. Help to create a class list.

6. Find several examples of the use of measures of central tendency in the newspaper and state whether your examples are a mean, a median, or a mode.

   Try to find at least one example of each.

If you have a lot of items to put in order you might want to use a sheet like the following to organise the numbers in ascending or decending order.

Grouping	Numbers
11-15	13
16-20	20, 18, 20, 17, 20
21-25	25

INVESTIGATION

It is "3rd and goal" on the 1-yd line with 10 seconds left in the football game.

Your team is trailing by 4 points and you need to score a touchdown.

You have decided to use a running play.

Max has had the following statistics on his runs:

15 yd, –3 yd, 0 yd, 20 yd, 100 yd, –1 yd, –5 yd.

Shane has had the following statistics:

2 yd, 3 yd, 0 yd, 2 yd, 4 yd, 1 yd, 2 yd.

The team statistician has calculated the following data for Max and Shane.

Player	Mean (yd)	Median (yd)	Mode (yd)	Range (yd)
Max	18	0	....	105
Shane	2	2	2	4

a. Who will you give the ball to? Why?

b. Compare your answer with others.

What sport is this?

1. Here are the salaries of 19 athletes, correct to the nearest $100 000.

   6 000 000, 1 000 000, 500 000, 500 000, 400 000, 400 000, 400 000, 300 000, 300 000, 300 000, 300 000, 200 000, 200 000, 200 000, 200 000, 200 000, 200 000, 200 000, 200 000.

   The mean is $631 578.95, the median is $300 000 and the mode is $200 000.

   a. In salary discussions which measure of central tendency would you use if you were:
      i. a player agent?   ii. an owner?
   b. Discuss your choices with others.
   c. Determine the mode of the choices made by the whole class.

2. Copy and complete the following sentences:
   a. The mean of a set of numbers shows us...
   b. The median of a set of numbers shows us...
   c. The mode of a set of numbers shows us...
   d. The range of a set of numbers shows us...

3. Which do you think is the most appropriate in the following situations, the mean, median or mode? Give a reason for your choice.

   a. The final mark on a report card, based on test and quiz marks throughout the term.

   b. Describing the price of houses in a city.

   c. Deciding what shoe sizes to order for your sports store.

   d. Fuel consumption rates for the school van during a 4-week period.

   e. Discussing salaries that people are paid in a certain profession.

PUT INTO PRACTICE

1. Ten players on a wheelchair hockey team scored the following numbers of goals:
   50, 47, 33, 30, 18, 31, 26, 13, 17, 19.

   a. Calculate the mean.

   b. Find the median.

   c. How would you finish this sentence?
   "The average player on the wheelchair hockey team scores about... ."

2. The Ladies Professional Golf Association paid out the following prize money to the top five players.
   $112 500, $69 819, $45 288, $45 288, $29 248.

   a. What was the mean amount, to the nearest dollar?

   b. What was the median amount?

   c. Why is the mean higher than the median?

3. The Trappers scored the following number of runs in each inning:
   0, 0, 3, 0, 2, 0, 1, 0, 0

   a. What is the range?

   b. What is the mode?

   c. If you decide to watch only one inning, what is the likely number of runs that the Trappers will score? Explain.

343

4. The points scored by the Pronghorns Women's Basketball team were:

62, 74, 80, 80, 78, 72, 67, 61, 94, 99, 98, 76, 104.

The measures of central tendency of these numbers are:
   Mean: 80,   Median: 78,   Mode: 80,   Range: 43.

About how many points would you expect that they would score in the next game?
Explain.

5. During a football series between the Stampeders and the Eskimos the gate attendances were:

18 492, 11 714, 17 723 and 20 019.

What was the mean attendance?

6. Elvis Stojko received the following scores in the Men's Qualifying free skate:

5.4, 5.3, 5.5, 5.5, 5.6, 5.1, 5.5.

   a. What is the median of these numbers?

   b. What is the mean of these numbers?

   c. If the highest and lowest scores are ignored, what are the mean, median and mode?

7.   a. Suggest reasons why the highest and lowest scores are dropped.

   b. Name another sport where this procedure is used.

8. The Oilers' top ten players scored the following numbers of goals during the season:

25, 31, 12, 16, 13, 15, 20, 14, 12, 13.

What was the median number of goals scored?

9. The player heights of a university volleyball team are:
   186 cm, 188 cm, 188 cm, 186 cm, 188 cm, 186 cm,
   188 cm, 185 cm, 190 cm, 187 cm, 186 cm, 187 cm,
   186 cm, 184 cm, 189 cm and 189 cm.

   The measures of central tendency are:
   Mean: 185 cm, Median: 187 cm, Mode: 186 cm,
   Range 6 cm.
   You are a sportscaster and you want to state the "average"
   height of the players.
   What will you say?   Why?

10. The Head of the Physical Education Department has
    asked you to help with the purchase of uniforms for the
    football team.
    Which of the following would be the best statistic to use
    in deciding on the uniform sizes? Mean, Median, Mode
    or Range.
    Explain your reasoning.

11. a. Record the previous day's low temperature for 7 or 8
       places listed in the newspaper or on the internet.

    b. Determine the mean, median, mode and range of this
       data.

    c. Do any of the places have temperatures that differ
       greatly from the mean, median or mode?
       If so, explain why there is a difference.

12. In his first football game Iain had gains of:
    10 yd, 3 yd, 0 yd, 12 yd, 12 yd, 1 yd, 2 yd and 0 yd.
    a.   Calculate his mean gain.

    b.   Draw a vertical bar graph of his gains.

    c.   Across the bars, draw a horizontal line that
          represents his mean gain.

    d.   What do you notice about this line?

PUT INTO PRACTICE

1. The following results for the 1500 m and the wheelchair 1500 m were posted at the Edmonton 2001 IAAF World Championships in Athletics.

Place	1500 m		Time (min:s)
1.	Hichman El Guerrouj	(Morocco)	3:30.68
2.	Bernard Lagat	(Kenya)	3:31.10
3.	Driss Maazouzi	(France)	3:31.54
4.	William Chirchir	(Kenya)	3:31.91
5.	Reyes Estevez	(Spain)	3:32.34
6.	Jose Antonio Redolat	(Spain)	3:34.29
7.	Rui Silva	(Portugal)	3:35.74
8.	Abdel_Kader Hachla	(Morocco)	3:36.54
9.	Gert-Jan Liefers	(Netherlands)	3:36.99

Place	1500 m wheelchair		Time (min:s)
1.	Aaron Gordian	(Mexico)	3:08.04
2.	Jeff Adams	(Canada)	3:08.13
3.	Saul Mendoza	(Mexico)	3:08.16
4.	Jun Hiromichi	(Japan)	3:08.24
5.	Ralph Brunner	(Germany)	3:08.58
6.	Tana Rawat	(Thailand)	3:09.03
7.	Jean Jeannot	(France)	3:09.17
8.	Heinz Frei	(Switzerland)	3:10.24
9.	Kelly Smith	(Canada)	3:10.37

a. Find the median time for each group of athletes.

b. Which group had the fastest times?

2. The amputee's 100 m and the 100 m results at the Edmonton Championships were as follows.

Place	100 m amputee		Time (s)
1.	Amy Winters	(AUS)	12.72
2.	Catherine Bader-Bille	(GER)	13.75
3.	Meaghan Starr	(AUS)	13.76
4.	Sabine Wagner	(GER)	14.35
5.	Mary Shea Cowart	(USA)	14.67
6.	Kelly Bruno	(USA)	14.92
7.	Andrea Scherney	(AUT)	14.94

Place	100 m		Time (s)
1.	Zhanna Pintusevich-Block	(UKR)	10.82
2.	Marion Jones	(USA)	10.85
3.	Ekaterini Thanou	(GRE)	10.91
4.	Chandra Sturrup	(BAH)	11.02
5.	Chryste Gaines	(USA)	11.06
6.	Debbie Ferguson	(BAH)	11.13
7.	Kelly White	(USA)	11.15

a. Determine the range of each group.

b. Which group of runners was closer together at the end of the race?

c. Calculate the difference between the two winning times.

d. Calculate the difference between the two median times.

Remember that:

$3 - 2 = +1$

$2 - 3 = -1$

The Plus/Minus statistic measures a team's strength in terms of goals for and goals against while a particular player is on the ice when the teams are at even strength.
It is also used with points for and against in basketball.

To calculate the Plus/Minus number we subtract the number of "goals against" from the number of "goals for".

This sometimes results in a negative number.

Example 1:

A player has played in 10 games.
There were six goals scored by her team while she was on the ice and three goals scored by the other team while she was on the ice.

What is the player's plus/minus statistic?

Solution:

Goals For – Goals Against $= 6 - 3$
                              $= 3$

She has a +3.

PUT INTO PRACTICE

1. a. Calculate the Plus/Minus number for each of the players in the table.

Player	Games Played	Goals For	Goals Against	+/– Number
Porter	31	8	34	–26
Micaela	31	15	21	
Darren	31	35	8	
Dan	30	35	12	
Brad	27	29	6	
Janet	31	35	14	
Tina	30	11	29	
Keith	3	1	3	

b. In No.1a it appears that Keith's Plus/Minus number is much better than Micaela's.
Is this a reasonable statement?
Explain.

c. Discuss your answer to No. 1b with others.

d. Calculate the mean, median and mode of the Plus/Minus numbers.

e. Do you think that the team is having a winning season?
Explain your answer.

CENTRAL TENDENCIES

COPYRIGHT © 2002 Rogue Media Inc. 349

2. a. Calculate the Plus/Minus number for each of the following basketball players.

Player	Games Played	Points For	Points Against	+/– Number
Marlene	5	292	217	
Sandy	4	200	151	
Mike	5	339	291	
Shannon	5	376	329	
Iain	5	349	320	
Wade	2	87	72	
Randa	4	117	103	
Rob	5	295	291	
Jennifer	1	11	11	
Jay	5	241	252	
Allan	2	87	108	
Chris	2	65	87	
Bryan	2	71	102	

b. Using these statistics, pick the top three players. Do not worry about the order.

c. Make a tally of the three choices from each person or group in the class.
Use this tally to determine the top three choices of the class.

d. How do your picks compare with the combined class picks?

Real World Project

You are ready to start Step 3 of your project.

THEOREM OF PYTHAGORAS

SQUARE ROOTS

GET THINKING

Mathematics is used when giving the dimensions of different playing areas and in providing the specifications for the dimensions of sports equipment
Discuss why this is important.

In this series of lessons you will learn about a relationship among the squares drawn on the sides of right-angled triangles. You will learn how to use this relationship and how useful it is.

For example, you can use it to make sure that a basketball court is square or that football or rugby goal posts are vertical

Before starting this you will need to know how to calculate the length of the side of a square.

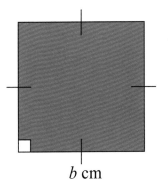

b cm

The **square root** of a number is the number which, when multiplied by itself, will give a perfect square number.

E.g., $\sqrt{25} = 5$ because $5 \times 5 = 25$.

Example:
Calculate the length of a side of a square whose area is 25 cm^2.

Solution:
For a rectangle, $A = bh$.
In a square, the base and height are equal.
Let the length of the base of the square be b cm.
$25 = bb$
$b^2 = 25$

To solve $b^2 = 25$ we need a number that can be squared to become 25.

We know that $5^2 = 25$ and so we know that $b = 5$.

This is called finding a **square root** of 25.

COPYRIGHT © 2002   Rogue Media Inc. 351

It is helpful to review the squares of some numbers before finding square roots.

1. Complete a copy of the table below.

Number	1	2	3	4	5	6	7	8	9	10	11	12
Number^2	1	4	9									

You will need this **list of squares** for the rest of this Tutorial.

2. From the list of squares you can see that:

$\sqrt{1} = 1$ because $1^2 = 1$,

$\sqrt{4} = 2$ because $2^2 = 4$ and

$\sqrt{9} = 3$ because $3^2 = 9$.

Use your list of squares to write an answer for each of the following.

a. $\sqrt{16}$ b. $\sqrt{25}$ c. $\sqrt{36}$

d. $\sqrt{49}$ e. $\sqrt{144}$ f. $\sqrt{64}$

g. $\sqrt{100}$ h. $\sqrt{121}$ i. $\sqrt{81}$

INVESTIGATION USING TECHNOLOGY

Another easy way to obtain the answer for $\sqrt{25}$ is to use the Square Root button on your calculator.

Learn how to use this button on your calculator by finding out what you have to do to 25 to get the answer 5.

On some calculators the $\sqrt{}$ key is on a button and you can use it directly.

On some calculators the $\sqrt{}$ key is just above the "x^2" button and you need to activate it by pushing the "Shift" or "Inv" or "2nd Fn" button first and then the "x^2" button.

You will also need to learn whether you key in "25" first and then push the Square Root button or whether you push the Square Root button first and then key in the "25".

3. Check your ability to use the $\sqrt{}$ button on your calculator by doing No. 2.

You can use your calculator to calculate the square root of any number that is small enough for your calculator to handle.

If you calculate a value for $\sqrt{200}$ you will find that it is approximately 14.142 135 62.

ESTIMATION

Before using your calculator it is helpful to have an estimate of the answer.

If you want to calculate $\sqrt{10}$ you should estimate first.
Look at your list of perfect squares and note that 10 is between 9 and 16.

So we know that $\sqrt{10}$ is between 3 and 4.
So the answer will be "three decimal something".

I.e., $\sqrt{10} = 3.\boxed{}$.

Number	3	4
Number^2	9	16

n	n^2
1	1
2	4
3	9
4	16
5	25
6	36
7	49
8	64
9	81
10	100
11	121
12	144

4. Use your list of squares to write each answer in the form: "whole number decimal something".

   E.g., $\sqrt{20} = 4.\boxed{}$.

   a. $\sqrt{11}$ b. $\sqrt{34}$ c. $\sqrt{50}$ d. $\sqrt{78}$ e. $\sqrt{95}$ f. $\sqrt{120}$

5. Use your calculator to calculate the value of the square root of each of the numbers in No.4.
   Round your answer to three decimal places.

6. Without a calculator, choose the correct approximate square root for each number.

   a. $\sqrt{18}$ 4.2426407,   5.9803862,   6.7157682;

   b. $\sqrt{50}$ 6.56777,   7.0710678,   8.98876;

   c. $\sqrt{86}$ 7.81854,   8.988754,   9.2736185;

   d. $\sqrt{95}$ 7.12345,   8.288632,   9.7467943.

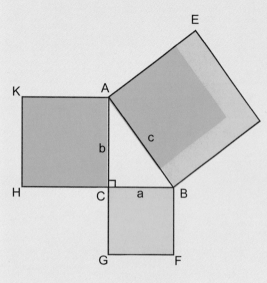

The **Theorem of Pythagoras** states that, in a right-angled triangle, the **Area of Square ABDE is equal to the Area of Square ACHK plus the Area of Square CBFG**.

Area Sq ABDE = Area Sq ACHK + Area Sq CGFB.

Another way of stating the theorem is:
The square drawn on the hypotenuse of a right triangle is equal to the sum of the squares drawn on the other two sides.

OR

The square of the hypotenuse of a right triangle is equal to the sum of the squares of the other two sides.

The easiest way to remember it is:
$$AB^2 = AC^2 + CB^2$$

The **hypotenuse** is the name given to the side that is **opposite** the **right angle**.
In the diagram, the **hypotenuse** is **AB** because it is opposite $\angle C$.

Another way is to use letters to represent the lengths of the sides.
We can say that the length of AB is c because AB is opposite vertex C.
Copy and complete:
The length of AC is b because AC is opposite vertex _____ .
The length of BC is a because BC is opposite vertex _____ .

$AB^2 = AC^2 + CB^2$ becomes $c^2 = a^2 + b^2$

INTERACTIVE

⊙ LESSONS

INVESTIGATION

1. Here is a picture.

   What is the Pythagorean relationship for the picture?

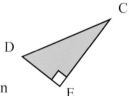

2. Draw the picture for the Pythagorean relationship:
   $g^2 = h^2 + j^2$

PUT INTO PRACTICE

This is a right-angled triangle.
The area of c^2 is the same as the sum of the areas of the squares drawn on the other two sides.

1. State the value of c^2 when the areas of the other two squares are 9 and 16.

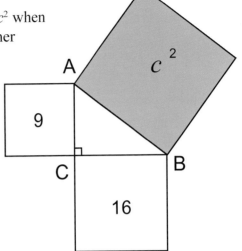

2. Calculate the value of r^2 when the other two areas are 9 and 25.

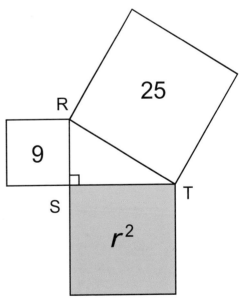

$$r^2 + 9 = 25$$

3. State the hypotenuse for each of the right-angled triangles above.

Example 1:

Calculate the length of AB.

$$c = ?$$

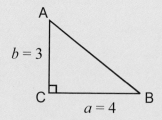

Solution:

$$AB^2 = AC^2 + BC^2$$
$$c^2 = b^2 + a^2$$
$$c^2 = 3^2 + 4^2$$
$$c^2 = 9 + 16$$
$$c^2 = 25$$
$$c = \sqrt{25}$$
$$c = 5$$
$$AB = 5.$$

Example 2:

Calculate the length of ST.

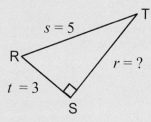

Solution:

$$RT^2 = RS^2 + ST^2$$
$$s^2 = t^2 + r^2$$
$$5^2 = 3^2 + r^2$$
$$25 = 9 + r^2$$
$$25 - 9 = 9 + r^2 - 9 \qquad \textit{Subtract 9 from each side.}$$
$$16 = r^2$$
$$r^2 = 16$$
$$r = \sqrt{16}$$
$$r = 4$$
$$ST = 4$$

4. Calculate the length of the hypotenuse.

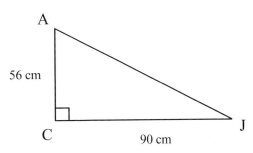

Copy and complete this solution.

$AJ^2 = AC^2 + \square^2$

$c^2 = \square^2 + a^2$

$\square^2 = 56^2 + 90^2$

$c^2 = \square$

$c = \sqrt{\square}$

$c = 106$

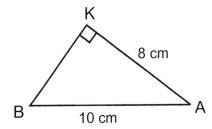

5. Calculate the length of BK.

K

8 cm

B   A
   10 cm

6. Calculate the length of the missing side in each triangle.

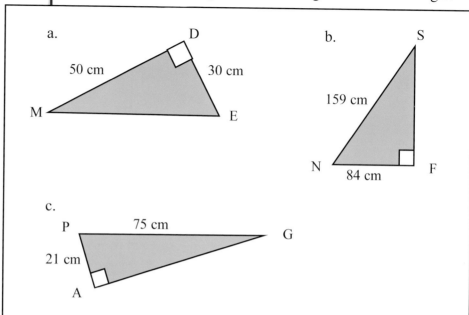

a.

50 cm D 30 cm

M   E

b.

S

159 cm

N 84 cm F

c.

P 75 cm G

21 cm

A

7. A climber is stranded on a climbing wall.
   You have a 24-ft ladder.
   For safety reasons, the foot of the ladder should be about
   6 ft away from the wall.

   a. Draw a diagram to represent this.

   b. How high up the wall can the ladder reach?
      Round your answer to one decimal place.

8. A student jogs along two sides of a field.
   She goes 120 yd south and 160 yd west.
   She could have walked "kitty corner" (along the diagonal)
   across the field.

   a. Draw a diagram to represent the two routes.

   b. Which is the shorter route?

   c. How much shorter is it?
      Round your answer to the nearest yard.

9. When a room is being constructed the diagonals are measured to ensure that the corners are "square".
If the diagonals are equal the room is said to be squared.

Measure your classroom to see if it is squared.

Step 1: Measure one length of the room.
Step 2: Measure one width of the room.
Step 3: Use the Theorem of Pythagoras to calculate the length of the diagonal that joins the length and width that you measured.
Step 4: Measure the diagonal to see if it matches your answer.
Step 5: Repeat Steps 1 to 4 for the other length, width and diagonal of the room.

10. On a 90° dogleg golf hole, Jean got a hole-in-one!
The first leg is 150 yd and the second leg is 200 yd.
What is the straight-line distance traveled by the ball?

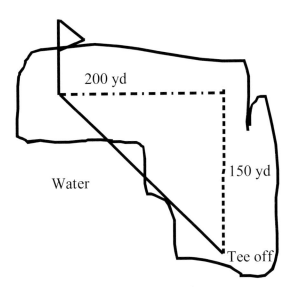

200 yd

150 yd

Water

Tee off

11. The catcher throws the ball from home to second.
How far is the throw, correct to one decimal place, if the
diamond has measurements as illustrated in the diagram?

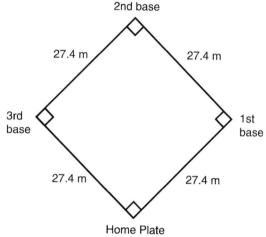

2nd base

27.4 m   27.4 m

3rd
base   1st
base

27.4 m   27.4 m

Home Plate

You are now ready
to start Step 4 of
your project.

12. A swimmer wanted to swim straight across a river that is
21 m wide.
He started out to swim straight across but, because of the
current, landed 10 m down stream on the opposite bank.

a. Draw a diagram to represent this situation.

b. How far did he travel, correct to the nearest metre?

13. A quarterback, **Q,** is standing exactly in the middle of her
own 25 yd line.
The field is 65 yd wide.
She passes to a player, **R,** who is on the sideline at his
own 45 yd line.
How far is the receiver from the quarterback?
Round your answer to the nearest yard.

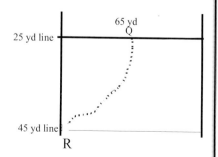

65 yd
Q
25 yd line

45 yd line
R

REVIEW

ADDITION OF INTEGERS

1. Calculate the value:

   a. $6 - 3$ b. $6 - 13$ c. $5 - 6$

   d. $13 - 4$ e. $2 - 16$ f. $29 - 31$

MEASURES OF CENTRAL TENDENCIES

2. Determine the mean, median, mode and range for the following sets of data:

   a. 10, 9, 13, 14, 9

   b. 7, 9, 16, 10, 6, 10, 7, 8, 7, 8, 7, 13

   c. 9, 7, 6, 5, 8, 10, 4, 7.

3. In a football game, a player gained 22 yd, 8 yd, 6 yd, 2 yd and 10 yd. He also had 0 yd on one play and losses of 3 yd and 1 yd on two plays.

   a. What are the mean, median and mode?

   b. Which of these best describes his performance? Why?

4. The members of a wrestling team have masses of 75 kg, 81 kg, 58 kg, 64 kg and 86 kg. Calculate the mean mass, correct to one decimal place.

5. In the games so far this season a soccer team has scored 3, 0, 5, 3, 2, 4, 1 and 2 goals.

   What is the range?

Mean:
Add the numbers.
Divide by the number of numbers.

Median:
Put the numbers in order.
Pick the middle number.

Mode:
Pick the most frequent number.

6. On the women's basketball team the starting players heights are 184 cm, 183 cm, 179 cm, 178 cm and 176 cm.

    a. What is the median height?

    b. The tallest player was replaced by someone who is 180 cm tall.

       How was the median height affected?

7. The Flames players had the following point totals for the season.
   70, 65, 54, 35, 33, 28, 23, 20, 20, 19,
   15, 13, 9, 8, 8, 7, 6, 5, 4, 4, 4, 4, 1, 0.

   What is the mode?

8. A rectangular swimming pool is 25 m long and 8 m wide.
   Mike swam diagonally from one corner of the pool to the other and back 5 times.

   How many metres did he swim?
   Round your answer to the nearest metre.

9. Dayna is flying a kite and has let out 200 m of string. Henri is standing directly beneath the kite and is 57 m from Dayna.

   How high is the kite above Henri?
   Round your answer to the nearest metre.

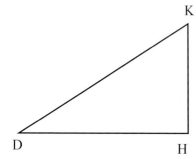

K

D   H

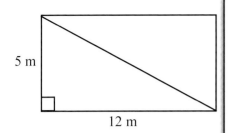

5 m

12 m

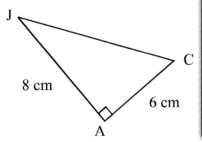

Triple play!

Area = Base × Height

Perimeter is the sum of the lengths of the sides.

J

8 cm

C

6 cm

A

10. Jill and Jean are playing catch in the back yard. The sides of the yard are 12 m and 5 m.

If they stand in the opposite corners of the yard, how far apart are they?

11. The bases are loaded and you are playing third base. A ground ball is hit to you. You tag the runner at third and step on third.

How far do you have to throw the ball to get the runner out at first base?
Round your answer to the nearest metre.

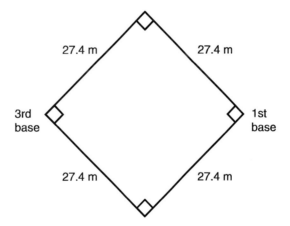

27.4 m   27.4 m

3rd base   1st base

27.4 m   27.4 m

12. a. Calculate the length of JC in the triangle AJC.

b. Calculate the perimeter of the triangle.

c. Calculate the area of the triangle.

d. Look at the number of centimetres in the perimeter and the number of square centimetres in the area.

What do you notice?

PROJECT

CHOOSING A COMMUNITY SPORTS FACILITY

Most citizens like having access to sports facilities in their communities.
A great deal of research and planning has to go into deciding which facilities would be suitable for a community.

Some of the questions that planners need to ask are:
What type of facility is required?
Where will the facility be located?
Who will be using it? (e.g. teens, seniors, all ages)
How much will it cost to build?
Who will be surveyed?
Are there opportunities for sharing costs with other groups?

Get Thinking

• Add at least one idea to this list.

• Compare your list with others and make a class list of questions.

STEP 1: INITIAL IDEAS

With your partner write a short paragraph describing some of the sports facilities you would like to see in your community.

Examples might include an ice arena, a swimming pool, a skateboard park or a fitness centre.

Give reasons for your choice.

STEP 2: RESEARCH

With your partner design a questionnaire to obtain information on what type of facility your class or school would like to see built, and where they would like it located.

How will you word your questionnaire to ensure you get accurate information?

a)   Will you list the choices and ask the participants to rank them in descending order of importance?
Will you include "None" or "Don't care" as options?

b)   Will you provide a list of locations to choose from or ask for locations?

c)   Will you conduct interviews or give out questionnaires to be completed by the participants?

d)   Do you have different ideas on how to collect the information you need?

STEP 3: SURVEY

a)   Collect and tabulate all the data.

b)   Decide how you will analyze the data.
     Will you use mean, median, or mode?
     Give reasons for your choice.

c)   Display your data in a suitable graph.

d)   Relate your findings to a map of the community, (obtainable from the town hall or a local realty office), to see if your survey matches the optimum location on the map.

e)   Do you see any connection between the type of facility chosen and the location in the community?

f)   Based on your survey, write your conclusions as to the type of facility and it's location.

STEP 4: VISUAL PRESENTATION

1. What will your facility look like?

    What should the capacity be?

    a)   Make sketches of different parts of your facility.

    b)   Make scale drawings of the important parts of your facility.
         Measurements may be expressed in metric or Imperial units.

2. Make a model of your facility.

ADVERTISING

GET THINKING

☐ How can understanding ratios help me decide where to order pizza?

☐ How did I choose my cellular phone plan? What would I do differently next time?

☐ 1995, Consumers Union reported that each year young people spend more than $70 billion of their own money and influence the spending of more than $196 billion of their parents' money.
How does advertisng affect the way that my household spends our family dollars?

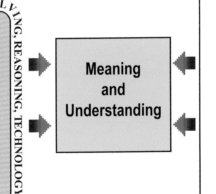

Content

- Area of a circle
- Ratio
- Proportion
- Decimals
- Percent
- Central tendency

MENTAL MATH, PROBLEM SOLVING, REASONING, TECHNOLOGY, VISUALIZATION, COMMUNICATION, CONNECTIONS, ESTIMATION AND

Meaning and Understanding

Intellectual Curiosity

What kind of consumer am I?

Do I mathematically evaluate the purchasing terms in order to make a decision or do I simply make fast purchases and resolve to deal with the consequences of quick decisions?

Real World Project

Buying Electronics

Research flyers for an electronic system;
investigate jobs that would allow you to pay for the system;
report your discoveries along with reasons for your final decision.

INTERACTIVE LESSONS

CONSUMER CHOICES

PIZZA

TUTORIAL 1

Enzo's Pizza

	Medium 12"		X-Large 16"	
	Single	Two	Single	Two
Cheese:	$9.99	$16.99	$13.39	$19.99
Each Additional Topping:				
	$1.50	$2.50	$1.95	$3.20

Bernie's Pizza

	Medium 12"		X-Large 16"	
	Single	Two	Single	Two
Cheese:	$10.50	$15.70	$13.50	$20.20
Each Additional Topping:				
	$0.95	$1.45	$1.25	$1.90

Example 1:

Calculate the cost of three 16" pizzas, with three additional toppings, at Enzo's.

Solution:

Two basic X-Large pizzas cost $19.99.
Their three additional toppings cost 3 × $3.20 = $9.60.
One single basic pizza costs $13.39.
It's three additional toppings cost 3 × $1.95 = $5.85.
The price is $(19.99 + 9.60 + 13.39 + 5.85) = $48.83.

1. The team decided to order pizza after the game.
   They couldn't decide whether to order
   four 12" pizzas or three 16" pizzas.

   a. Calculate the cost of four mediums pizzas, with three additional toppings, at Enzo's.

   b. Calculate the cost of four medium pizzas, with three additional toppings, at Bernie's.

   c. Calculate the cost of three X-large pizzas, with three additional toppings, at Bernie's

   d. They noticed that 4 medium pizzas cost about the same as 3 X-large pizzas.
      They went to Bernie and asked his advice about which combination to order.
      He reminded them that they needed to consider the area of a circle.
      They knew that the area of a circle was given by

      $A = \pi r^2$ where r represents the radius.
      First they decided to calculate the area of one 12" pizza.
      Copy and complete their solution.

      > The diameter (d) of the medium pizza is 12" so the radius (r) is $\square$".
      >
      > $$A = \pi r^2$$
      > $$A = \square (6)^2$$
      > $$A = \square \pi$$
      > $$A = \square$$
      >
      > The area covered by one medium pizza is about 113 in^2.

      Calculate the area covered by four medium pizzas.

   e. Calculate the area covered by three X-large pizzas.

   f. Which combination would you advise the players to buy? Why?

2. A group decided that they could eat at least one medium pizza and one X-large pizza.
They agreed that they want four additional toppings.

   a. Calculate the cost of the two pizzas at each of the pizzerias.

   b. Suggest a combination of pizzas, with four additional toppings, that they can order that will give them more pizza for less money.

3.   a. Obtain at least two sets of pizza prices from your area.

   b. Compare the prices of a medium pizza with three additional toppings.

   c. Check to see if the mediums from each place are the same size.

   d. Where would you order the pizza?
Why?

4. You need to order pizzas for your class.
You would like to have two slices per person.
You want four additional toppings.

   a. Calculate the cost of these pizzas in your area.

   b. How many slices would be left over?

5. If you were Bernie from Bernie's Pizza, how might you increase your business through the use of a good advertisement?

Develop an advertisement to do this using technology or other means.

Real World Project

You are now ready to start Step 1 of your project.

INVESTIGATION

Here are some details of costs of four new cellular phone plans:

	Callus	Bing Mobility	Coggers	Bowser
Monthly Fee	$25	$25	$20	$20
Activation Fee	$25	$35	$25	$0
System Access Fee (per month)	$6.95	$70/year OR $6.50/month	$6	$6.95
Air Time Included (min)	150	200	150 OR 100 weekdays and 250 weekends	200
Additional Time (¢/min)	25	25	25	20

Additional Features

	Callus	Bing Mobility	Coggers	Bowser
Call Forwarding (per month)	$2 up to 3000 min	Included	$2 up to 2500 min	1000 min free $0.10 each additional minute
Call Waiting	Included	Included	$2/month	Included
Caller I.D. (per month)	$3	$3	$4	$3
Roaming Charges (outside coverage area)	$0.25/min	$0.20/min	$0.15/min	$0.10/min

1. You are interested in getting a cell phone plan.
   After doing some analysis you have decided that you will average 0.5 hours per day during the week.
   You think that you will likely double your weekday use on the weekends.

   a. Calculate the cost of 6 months of each plan.

   b. Which one would you pick?
      Why?

   c. If you think that you will use about 30 min of "roaming time" each month how much will that add to the 6-month cost of the plan that you chose?

2. a. Research information on plans in your area.

   b. Choose the plan in your area that would be best for 560 min over 60 days in the summer.

   c. Choose the plan in your area that would be best for your requirements over 60 days in the summer.

1. Pre-paid plans are available.
   These pre-paid plans expire when either all the air minutes are used or when the time expires.
   Most plans allow you to carry over any unused air minutes if you renew the plan before the time expires.

   Kent plans to get a cell phone for 60 days in the summer to use while he is working.
   Here are details of pre-paid plans offered by four companies.

Real World Project

You are now ready to start Step 2 of your project.

Plans	Gold Plan $10		Silver Plan $25		Bronze Plan $50	
Details	Valid For	Local Air Time	Valid For	Local Air Time	Valid For	Local Air Time
Company I	30 days	25 min	60 days	75 min	60 days	170 min
Company II	30 days	30 min	90 days	70 min		
Company III	30 days	30 min	60 days	75 min	90 days	150 min
Company IV	30 days	25 min	90 days	75 min		

a. What will be the total cost of each company's plan if Kent estimates that he will need 560 min in order to contact his parents for rides and other items during the summer?
   Is it better to get two 30-day plans rather than a 60-day plan? Why or why not?

b. Estimate what your requirements would be for 60 days in the summer.

c. Which of these four plans would best fit your requirements? Why?

Company I:
The $50 plan costs twice as much as the $25 plan but it gives more than twice as many minutes.
The $50 plan costs five times as much as the $10 plan but it gives more than five times as many minutes.
Kent should get close to 560 min with $50 plans and then top it up with other plans.

A lot of advertisements involve percent discounts. Here is a review of percent.

Example 1: A $70 sweater was advertised at "30% off". Calculate the amount of the discount.

Solution: 30% of 70

$$\frac{x}{70} = \frac{30}{100}$$

$$= \frac{30}{100} \times 70 \qquad \textbf{OR} \qquad 100x = 70 \times 30$$

$$= 0.30 \times 70 \qquad\qquad\qquad x = (70 \times 30) \div 100$$

$$= 21 \qquad\qquad\qquad\qquad = 21$$

The discount is $21.

Example 2:

At a competing store, a $60 sweater was advertised at a sale price of $40.
Calculate the percent of the discount and compare the rate of discount to that in the first store.
Round the answer to the nearest percent.

Solution:

The discount is $60 – $40 = $20.

$$\frac{20}{60} = \frac{x}{100}$$

$60x = 20(100)$
$60x = 2000$
$x = 2000 \div 60$
$x = 33.3\ldots$
The rate of discount is about 33%.
This is a better rate of discount.

1. Calculate the following discounts.
   a. 8% of $160   b. 25% of $140   c. 40% of $395

2. a. $9.75 is what percent of $65?
   b. $39.60 is what percent of $198?

3. Here are some excerpts from a sales flyer from a leather store.

Up to 70% off everything.		
Women's Miranda Coat:	Regular Sale Price	$495
	Sale Price	$199
Men's Metro Jacket:	Regular Sale Price	$525
	Sale Price	$199
Women's Astoria Coat:	Regular Sale Price	$425
	Sale Price	$149
Men's Boulevard Jacket:	Regular Sale Price	$425
	Sale Price	$199
Women's Village Coat:	Regular Sale Price	$495
	Sale Price	$169
Men's Urban Explorer Jacket	Regular Sale Price	$595
	Sale Price	$229
Every Leather Jacket is on Sale!		

a. What is the percentage discount on each item? Round the answers to the nearest whole percent.

b. Is the advertisement misleading? Why or why not?

c. Calculate the price of each item at a 70% discount.

4. Arthur looked at the advertisement on the left and said: "I am going to wait until the second week because then the items will be free!"
Is Arthur correct? Why or why not?

You may want to consider what the final price on a $100 item is.

Real World Project

You are now ready to start Step 3 of your project.

Annual Odds and Ends Two-Week Sale!

50% off on selected items all week.

An additional 50% off on these items in the second week!

Hurry In!

PUT INTO PRACTICE

1. At Jake's Fast Foods you can buy a Combo, with a large burger, fries and a drink, for $5.99.
   Individual prices are:

Large Burger	$2.99
Fries	$1.99
Drink	$1.99.

   You want the large burger and fries but don't want the drink.
   Should you order the Combo?
   Why or why not?

2. A 10-lb (4.54 kg) bag of Royal Gala Apples is priced at $7.88.
   New Crop Red Delicious Apples are on sale for $0.98/lb or $2.16/kg.
   a. The store manager has decided that the Royal Gala apples should be priced the same way as the Red Delicious apples.
      What is the price per pound and per kilogram of the Royal Gala apples?

   b. What type of apple would be a better buy?
      Why?

3. a. Black out the actual cost of items in several advertisements.

   b. Have others estimate the costs of the products or services.

   c. For each product or service subtract the actual cost from the estimated cost.

   d. Add the integers that you calculated in No. c.
      (An answer close to 0 indicates good estimating skills.)

4. A magazine advertises prices as follows:
   One-year subscription (10 issues) is $21.39 including GST.
   Two-year subscription (20 issues) is $40.13 including GST.
   News-stand price is $4.25 per issue.

   a. How much do you save on a one-year subscription compared to buying the magazine from the news-stand for one year?

   b. Compare the costs of a two-year subscription to buying them at a news-stand.

   c. Why might it be better to buy the magazine at the news-stand?

5. a. In the classified advertisements of a newspaper find five cars of a certain model and a specific year.

   b. Calculate the mean price.

   c. Find the median price.

6. Joshua needs 8500 flyers printed.
   Bruno's Copy Centre charges:
   3¢ each for the first 1000
   2¢ each for the next 4000 and
   1.5¢ each for the next 6000.
   Reine's PrintWerx charges a set-up fee of $35 and 1.5¢/copy.

   a. Which should he choose?
      Why?

   b. Which should he choose if he wants 4500 flyers?
      Why?

7. The cost of a 3-Pickup Electric Guitar is $374.48 including tax.
The cost of a 60-watt amplifier with 12" speakers is $374.49, including tax.
The amplifier sells for $353.09 with the purchase of any electric guitar.

   a. Since you need both items how much will you save by buying the two items together?

   b. You can make 12 equal payments, interest free on approved credit.
   What would each of these payments be if you bought the amplifier and guitar together?

8. Flyers from two different stores are delivered to your door.

ZABA'S

Quick Dinner
225 g
59¢

Regular Chips
400 g
2/$5

ANECCA'S

Quick Dinner
12-pack (225-g boxes)
$7.99

Regular Chips
180 g
3/$3.99

You need to change the dollars to cents or the cents to dollars.

a. Which store gives you the best price for one Quick Dinner?

b. Which store gives you the best deal for Regular Chips?

You might want to calculate the cost per 100 g.
You can start like this:

Two bags cost $5. 800 g costs $5.
$$\frac{\$x}{100 \text{ g}} = \frac{\$5}{800 \text{ g}}$$

9.

| Save 78¢ on two! | Toothpaste A | 130 mL | 2/$3. |
| Save $1.68 on three! | Toothpaste B | 75 mL | 3/$3.99. |

Calculate the cost per 100 mL of each.
Round your answer to the nearest cent.

$$\frac{x¢}{100 \text{ mL}} = \frac{300¢}{260 \text{ mL}}$$

10. You want to buy Play Centre 2.
You particularly want to buy the Grand Canuck 3 game for the Play Centre 2 system.

The Shop	Ready Shop	Cool Trading
Play Centre 2 Grand Canuck 3 included **$499.99**	Play Centre 2 Grand Canuck 3 Ready to Roll 2 Omni included **$599.99**	Play Centre 2 **$446.83** Grand Canuck 3 **$69.97**

a. Where should you buy?
Why?

b. If your friend buys the most expensive system, how much more is it than the cost of the system that you chose?

K2 Golden	$539.99
K2 BigBert	$539.99
Ride Team	$409.99
Jaguar	$399.99
Jaguar Plus	$399.99
San Jose Y Arrow	$399.99
Z-type Stealth	$399.99
Mariachi Wide	$389.99
Altera Board	$369.99
Pacer	$339.99
Pacer Wide	$339.99
Xtra Big	$309.99
Z-Boogie	$239.99
Izezk8	$89.99

Real World Project

You are now ready to start Step 4 of your project.

11. a. Determine the mean, median, mode and range of prices for the snowboards listed on the left.

   b. Which of these numbers is more appropriate to use when discussing the price of snowboards?
   Why?

12. You are going to start snow boarding.
   The items that you require are:
   board, bindings, boots, goggles, helmet, jacket, pants, socks, gloves, lock and bag.
   Research prices at your local sport shop or on the internet.

   Calculate:
   a. the least that you could spend

   b. the most that you could spend.

   c. The job that you have pays $8/h.

   How many hours would you have to work in order to pay the minimum amount?

   How many hours would you have to work to pay the maximum amount?

1. You have $100 to purchase 10 food items advertised in a grocery flyer.
   What would you buy?

2. a. Find an advertisement in the newspaper that lists a sale price and a regular price.
   Calculate the percentage discount.

   b. Try to find another advertisement that advertises the same item and that shows the regular price and a discount rate.
   Calculate the selling price.

   c. Decide where you will buy.
   Write your reasons.

3. a. Calculate the cost of a can of pop at two 12-packs for $8.

   b. Individual cans cost 50¢.
   How many individual cans can you buy before it is cheaper to buy a 12-pack?

4. A magazine for people, aged 9 to 13, sells for $3 per single issue.
   You can order 10 issues for $27.99 + GST = $29.95 as a gift subscription.
   The advertisement states that parents will be getting 6 issues of Family Magazine free.
   Family Magazine normally sells for $3 per single issue.
   This is supposed to be a saving of over 38%.

   Is this correct?
   Show your calculations.

PROJECT

BUYING ELECTRONICS

People of your age are one of the biggest markets for electronic sales. Because of this, you are constantly exposed to electronics advertising and many of the advertisements are directed towards your age group.

If you are going to make wise consumer choices you will need to do some research before you make your decisions.

You should ask yourselves the following questions when buying a system:

Do I want a package (all components are together)?
Do I want to buy it piece by piece?
Do I need a stand for this equipment?
Do I have to pay a sales tax?

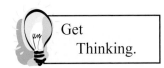

STEP 1: INITIAL IDEAS

With another student write a brief description of what type of system you would like.
Detail the items you want in the system.
Estimate the cost to buy this system.

STEP 2: RESEARCH

Obtain several flyers, catalogues or brochures advertising electronics.

CONSIDER THE FOLLOWING:

1. Package or piece by piece.
2. Price of the items (comparison of prices between items of same quality).
3. Quality.
4. Tax.

STEP 3:   AFFORDABILITY

Check the newspaper to see which jobs you qualify for.
Examine the salary paid for doing these jobs.

Investigate the length of time that you have to work in order to be able to afford your system.

Estimate how much of your salary will be "take-home pay" and how much you will spend for other items (i.e., movies, food).

STEP 4:   CONCLUSION

Write a short report detailing what you discovered about the system that you would like to buy and a description of the job and hours that you would need to work to pay for it.

Conclude with a decision as to whether you would buy this one, choose a less expensive system or wait until you could afford your first choice. Include the reasons for your decision.

> Use pictures from flyers
> to illustrate your report.

GLOSSARY

acute angle

an angle whose measure is less than 90°

acute triangle

each of the three interior angles measures less than 90°

algebraic modeling

representing a pattern or relationship by an algebraic expression or an equation (formula)

altitude

a line segment showing the height of a figure, e.g., in a triangle, an altitude is found by drawing, from a vertex, a line that is perpendicular to the opposite side

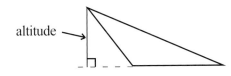

angle

an amount of rotation

arithmetic mean

the quotient when you divide the sum of the numbers by the number of numbers, e.g., the mean of 2, 3, 5, 10 is 5 because $(2 + 3 + 5 + 10) \div 4 = 5$

average

see **arithmetic mean**

bar graph

a graph with horizontal or vertical bars, of equal width, that represent data,

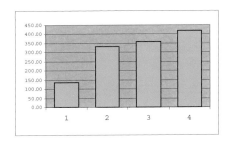

bisector

a line that divides an angle or a line segment into two equal parts

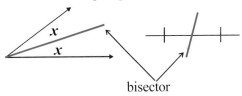

broken-line graph

a graph with line segments joining points that represent data

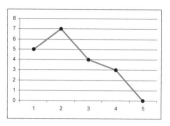

capacity

the volume of material that a container can hold, e.g., 2 L

cartesian coordinate grid

a graph that contains an horizontal axis and a vertical axis

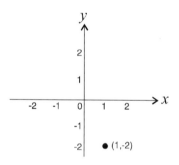

census

surveying an entire population, see also **population**

circle graph

a graph in which a circle (pie) represents the whole and the sectors (pie-shaped pieces) represent the data

clustering

a strategy used for calculating with numbers that cluster around one particular value, e.g., 54, 56, 58, 58.7, 61.345 all cluster around 60

coefficient

the number by which a variable is multiplied, e.g., the coefficient of x in $8x$ is 8

complementary angles

two angles whose sum is 90°

composite number

a number that has factors other than itself and 1; 6 is composite but 7 is not; see also **prime number**

congruent figures

figures that have the same size and shape

coordinate graph

a grid that has data points named as ordered pairs of numbers, e.g., (1, –2), see also **cartesian coordinate grid**

coordinate plane

see **cartesian coordinate grid**

coordinates

an ordered pair of numbers used to describe a location, e.g., (1,–2), (0,0) is the address of a point that is 1 unit to the right and 2 units down from the origin (0,0).

data
information

database
organized information

degree
a unit for measuring angles ($\frac{1}{360}$ of a complete rotation), e.g., $90° = \frac{1}{4}$ of a complete rotation

diameter
a line segment that joins two points on the circumference of a circle and passes through the centre of the circle

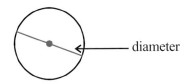
diameter

equation
a mathematical sentence with a left side equal to a right side, e.g., $x + 1 = 6$

equivalent fractions
fractions that represent the same value

e.g., $\frac{2}{3} = \frac{8}{12}$

equivalent ratios
ratios that represent the same relationship, e.g., $1:2:3 = 5:10:15$

evaluate
to determine a value of

exponent
a superscript that usually means repeated multiplication, e.g., $9^3 = 9 \times 9 \times 9$

expression
a mathematical phrase (one or more terms without an equal sign), e.g., $x + 1$

extrapolate
to estimate values lying outside the range of given data, e.g., extend a line in a graph, see also **interpolate**

factor
a number or expression that will divide exactly into another number or expression, see also **to factor**

first-degree equation
an equation in which the variable has only the exponent 1, e.g., $3x + 4 = 5$

first-degree polynomial
a polynomial in which the variable has only the exponent 1, e.g., $3x + 4$

formula
a symbolic way to represent a general rule or relationship, e.g., perimeter (P) of a rectangle with length (l) and width (w) is given by $P = 2(l + w)$

graph
a representation of data in pictorial form

height
see **altitude**

hexagon
a polygon with 6 sides

 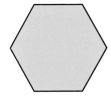

histogram

a graph, in which each bar represents a range of values, and the data are arranged in order

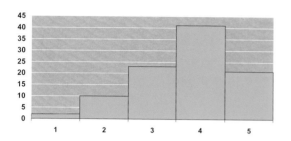

hypotenuse

the side of a right triangle opposite the right angle, see also **leg**

improper fraction

a fraction whose numerator is greater than or equal to its denominator, e.g., $\frac{7}{3}$, $\frac{3}{3}$

independent variable

a variable that does not depend on another for its value, see also **dependent variable**

integers

...,−3, −2, −1, 0, +1, +2, +3,...

interpolate

to estimate values lying between points representing given data, see also **extrapolate**

isosceles triangle

a triangle that has two equal sides

leg

a side of a right triangle that is not the hypotenuse, see also **hypotenuse**

linear dimension

measure of length

linear relation(ship)

a relation(ship) between two variables that can be represented by a straight line on an ordinary coordinate graph

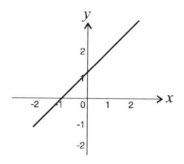

mass

the amount of matter in an object, e.g., 5 kg

mean

see **arithmetic mean**

measures of central tendency

mean, median and **mode**

median

the middle number of an odd set of numbers when they are listed in order

median

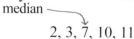

2, 3, 7, 10, 11

or the average of the two middle numbers of an even set of numbers
e.g. the median of 2, 3, 5, 10 is 4

mixed number

a number that is the sum of a whole number

and a fraction, e.g., $4\frac{5}{6}$

mode

the most frequent number(s) of a set; e.g., the mode of 2, 3, 5, 3, 11 is 3, the modes of 2, 3, 5, 3, 5 are 3 and 5, and 2, 3, 5, 10 has no mode

monomial

an algebraic expression with only one term, e.g., $7x^3$

multiple

the product of a given number and a whole number, e.g., 9, 18, 90 are multiples of 9

natural numbers

1, 2, 3, 4,...

number line

a 1-dimensional graph on a line

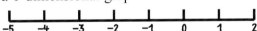

obtuse angle

an angle that measures more than 90° and less than 180°

order of operations

the punctuation rules of mathematics, e.g., BEDMAS (Brackets, Exponents, Division & Multiplication, Addition & Subtraction)

perfect square

a number or expression that is formed by multiplying a number or expression by itself, e.g., $64 = 8^2$

perpendicular bisector

a line that passes through the midpoint (m) of a line and intersects it at 90°

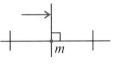

perpendicular lines

two lines that intersect at a 90° angle

pictograph

a graph that illustrates data using pictures or symbols

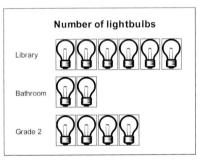

= 2 lightbulbs

plane shape

a 2-dimensional figure

polygon

a closed figure formed by three or more line segments, e.g., triangles, quadrilaterals

polynomial

an algebraic expression that contains only whole number powers of a variable
e.g. $2x^2 + 3x + 4$

population
the total number of individuals or items under consideration in a surveying activity, see also **census**

power
a term written in exponential form,
e.g., 3^5 is 3 to the power of 5
x^2 is x to the power of 2

primary data
information that is collected directly, e.g., interviews

prime factorization
an expression showing a composite number as a product of its prime factors,
e.g., $30 = 2 \times 3 \times 5$

prime number
a natural number greater than 1 that has only two factors, itself and 1, e.g., 11,
see also **composite number**

product
the answer to a multiplication question

proper fraction
a fraction whose numerator is smaller than
its denominator, e.g., $\dfrac{3}{7}$,
see also **improper fraction**

proportion
an equation showing that two ratios are equal, e.g., $3:5 = 6:10$

Pythagorean Theorem
see **Theorem of Pythagoras**

quadrilateral
a polygon with four sides

radius
a line segment drawn from the centre of a circle to any point on the circumference of a circle

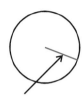

range
the difference between the largest and smallest number in a set of numbers

rate
a comparison of two numbers with different units, e.g., 100 km:2 h, see also **ratio**

ratio
a comparison of numbers with the same units, see also **rate**

regular polygon
a polygon with equal sides and equal angles

relation
a relationship between variables that can be expressed as a table of values, a graph or an equation

right triangle
a triangle containing a 90° angle

rhombus
a quadrilateral with four equal sides

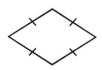

rounding
a systematic process of replacing a number by an approximate value of that number, e.g., $149 \doteq 100$, correct to the nearest hundred

sample
a small group chosen from a population that is used in order to make predictions about the entire population

scale drawing
a drawing in which the lengths are a reduction or an enlargement of actual lengths

scalene triangle
a triangle with three unequal sides

scientific notation
often used on calculators to show very large or very small numbers, e.g., 45 000 000 000 000 might look like 4.5 E13   (4.5×10^{13})

secondary data
information that is not collected directly, e.g., from a database, see also **primary data**

similar figures
figures that have the same shape (but may be different sizes)

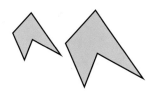

simple interest
the periodical rent (monthly, yearly, etc.) paid for the use of money, calculated using $I = Prt$ where P is the principal, r is the rate of interest, and t is the time

solid
a 3-dimensional figure

substitution
the process of replacing a variable by a value

supplementary angles
two angles whose sum is 180°

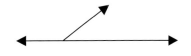

survey
a method of obtaining information by interviews or questionnaires

table of values
a table used to record the relationship between two variables

tally chart
a chart that uses tally marks to count data and record frequencies

term
each of the quantities in a ratio or an algebraic expression

Theorem of Pythagoras
the formula that shows that the area of the square drawn on the hypotenuse of a right-angled triangle is the sum of the areas of the squares drawn on the other two sides, e.g., $a^2 = b^2 + c^2$

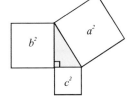

to factor

> to express a number as the product of two or
> more numbers, see also **factor**

trapezoid

> a quadrilateral with only
> one pair of parallel sides

variable

> a symbol used to represent an unspecified
> number, e.g., $7x - 8y + 9$ has variables x, y

vertex

> the point where two sides of a polygon meet

volume

> the amount of space occupied by a solid or a
> liquid, e.g., 2 cm^3

PUZZLES AND PATTERNS

ORDER OF OPERATIONS

ORDER OF OPERATIONS   TUTORIAL 1

Inv 1: (page 5)

Calculate the cost of each kind and add the answers; $3×5.49 + 7×1.29 + 4×5.99 = \$49.46$

PIP: (page 7)

1a. 26   b. 15   2a. (43+7)×2   b. 8+9–2–4 or ...

3. $220   4. 584

5. $25.59   6. $55.75   7. (6×3) – 8 = 10   8. (3+6) × 5 = 45   9. $2.10   10. 15 + (3×6) – 10 = 23

INTEGERS

INTEGERS   TUTORIAL 1

PIP: (page 10)

1a. +3   b. –10   c. +70   d. +6%   e. –2

  f. +500   g. +3   h. 0

2a. 7 below par   b. 1 below par   c. 4 over par   d. 9 over par

  e. par   f. 3 below par   g. 8 over par   h. 2 below par

3a. –4   b. +3   c. +18   d. –10

4a. A: –3, B: 0, C: +4;   b. D: +3, E: +1, F: -2;

  c. G: –5, H: –1, J: +2.

5a.

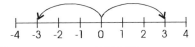

b.

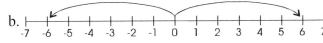

c.

d.

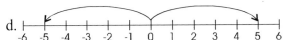

COMPARING INTEGERS   TUTORIAL 2

PIP: (page 11)

1a. +4	b. –3	c. +5	d. +6
2a. +7	b. –5	c. –12	d. –2
3.a. –3	b. +5	c. +2	d. +6
4a. –4	b. –3	c. –7	d. –3

5a. –2, –7;   b. +2, –3   c. +3, –3000

6a. +9, +7, –2, –3;   b. +1, –2, –5, –9;   c. –2, –4, –5, –9.

7a. –5, 0, +2, +6;   b. –6, –4, –3, –2.

8a. <   b. >   c. <   d. >

9a. +6 > +4   b. T   c. +2 > +1   d. –10 < –4   e. –2 < 0

   f. +1 > 0

10a. Neon   b. –249°C, –210°C, –71°C, –39°C, 0°C.

11a. Well   b. Winn   c. Winn, Mont, Calg, Mosc, Van, Lond, Hong K, Well.

12. a, b, e.

COMPARING INTEGERS   TUTORIAL 3

Inv: (page 13)

5 pairs of red and white tiles cancel. There are 2 whites left. +5 and –7 combine to be –2.

PIP: (page 14)

2. It will be less.   3. It will be greater.

4a. 5   b. –8   c. any integer from –8 to 8   d. –13   e. –3

ADDING INTEGERS   TUTORIAL 4

PIP: (page 15)

1a. $(+4) + (–2) = +2$ b. $(+4) + (–6) = (–2)$ c. $(+3) + (–2) = (+1)$

   d. $(+2) + (–5)= (–3)$ e. $(+3) + (–1) = (+2)$ f. $(+3) + (–3) = 0$

2a. $(+2) + (–3) = (–1)$ b. $(–4) + (+3) = (–1)$ c. $(+4) + (–1) = (+3)$

   d. $(+2) + (-2) = 0$

3a. +1   b. +7   c. –2   d. –3

4a. +1   b. –3   c. 0   d. +8   e. –5   f. +2   g. –4   h. –3

5a. $(–6) + (+4) = (–2)$ b. $(+3)+(–2) = (+1)$ c. $(–5) + (–3) = (–8)$

   d. $(+4) + (+1) = (+5)$ e. $(+8) + (–4) = (+4)$ f. $(–4) + (+8) = (+4)$

   g. $(–50) + (–30) = (–80)$ h. $(–20) + (+15) = (–5)$

6a. +3   b. –15   c. +4   d. –12   e. +8   f. –5   g. 0   h. +2

   i. –10   j. 10   k. –110   l. +6

ADDING INTEGERS   TUTORIAL 5

Inv: (page 16)

a. +7   b. –5   c. +2   d. 0

396

PIP: (page 16)
1a. –7   b. +2   c. –1

2a.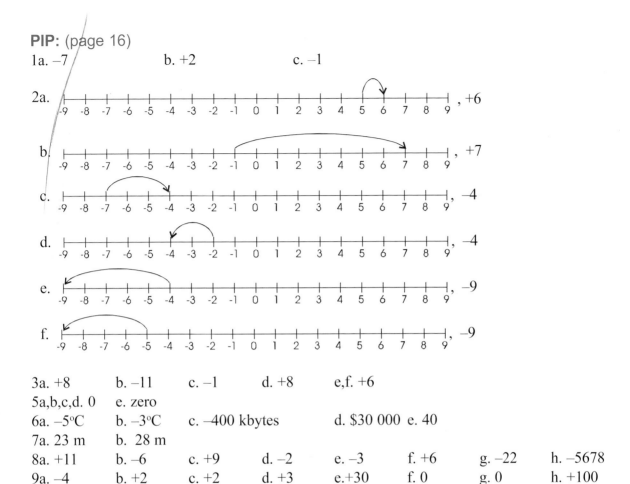

3a. +8   b. –11   c. –1   d. +8   e,f. +6
5a,b,c,d. 0   e. zero
6a. –5°C   b. –3°C   c. –400 kbytes   d. $30 000   e. 40
7a. 23 m   b. 28 m
8a. +11   b. –6   c. +9   d. –2   e. –3   f. +6   g. –22   h. –5678
9a. –4   b. +2   c. +2   d. +3   e.+30   f. 0   g. 0   h. +100
 i. +2   j. –1

SUBTRACTING INTEGERS   TUTORIAL 6

Inv: (page 19)
(–5) – (–3) = –2
PIP: (page 21)
2a. –3   b. +3   c. +11   d. –1   e. –2   f. +13   g. 4   h. –14
3a. (+5) + (–2), +3   b. (–3) + (–6), –9   c. (–6) + (–7), –13   d. (+7) + (+9), +16
 e. (+3) + (–8), –5   f. (–6) + (+1), –5   g. (–6) + (–6), –12   h. (+6) + (+6), +12
 i. (–1.2) + (+1.2), 0   j. 0 + (+2), +2   k. (–4) + (+6), +2   l. (+7) + (+5), +12
 m. (–9) + (–6), –15   n. 0 + (–2), –2   o. 0 + (–2), –2
4a. +13   b. +1   c. +9   d. –11   e. +10   f. –17   g. +1   h. – 1   i. –1
 j. –14   k. +3   l. –4   m. 0   n. 0   o. 0
5a. +4   b. –1   c. –10   d. +2   e. 0   f. –8
6. Subtracting an integer from a smaller integer gives a negative answer.
   Subtracting an integer from a larger integer gives a positive integer.

7a. When a positive integer is subtracted from a smaller positive integer the answer will be negative.　　　b. T　　　c. The answer will always be positive.

d. When a negative integer is subtracted from a smaller negative integer the result will be negative.

9a. +65　　b. +51　　c. +54　　d. –34　　e. +146　　f. –109　　g. 0　　h. –100
i. +100

10a. –4　　b,c. +2　　d. +3　　e. +30　　f,g. 0　　h. 100　　i. +2　　j. –1

MULTIPLYING INTEGERS　　　TUTORIAL 7

Inv: (page 26)

The product of a positive and a negative integer is negative.　The product of two negative integers is positive.

PIP: (page 27)

1.

QUESTION	TILE PICTURE	PRODUCT
$(+5) \times (-1)$	☐ ☐ ☐ ☐ ☐	–5
$(-5) \times (-1)$	☒■ ☒■ ☒■ ☒■☒■	5
$(-3) \times (+1)$	☐☒ ☐☒ ☐☒	–3
$(-3) \times 0$	☒☒ ☒☒ ☒☒	0

2.

I	II
+12	–15
+8	–10
+4	–5
0	0
–4	5
–8	10
–12	15

3. positive, negative, negative, positive, positive, negative.

4a. –12　　b. –12　　c. +2　　d. +16　　e. +10　　f,g. 0　　h. –24　　i. +21

5a. neg　　b,c,d. 0　　e. pos　　f. neg　　g. pos　　h. 0　　i. pos　　j. neg
k. neg　　l. neg　　m,n. 0

6a. The product is always negative.
b,c. T
d. The product is positive.　　e. T.

7. –30, –24, –24, –12, 0.

8.

×	–3	–2	–1	0	1	2	3
2	–6	–4	–2	0	2	4	6
–2	6	+4	2	0	–2	–4	–6
4	–12	–8	–4	0	4	8	12
–4	12	8	4	0	–4	–8	–12
6	–18	–12	–6	0	6	+12	18
–6	18	12	6	0	–6	–12	–18

USING TECHNOLOGY   TUTORIAL 8

2a. –120   b. –190   c. +85   d. –860   e. +1260   f. –990   g. –868   h. –182
  i. –289   j. –336   k. +450
3a. 1   b. –1   c. 1   d. –1   e. 1   f. –1
8ai. neg   ii. pos   iii. 0   bi. pos   ii. neg   iii. 0

DIVISION AND MULTIPLICATION   TUTORIAL 9

PIP: (page 32)

1.

Division Statement	Result
(+6) ÷ (+3)	+2
(+3) ÷ (+3)	+1
(–3) ÷ (+3)	–1
(–6) ÷ (+3)	–2
(–8) ÷ (+2)	–4

2a. pos   b. neg
3a same   bi. neg   ii. pos
4a. 3   b. original number
5a,b. 3   c,d. –3   6a,b. 3   c,d. –3
7a,b. 3   b. c,d. –3
8a. pos   b. neg,   c. neg,   d. pos.

DIVIDING INTEGERS   TUTORIAL 10

PIP: (page 35)

1a. +3   b. +5   c. –4   d. –6   e. +6   f. +9   g. +1   h,i. –1
2a. –4   b. +8   c. +2   d. –8   e. +5   f. –6   g. +1   h,i. –1
3a. +5   b. +5   c. –4   d. –6   e. +6   f. +9
4a. +3   b. –6   c. +8   d. –11   e. –6   f. +3   g. –7   h. +4
  i. +8   j. –13   k. –0.270   l. –64.146   m,n. 0   o,p. –1
5a. If the signs are the same, the answer is positive. If the signs are different, the answer is
  negative.   b. –1 c. 0
6a. –4   b. –24   c. –3   d. +12   e. +7   f. –56   g.–18   h. +2
  i. –3

USING INTEGERS   TUTORIAL 11

PIP: (page 37)

1ai. +$650   ii. –$120   iii. +$300   iv. –$15   v. +$1000
  vi. –$393   b. 58
2. 1140 m   3. –5°C   4. $6000
5a.   b,c. –3

6a.

Day	Opening Price ($)	Closing Price ($)	Daily Change ($)
Mon	23	21	−2
Tues	21	24	3
Wed	24	52	28
Thurs	52	19	−33
Fri	19	21	2

b,c. −2

PATTERNS

RECOGNIZING PATTERNS   TUTORIAL 1

Inv: (page 39)

a. plants + 1 means legs +4   b. 16, 20   d. 288   e. 61

PIP: (page 41)

1a. 19   b. 9 more cubes in all   c. $a = t + 9$
  di. 21   dii. 32   diii. 49   ei. 104   eii. 36   eiii. 163

2a. 18   b. 2 more than twice the number of tables   c. $p = 2t + 2$
  di. 32   dii. 76   diii. 226   ei. 23   eii. 14   eiii. 46

3a. 9, 11, 13 b. 1 more than twice the number of triangles   c. $n = 2t + 1$
  di. 39   dii. 69   diii. 427   ei. 28   eii. 95   eiii. 37

4a. 28   b. number of bricks is previous number of bricks plus the number of steps

  c. 153   d.

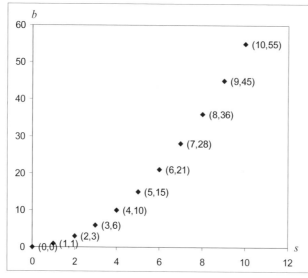

5a. 10   b. 15

VISUALIZING PATTERNS   TUTORIAL 2

PIP: (page 45)

1ai. (1,1)   aii. (10,0) aiii. (3,1) aiv. (8,9) av. (3,6)
  bi. K   bii. B   biii. J   biv. D   bv. F   bvi. O

GRAPHING PATTERNS TUTORIAL 3

Inv: (page 46)

28

PIP: (page 47)

1.a.

Number of Towers	Number of Blocks
4	15
5	19
6	23

b. (1, 3), (2, 7), (3, 11), (4, 15), (5, 19), (6, 23);

c. The number of blocks is 1 less than 4 times the number of towers.　　　　d. $B = 4T - 1$;

e. Yes.

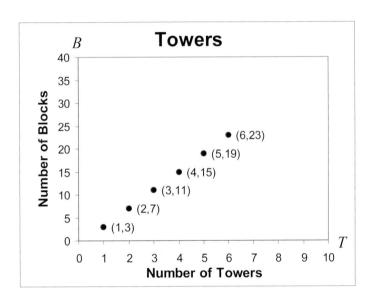

f,g. 39

2. 5

3a.

People	Shakes
5	10
6	15
10	45

b.

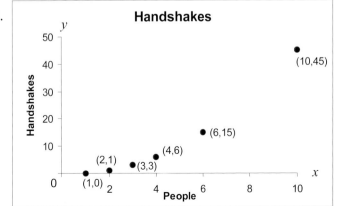

c. No.

POINTS OR LINE   TUTORIAL 4

Inv: (page 49)

a. Earnings are $20 more than $8.50 times the number of customers. $e = 8.5c + 20$

b.
c	4	5	6
e	54	62.5	71

c. No. The number of customers can only be a whole number.

PIP: (page 51)

1a. continuous   b. $70   c. $110   d. 15 min   e. $20 more than $2/min

2a. 3 kg   b. $m = 3n + 5$ e. No

2c.

Number Of Melons	Mass (kg)
0	5
1	8
2	11
10	35

2d.

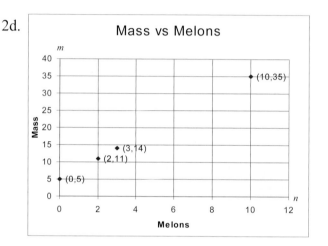

3a. $W = 15 + 3S$ b. $W = 15 + 1.5S$ 4. $F = 32a + 40K$

PUZZLES

MAGIC SQUARES TUTORIAL 1

Inv: (page 53)

1a,b,c. 15   d. same   e. 3   2a. Yes.   b. 5

PIP: (page 54)

1a. 2, 5, 8, 11, 14, 17, 20, 23, 26;

b.
23	2	17
8	14	20
11	26	5

c. Yes   d. $42 = 3 \times 14$ 3b. $3n + 12$

4. Magic sum is 51.   5. Magic sum is 72.   7. No.   8a,b. 4096 c. same   d. Yes.

9a. 2, 6, 18, 54, 162, 486, 1458, 4374, 13 122;
2: b,c. 4 251 528   11. Magic product is 531 441.

NUMBER TRICKS TUTORIAL 2
Inv: (page 59)
1
PIP: (page 61)
1. 2   2. 0   3. 81

CALENDAR MATH TUTORIAL 3
PIP: (page 62)
1a. add 7   b. 24   4. 48

REVIEW
(page 64)
1a. 12   b. 7   c. 11   d. 24
2a. 43   b. 22   c. 69   d. 207   3a. 6   b. 153
4. 4 J, 3 T, 5S; …

5a.

Circles	Triangles
7	3
9	4

b. $c = 2t + 1$ d. 25

6a.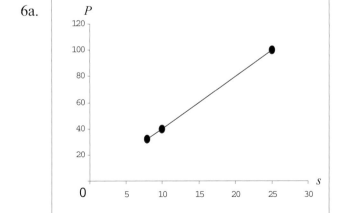

b. Perimeter is 4 times the length.
c. $P = 4s$.

7a. $\dfrac{n}{9} = 10$ b. $7 + 4n = 51$
    c. $6n - 4 = 20$
8a. C   b. D   c. B   d. A
9a. $1445
10. 775   11. 28
12a. G: 9, L: –10   b. G: 1, L: –100
    c. G: –1, L: –1000.
13a. +3   b. +9   c. –18   d. –2
    e. –10   f. –6   g. +16   h. +4
    i. –8   j. –16   k. –48   l. –3

14. A: +$667, B: –$667, C: $0   15. +$61   16. –$184.50

ENTERTAINMENT

DECIMALS

ROUNDING   TUTORIAL 1

Inv: (page 72)

4	4	3.5	3	4	4

PIP: (page 72)

1a. 3   b. 4   c,d. 3   e,f. 4   g. 3   h. 4

2a. 12   b,c. 13   d. 103   e,f. 104   g,h. 1003

3a. 30   b. 40   c,d. 30   e,f. 40   g. 30   h,i. 40

j,k,l. 30   m. 40   n. 30   o. 40   p. 90   q,r. 100

4a. 12   b,c. 13   d. 103   e,f. 104   g. 1003   h,i,j,k,l. 15

5a,b,c. 10   d,e,f. 100   g. 1000   h. 10   i,j. 20   k,l. 10

6a. 300   b,c. 400   d. 100   e. 900   f,g. 1000   h. 300

7a,b,c,d. 650

MONEY ADDS UP   TUTORIAL 2

PIP: (page 74)

1a. $10.95   b. $25.39   c. $11   d. $23.56

2a. $5.45   b. $2.16   c. $4.58   d. 83¢

3a. $3   b. $10   c. $14   d. $3   e. $4   f. $2

4a. $2,13   b. $10.26   c. $14.66   d. $2.54   e. $3.62   f. $2.55

5a. $7   b. $20   c. $17   d. $13

6a. $6.69   b. $16.84

ADDING & SUBTRACTING DECIMALS   TUTORIAL 3

Inv: (page 77)

8	2	6	6.06	6.06	6	Yes

PIP: (page 77)

1a,g. 0.9   b,h. 0.6   c,i. 3.7   d,j. 4.25   e,k. 12.11   f,l. 4.7

2a. 49.89   b. 21.3   c. 23.98   d. 215.55   e. 118.12   f. 509.15

 g. 0.64   h. 1215.1

3a. 14.63   b. 10.9   c. 194.53   d. 41.89   e. 16.85   f. 8.974

 g. 13.85   h. 1.367   i. 30.211   j. 1.565   k. 1.111   l. 33.535

4a. 2.7 m   b. $1.22   c. $62.44   d. 21.975 cm, 21.475 cm   e. $19.

SPENDING MONEY   TUTORIAL 4

PIP: (page 81)

1a. T-shirt   b. hats   2. $20   3. $39.96

MULTIPLYING A DECIMAL   TUTORIAL 5

Inv: (page 82)
1a,b. 2   c. same   2a,b. 1   c. same
3. same number of decimal places in the answer as in the question

PIP: (page 84)
2a. 18.9   b. 56.8   c. 92.8   d. 63.5   e. 5.04   f. 24.56
  g. 13.44   h. 7.209   i. 4.01   j. 0.927   k. 13.02   l. 7.281
3. $70.80
4a. $62.28, $6   b. $20.76   c. $83.04, $8   d. 1
5a. $990   b. $143.75   c. $2727.50

MULTIPLYING BY TENS   TUTORIAL 6

Inv: (page 85)

1.	A	B	C
	5000	300	240
	500	30	24
	50	3	2.4
	5	0.3	0.24
	0.5	0.03	0.024
	0.05	0.003	0.0024
	0.005	0.0003	0.000 24

2a. larger   b. right   c. same   3a. smaller   b. left   c. same

PIP: (page 86)
1a. 500   b. 64.8   c. 41.6   d. 730   e. 3040   f. 1004
2a. 0.04   b. 0.034   c. 0.62   d. 1.28   e. 0.74   f. 0.0018
  g. 0.088   h. 0.004   i. 0.003   j. 0.000 96   k. 0.007   l. 0.000 36
3a. $9   b. $90   c. $900   4. 2.3 L

MULTIPLYING DECIMALS   TUTORIAL 7

Inv: (page 87)
12   1   1   2   Yes   11.18
PIP: (page 88)
1a. 10.498 765 4312   b. 3.060 802 469 083   c. 2.521 309 876 39
  d. 851.0261234202
2. a,d,f.   5a. 4.37   b. 10.24   c. 4.048   d. 1.462   e. 0.332   f. 2.001
6. H: 68.4 cm, D: 90.3 cm   7a. $7.82   b. $7.04   c. $6.26

DIVIDING BY TENS   TUTORIAL 8

Inv: (page 90)

1.

A	B
0.003	0.0012
0.03	0.012
0.3	0.12
3	1.2
30	12
300	120
3000	1200

2a. smaller   b. left   c. same
3a. larger   b. right   c. same

PIP: (page 91)

1ai,ii. 0.5   bi,ii. 0.05   ci,ii. 0.005   2. same
3ai,ii. 50   bi,ii. 500   ci,ii. 5000   4. same
5a. 0.27   b. 0.035   c. 0.004   d. 58.7   e. 6.97   f. 30.4
6a. 640   b. 7000   c. 68 300   d. 4000   e. 67 000   f. 370
7a. 0.4132   b. 0.2195   c. 19.2   d. 49.5   e. 82 000   f. 80
8. d, f

DIVIDING DECIMALS   TUTORIAL 9

Inv: (page 93)

$6 or $7 $6.50 $6.50

PIP: (page 94)

1a. 3.3   b. 12.5   c. 0.8   d. 17.53   e. 8.4   f. 7.75
4. $5.75   5. $6.15   6. $11.25   7. $7.84   8. $12.93 or $12.94
9. $1 254 328   10. 12

GRAPHS

READING AND INTERPRETING GRAPHS

Inv: (page 96)

2a. half   b. $25   c. Clothes, Food and Snacks   d. about $6

  e. about $19

3a.

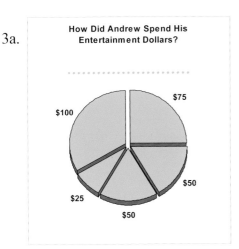

b. $300

4a. 60   b. 54-40

  c. The Wilkinsons   d. 30

5.

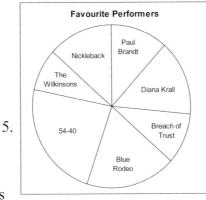

Bands	Frequency
Paul Brandt	7
Diana Krall	9
Breach of Trust	6
Blue Rodeo	11
54-40	14
The Wilkinsons	5
Nickleback	8
Total	**60**

PIP: (page 99)

3a. A histogram has the vertical columns
  joined. The information on the horizontal axis is continuous.
  b. horizontal groups of 500 km, vertical groups of 20 people   c. 0-500 km

4a. Arts   b. Science or Sports

5a. 36   b. Arts   c. Health   d. Education   e. 6

8a. 2 plays   10b. 66

12a. sets and studios; director, story and rentals   c. about $2.5 million

14a. The average number of movies attended each year.   b. 12-17's   c. over 65's

15a. Japan and Switzerland   b. South Africa and Singapore

REVIEW

(page 113)

2a. 10.1   b. 25.39   c. 6.619   d. 44.05   e. 198.385   f. 7.4254

  g. 7844.6240   h. 7844.6253   i. 7844.694 3

3a. 2.5   b. 1.5   c. 11.4   d. 6.9   e. 11.4   f. 10.9   g. 9.8

4a. 66.8   b. 163.835   c. 2116.50   d. 0.0537 6

7a. $8.03   b. $6.73   8. $30.75   9. 6.174

10a. Sit Coms   b. Game Show or Survival

11a. 9 pm, midnight, 1 am   b. 18

HOME

FRACTIONS
FRACTION CONCEPTS TUTORIAL 1
Inv: (page 122)

1.

Poster	Which Envelope?	Sketch of Poster Showing Fold Lines	Folded Poster is What Fraction Of Original Size?
A	38 cm × 23 cm		$\frac{1}{2}$
B	38 cm × 23 cm		$\frac{1}{3}$
C	24 cm × 12 cm		$\frac{1}{4}$

3a,b.   3c. 8

PIP: (page 124)

1a. 2 b. 3 c. 4 d. 6 e. 10 f. 5

2a. 6 b. 10 c. 5

3a. $\frac{1}{4}$ b. $\frac{1}{7}$ c. usually $\frac{1}{3}$ d. $\frac{1}{6}$ e. $\frac{1}{20}$

408

Inv: (page 125)

Shape Used To Cover Double Hexagon	Diagram	No. of Shapes Needed To Cover It	Fraction Represented By:	
Hexagon		2	One hexagon $\frac{1}{2}$	2 hexagons 1
Trapezoid		4	One trapezoid $\frac{1}{4}$	3 trapezoids $\frac{3}{4}$
Rhombus		6	One rhombus $\frac{1}{6}$	5 rhombi $\frac{5}{6}$
Triangle		12	One triangle $\frac{1}{12}$	7 triangles $\frac{7}{12}$

PIP: (page 126)

4a. $\frac{5}{12}$ b. $\frac{3}{4}$ c. $\frac{5}{6}$ d. $\frac{9}{12}$ or $\frac{3}{4}$

6a. $\frac{3}{4}$ b. $\frac{5}{6}$ c. $\frac{1}{2}$

7.

Proper	Improper
a, c, d	b, e, f, g

MIXED NUMBERS & IMPROPER FRACTIONS TUTORIAL 2

Inv: (page 127)

1a. 6   c. 6, 6   2a. 12   c. 12, 12   3. 36, 36, 36

PIP: (page 128)

1a,c. 10   2a,c. 15   3a. quarter, quarters, $1\frac{3}{4}$ b. sixth, sixths, $1\frac{2}{6}$ or $1\frac{1}{3}$

4a. $2\frac{1}{4}$ b. $2\frac{5}{12}$ 6a. $\frac{9}{4}$ b. $\frac{3}{2}$ c. $\frac{16}{5}$ d. $\frac{7}{3}$ e. $\frac{19}{8}$

7a. 10   b. 12   c. 5   8b. 2 wholes, 1 quarter   c. $2\frac{1}{4}$

9b. 1   c. 5   d. $1\frac{5}{8}$ 10. $2\frac{1}{2}$

11a. $3\frac{1}{2}$ b. $1\frac{1}{3}$ c. $2\frac{2}{3}$ d. $2\frac{3}{4}$ e. $2\frac{3}{10}$

12a. $\frac{3}{2}$ b. $\frac{14}{3}$ c. $\frac{9}{4}$ d. $1\frac{1}{3}$ e. $4\frac{1}{2}$ f. $2\frac{3}{4}$ g. $\frac{17}{8}$ h. $\frac{31}{8}$

EQUIVALENT FRACTIONS   TUTORIAL 3

Inv: (page 133)

1b. two regions for each, equal   c. four for each, equal   d. equal

2c. four   e. eight   f. equal

PIP: (page 135)

2a. 80   b. 125   c. 10   d. 6   e. 12   f. 18

3ai,ii. $\frac{1}{8}$ iii. $\frac{7}{10}$ iv. $\frac{7}{8}$ v,vi. $\frac{3}{4}$ b. i and ii, v and vi

ADDING & SUBTRACTING FRACTIONS TUTORIAL 4

Inv: (page 138)

1b,c. $\frac{3}{4}$ 2b. $\frac{5}{6}, \frac{5}{6}$ 3b. 1   ci. 1   c.ii. $\frac{1}{6}$

PIP: (page 139)

1a,b. $\frac{1}{4}$

2a. $\frac{2}{3}$ b. $\frac{3}{5}$ c. $\frac{7}{10}$ d. $\frac{11}{100}$ e. $\frac{3}{5}$ f. $\frac{4}{5}$ g. 1   h. $\frac{3}{10}$

3a. $\frac{5}{6}$ b. $\frac{1}{10}$ c. $\frac{1}{4}$ d. $1\frac{1}{3}$

4ai. You add them.   ii. unchanged   bi. You subtract them.   ii. unchanged

Inv: (page 140)

3 triangles   3   4 triangles   12   7

5a. $\dfrac{1}{2}$ b. $\dfrac{7}{8}$ c. $3\dfrac{7}{8}$ d. $\dfrac{37}{100}$ e. $\dfrac{23}{100}$ f. $\dfrac{1}{6}$ g. $1\dfrac{1}{8}$ h. $1\dfrac{5}{8}$

i. $1\dfrac{1}{4}$ j. $\dfrac{5}{12}$ k. $\dfrac{1}{2}$ l. $4\dfrac{1}{6}$

6a. $1\dfrac{1}{6}$ b. $1\dfrac{9}{10}$ c. $3\dfrac{11}{12}$ d. $\dfrac{1}{6}$ e. $\dfrac{9}{10}$ f. $1\dfrac{5}{12}$

$\dfrac{1}{2}$ h   8. $3\dfrac{1}{3}$ h   9. $1\dfrac{1}{3}$ pizza   10. $1\dfrac{5}{12}$ h   11. 23 h

MULTIPLYING FRACTIONS   TUTORIAL 5

Inv: (page 145)

1. $\dfrac{12}{32}$ or $\dfrac{3}{8}$ $\dfrac{3}{8}$ 2a. $\dfrac{1}{6}$ bi. It is 1×1.   ii. It is 2×3.   c,d. $\dfrac{1}{6}$

3a. $\dfrac{3}{10}$ bi. It is 1×3.   ii. It is 2×5.   c. $\dfrac{1}{2}\times\dfrac{3}{5}, \dfrac{1\times3}{2\times5}$ d. $\dfrac{1\times3}{2\times5}=\dfrac{3}{10}$

4a. $\dfrac{1}{4}$ b. $\dfrac{1}{3}\times\dfrac{3}{4}, \dfrac{1\times3}{3\times4}$ c. $\dfrac{1\times3}{3\times4}=\dfrac{3}{12}$ d. equal

5. Multiply the numerators and multiply the denominators. Write the answer in simplest form.

PIP: (page 148)

1. $\dfrac{4\div2}{10\div2}$ $\dfrac{2}{5}$ 2. 16   8,8 $\dfrac{2}{5}$

3a. $\dfrac{1}{16}$ b,c. $\dfrac{1}{12}$ d. $\dfrac{1}{6}$ e. $\dfrac{1}{2}$ 4a. $\dfrac{1}{7}$

5a. $3\dfrac{1}{2}$ b. 3   c. $3\dfrac{1}{2}$ d. 3.5   e. $2\dfrac{11}{12}$ f. $2\dfrac{17}{30}$

6. 6   7. $\dfrac{1}{3}$ 8. 14

DIVIDING FRACTIONS   TUTORIAL 6

PIP: (page 151)

1ai,ii. 2   bi,ii. 6   ci,ii. 8   2. 5   3. 6   4. 9

1a. 2   b. 6   c. 12   2. 15

PIP: (page 154)
5. 10   6. 5   7. 30

Inv: (page 155)
4 3 trapezoids   4   4   4

PIP: (page 155)
8. 6   9. 2   10. 3

Inv: (page 156)
To divide by a fraction multiply by the fraction obtained by interchanging the numerator and denominator.

PIP: (page 157)
12a. $\frac{2}{3}$ b. $1\frac{1}{2}$ c. $1\frac{1}{3}$ d. $\frac{4}{5}$ e. $2\frac{2}{3}$ f. 4   g. $1\frac{1}{2}$ h. $3\frac{1}{3}$

i. $2\frac{1}{10}$ j,k. 10   l,m. 60   n. 1.5

13. g and n, j and k, l and m

MEASUREMENT

USING AN IMPERIAL RULER TUTORIAL 1

PIP: (page 160)

4a. $1\frac{3}{8}$"   b. $2\frac{15}{16}$"   c. $1\frac{1}{4}$"   d. $3\frac{1}{16}$"   e. $\frac{1}{2}$"

5a. 36"   b. 20"   c. 27"   6a. 5'   b. 6' 8"   c. $4\frac{1}{3}$'

ADDING & SUBTRACTING IMPERIAL MEASURES TUTORIAL 2

PIP: (page 165)

1a. $\frac{7}{8}$ b. $\frac{7}{8}$ c. $\frac{1}{8}$ d. $\frac{5}{8}$

2a. $3\frac{7}{8}$"   b. $\frac{15}{16}$"   c. $4\frac{7}{12}$'   d. $1\frac{1}{12}$'

3. Yes   4. 4' 6"   5. Jen, $\frac{2}{3}$ mi

412

LINEAR MEASUREMENT   TUTORIAL 3

PIP: (page 168)

1.

Item	Measurement Tool Used
a. Width of your small finger	Tape or ruler
b. Width of two fingers	Tape or ruler
c. Length of your foot	Tape or ruler
d. Length of your large stride	Tape or ruler
e. Length of your regular stride	Tape or ruler
f. Length of a standard paper clip	Ruler or tape
g. Thickness of a dime	Ruler or micrometer

5a. 8   b. 3

6a. 3", 7. 6 cm

 b.13:, 22.9 cm   c. 4' 2", 126.9 cm

CONVERSIONS BETWEEN SI AND IMPERIAL UNITS   TUTORIAL 4

PIP: (page 171)

1a. 0.621   b. 3.281   c. 0.914
 d. 0.305   e. 1.094   f. 0.621
2a. about   3. 3109 km   4. 20 m × 46 m

5. CFL, 0.5 m, 0.6 yd

6a. 209 yd   b. 626 ft, 7512"   c. 9"

PERIMETER TUTORIAL 5

PIP: (page 174)

1a. 24 cm   b. 48 cm   c. 32 cm   d. 46.5 cm   e. $40\frac{1}{2}$ "

3. 16
4a. 20.7   b. 3   c. 2   5. 145 ft

AREA   TUTORIAL 6

Inv: (page 176)
2a. 42 cm^2 b. 24 cm^2 c. 16 cm^2 d. 15 cm^2
3. 6   7   6×7=42   base   height bh
PIP: (page 177)
1. 12   2a. about 1100 cm^2 6. 115.5 ft^2
4a. 31.5 × 20.0   b. 630.4 pi^2 c. 631 or 32 × 20 = 640

5.

P	A	B	N
b, d, g	a, e, f	h	c

WORKING WITH AREA TUTORIAL 7

PIP: (page 180)
1a. 30 squares   b. 40 squares   c. 36 squares   d. 30 squares
 Multiply the length of the base by the height.

2.

Rectangle			Parallelogram		
Base	Height	Area	Area	Base	Height
5	2	10	10	5	2
$2\frac{1}{2}$	6	15	15	$2\frac{1}{2}$	6
10	5	50	50	10	5
3	$6\frac{1}{2}$	$19\frac{1}{2}$	$19\frac{1}{2}$	3	$6\frac{1}{2}$

3a,b,c,d. 40   e. 20   f. 21
Inv: (page 182)

Area of the triangle is half the area of the parallelogram $A_t = \frac{1}{2}A_p$ 18 squares

PIP: (page 183)
4a. 12 squares   b. 25 squares   c. 12 squares   e. 12 squares
5a,b,c. 20   6. equal
7. rectangular garden
8a. 250 ft²   b. 275 ft²   c. 19   d. $855   e. 25 ft²   f. 1   g.i. $300   ii. $325
6a. 9.354 ft² b. 6 L   c. $67.85   d. Yes   e. $20   f. $187.85
11a. 9 m   b. 50 m   c. $263.33 or $278.82 12a. 2.4 m b. 4346 cm²
13a. 2700 cm²   b. 4636 cm²   c. 1936 cm²   d. 274 cm
14a. 21 ft²   b. $183.75 c. $105   d. $288.75   15a. 27   b. $5008.50   c. $965
16a. 50.84 m²   b. 57.6 m² c. 6.76 m²   17a. 3   b. 6¢.

18. 6.384 m² 19. $12\frac{1}{2}$"   20a. square b. 400 m²

VOLUME   TUTORIAL 8
Inv: (page 194)
1a. 6   b. 12   c. 18   d. 36
 e. 48, number of cubes in one layer times the number of layers   f. 48 cm³
3a. 18   b. 5   c. 90   d. 90 in³
Examp: No, because of Order of Operations.
PIP: (page 195)
3c. same number

4a. 7"   b. 1666 in^3 c. 4998 in^3 d. 82 L   e. 4   f. $7.92
5a. 216 000 cm^3 b. 12 min   6a. 0.75 m^3 b. 1 yd^3

7.

A	VC	B	N
e,	a, d	b	c

MASS   TUTORIAL 9

PIP: (page 198)
4a. 30.87 lb b. 10.5 h   5a. 25 kg   b. 4.54 kg c. 6
6a. Kyle, 25 lb or 11.4 kg   7a. 228 ft^2 b. 3   c. 861 ft^2 d. 10
8. 1.362 kg   9a. 181.6 kg   b. 10   10. $2.69/kg
11a. $6.90/kg   b. $7.54/kg   c. $10.05/kg   d. $8.50/kg

REVIEW

(page 201)

1a. $\dfrac{1}{2}$ b. $\dfrac{3}{4}$ c. $\dfrac{3}{5}$ d. $\dfrac{6}{10}$ e. $\dfrac{3}{4}$ f. $\dfrac{3}{8}$ g. $\dfrac{1}{4}$ h. $\dfrac{3}{16}$

2a. $\dfrac{2}{5}$ b. $\dfrac{3}{5}$ c. 1   d. $1\dfrac{2}{5}$

4a,b. $1\dfrac{1}{4}$ c. $1\dfrac{2}{3}$ d. $25\dfrac{1}{2}$ e. $5\dfrac{1}{10}$ f. $5\dfrac{1}{100}$ g. $2\dfrac{1}{4}$ h. $2\dfrac{2}{3}$ i. $26\dfrac{1}{2}$ j. $6\dfrac{1}{10}$

5a. $\dfrac{7}{4}$ b,c. $\dfrac{5}{2}$ d. $\dfrac{27}{8}$ e. $\dfrac{43}{10}$ f. $\dfrac{591}{100}$ g. $\dfrac{17}{6}$ h. $\dfrac{23}{6}$

6a,b. $\dfrac{3}{4}$ c. $\dfrac{3}{8}$ d. $\dfrac{5}{8}$ e. $1\dfrac{1}{8}$ f. $1\dfrac{5}{8}$ g. $\dfrac{37}{100}$ h. $\dfrac{1}{12}$ i. $\dfrac{13}{30}$

   j. $\dfrac{7}{16}$ k. $\dfrac{1}{100}$ l. $13\dfrac{15}{16}$

7a. $\dfrac{1}{9}$ b. $\dfrac{1}{8}$ c. $\dfrac{8}{15}$ d. $\dfrac{9}{20}$ e. $\dfrac{3}{4}$ f. 4

8a. 1   b. 2   c. $\dfrac{5}{6}$ d,e. $\dfrac{5}{16}$ f. $\dfrac{5}{8}$

9a. $1\dfrac{3}{16}$"   b. 6"   c,d. $5\dfrac{3}{8}$"   e. 5   f. 14   g. 3

10a. 0.394   b. 1.094   c. 3.281   d. 1.308   e. 0.002   f. 2.205   g. 0.305   h. 0.914
   i. 2.54   j. 0.454   k. 454   l. 12

11. 12 yd or 36 ft   13. 2625 ft or 875 yd; 4922 ft or 1641yd; 9.3 mi; 12.4 mi; 186 mi/h

14a. 28 cm   b. 15.2 cm c. $19\frac{1}{2}$ ft   d. $49\frac{1}{8}$"   e. 199.2 yd h. 79.8 mi

15a. 25.6 m b. 84 ft   c. 14

16a. 150 cm²   b. $2\frac{1}{4}$ ft²   c. 138.32 m²   d. 19.22 ft   17a. 0.346 m²   b. 60 in²

18a. 115 ft² b. $394.80 19a. 36.15 m²   b. $91\frac{1}{4}$ ft²

20a. 18 m² b. 5   21. 0.675 m³

FOOD FARE

EQUATIONS

SOLVING 1-STEP EQUATIONS   TUTORIAL 1

PIP: (page 217)

3a. 7	b. 4	c. −1	d. −3	e. 2	f. −1	g. 8	h. −6
4a. 8	b. 10	c. 7	d. −12	e. −3	f. −6	g. −10	h. −8
5a. 12	b. −58	c. 80	d. 23	e. −3	f. −90	g. 52	h. −42
6. 75							

1-STEP EQUATIONS- PROBLEM SOLVING   TUTORIAL 2

Inv: (page 220)

How much money she needs and how many hours of work are required.
St 1: Let the number of hours be h.
St 2: $6.5h = 304.95 - 155$
St 3: $6.5h = 149.95$, $6.5h \div 6.5 = 149.95 \div 6.5$, $h = 23.07$
St 4: She will have to work another 23 h.

PIP: (page 221)

1. 12   36   9   9 $9 \times \$2.75 = \$24.75$
2. $1.35   3. $35.20   4. 7 cans   5. $7.05/h   6. 20 h   7. 2cups
8. 93¢   9. $17.15

VERIFYING ANSWERS TO 1-STEP EQUATIONS   TUTORIAL 3

Inv: (page 224)

$$4 \times \frac{x}{4} = 4 \times 5, x = 20 \qquad LS = \frac{(20)}{4} = 5 = RS \qquad x = 20$$

1a. T   b. 1   c. 8   d. T   e. 1   f. T
2a. 9   b. 20   c. 2   d. 3   e. – 40   f. –15   g. –2   h. 27

SOLVING 2-STEP EQUATIONS   TUTORIAL 4

Inv: (page 227)
Insp: 10, 5, 5   AlgTile: 2, 10/2, 5   Rep: 3, 10, 5, 5
RevOper: 3, 3, 3, 10, 2x, 10, 2, 5
PIP: (page 229)
1a. 6   b. 1   c. 6   d. 18   e. 5   f. 3   g. 5   h. –4   i. 4

2.

–9	–8	–7	–6	–5	–4	–3	–2	–1	0	1	2	3	4	5	6	7	8	9
R	O	A	S	T	T	U	R	K	E	Y	W	I	T	H	S	A	G	E

3.

15	2	18	23	10	3	12		25	14	16	24			
B	A	N	N	O	C	K		W	I	T	H			
17	20	9	6	11	8	21	13	4		5	19	1	22	7
S	A	S	K	A	T	O	O	N		J	E	L	L	Y

VERIFYING ANSWERS TO 2-STEP EQUATIONS   TUTORIAL 5

PIP: (page 233)
1a. T   b. –7   c. T   d. T   e. –54   f. T

PROBLEM SOLVING WITH 2-STEP EQUATIONS   TUTORIAL 6

Inv: (page 235)

St 1: Let the number of doughnuts be d.   St 2: $\dfrac{d}{5}+1 = 14$

St 3: $\dfrac{d}{5}+1-1=14-1$, $\dfrac{d}{5}=13$, $5\times\dfrac{d}{5}=5\times13$, $d=65$

St 4: There were 65 doughnuts left over.
PIP: (page 235)
1. $1.89   2. $13   3. $7.50   4. $1.19   5. 6 h   6. $57   7. 40
8. 20   9. 4   10. 450 cans

RATIO, RATES, PERCENT
RATIO TUTORIAL 1

Inv: (page 240)

$$\frac{2}{3} = \frac{4}{6} = \frac{6}{9} = \frac{8}{12}$$

PIP: (page 241)

1.a.  3:5

b.  5:3

c.  4:7

d.  4:8 or 1:2

2a. 8:6 or 4:3   b. 7:3   c. 2:6 or 1:3   d. 6:2 or 3:1
   e. 8:26 or 4:13   f. 8:18 or 4:9

4a.  3:1:2

b. 2:3:1

c. 4:2:2 or 2:1:1

d. 1:2:3:1

5. W: 25 kg, O: 15 kg, C: 20 kg

Inv: (page 244)

a. 8

b. 80 + 8 + 37 = 125   16, 5   480   8   750   48   (480+48)
   (750–528) 222

Inv: (page 246)

a. 5:6   5   42, 42   5   35   35

b. 200, 200   40   240
PIP: (page 247)
6. 833 mL   7a. 1:3   b. 1:4   c. 76 mL

RATIO TUTORIAL 2

Inv: (page 249)
s, 23   39, 39   299   299
PIP: (page 250)
1a. A:B:F: = 6:2:1   b. A: 540 mg, B: 180 mg, F: 90 mg
2a. 3:2   b. 2:3:4   c. 2:3:1:4   d. 2:1:4:3   e. 4:1   f. 5:12:8   g. 9:10:20   h. 8:6:3:2:1

4. 7   18   3, 2, 18 $\dfrac{5\times3}{6\times3}$, $\dfrac{7\times2}{9\times2}$ 15, $\dfrac{14}{18}$

5. 0.75, 0.875

6a. 3:5   b. $\dfrac{10}{23}$ c. 8:11   d. $\dfrac{4}{5}$ e. $\dfrac{11}{32}$ f. 3:8   g. $\dfrac{6}{10}$ h. $\dfrac{7}{8}$
7a. C:S:N:G:T = 3:8:4:9:24   b. 225 g
   c. C: 75 g, N: 200 g, S: 100 g, G: 225 g   d. 750 g
8a. C:N:T = 3:1:4   b. 285 g   c. 95 g
9a. R:C:W:T = 2:4:6:12   bi. 32   bii. 48
10a. C:R:N:15 = 9:4:2:15   b. 20 000 kg or 20 t   11a. F:B = 72:1   b. 360

RATE   TUTORIAL 3

Inv: (page 255)
   a. an average of 80 words each minute   b. 50 L flow each minute
   c. an average of 80 km each hour   d. beats 78 times each minute
   e. A cubic centimetre has a mass of 19.3 g.
PIP: (page 258)
1a. 60 km/h   b. 4 recipes per person   c. 8 people per table
   d. 140 pages per book   e. 12 bags per box   f. 8 eggs per carton
   g. 37 students per class   h. 13 L per container

2a.
Words typed	125	250	375	1000
Minutes	1	2	3	8

b.
Fuel used (L)	12.2	36.6	244	61
Time (h)	1	3	20	5

c.
Tables	1	2	5	33
Chairs	8	16	40	264

d.
Glasses	1	2	5	15
Volume (mL)	180	360	900	2700

3. 5 min/pizza, 48 pizzas   4a. $1462.50   b. $53.25/h
5a. 2.5 blocks/min   b. 375

6a. $3.74/meal   b. 49¢/drink   c. $10.65/h
d. 12¢/cookie or $1.44/dozen   e. 5 words/cake   f. 3 burgers/player
g. 16 cookies/tray
7. 2 pies/h   b. 148   8. rabbit, 2.77¢/g

PERCENT   TUTORIAL 4

PIP: (page 262)

1a. $\dfrac{57}{100}$ b. $\dfrac{4}{5}$ c. $\dfrac{1}{4}$ d. $\dfrac{39}{100}$

2a. 47%   b. 23%   c. 225%   d. 86%   e. 70%   f. 120%

3a. 3:25, $\dfrac{3}{25}$ b. 4:125, $\dfrac{4}{125}$ c. 1:10, $\dfrac{1}{10}$ d. 147:100, $\dfrac{147}{100}$ e. 1:200, $\dfrac{1}{200}$

f. 3:400, $\dfrac{3}{400}$ g. 3:500, $\dfrac{3}{500}$ h. 21:25, $\dfrac{21}{25}$ i. 127:200, $\dfrac{127}{200}$

j,k. 37:40, $\dfrac{37}{40}$ l. 1:100, $\dfrac{1}{100}$

4a. 57%   b. 50%   c. 37.5%   d. 80%   e. 75%   f. 80%   g. 52%   h. 100%
i. 2430%   j. 65%   k,l. 100%

5.

		Fraction	Decimal	Per cent
	a.	$\dfrac{3}{5}$	0.6	60%
	b.	$\dfrac{1}{8}$	0.125	12.5%
	c.	$3\dfrac{9}{20}$	3.45	345%
	d.	$6\dfrac{1}{4}$	6.25	625%

6a. 0.63   b. 0.6   c. 4.5   d. 0.932   e. 1.45   f. 0.875   g. 0.75   h. 0.1875
i. 0.45   j. 0.123
7a. 35   b. 3.8   c. 162   d. 1.08
8a. 50%   b. 60%   c. 72%   d. 200%   9a. 50   b. 3   c. 12

420

PERCENT PROBLEMS TUTORIAL 5

PIP: (page 273)

1a. $6   b. 62.5 L   c. 10.8 g   d. 7 dinners
2a. 15%   b. 12.5%   c. 25%   d. 20%
3ai. 38.4 m³ aii. 259.2 m³   b. 10.6%
4a. $157.50 b. $47.25   c. $110.25   5. $6.75

6a. $\dfrac{1}{10}$ b. 25%   c. 31.25%   d. 53:27   e. $100   7. $4590   b. $2754

8a. $\dfrac{1}{50}$ b. 58 800 bushels   c. 147 acres   d. $153 615

9a. $4800   b. $2880   c. $3125   d. $405
10a. 50 ft   b. 2700 ft² c. 1600 ft² d. 125 ft² ei. 9%   ii. 450 ft²
11. $1.34, 2680%

PROPORTIONS   TUTORIAL 6

Rachel   Add 3 cups of water.

Inv: (page 280)

$\dfrac{w}{17.5}=\dfrac{2.5}{3.5}$, $17.5\times\dfrac{w}{17.5}=17.5\times\dfrac{2.5}{3.5}$, w=17.5×2.5÷3.5, w=12.5, The width will be 12.5 cm

PIP: (page 281)

1a. 4, 4   3, 3   3 × 4 ÷ 12   1
b. 30, 30   5, 5, 1   5 × 30 ÷ 25

2a. 8   b. 33   c. 0.9375 or $\dfrac{15}{16}$ d. 2   e. 14   f. 2

3. 6 mL   4. 3.75 cm   5a. 3.48 m b. 150 m   6a. 10.5 cmb. 1.4 cm
7a. 25   b. 240   8. 4 mL   9. 96

REVIEW

(page 284)

1. 5 cups   2a. 4   b. 8 cups   3. 0.5 tbsp or 1.5 tsp

4a. 375°F   b. $1\dfrac{1}{2}$ tbsp   5. 8 min   6. 75 tbsp, $3\dfrac{3}{4}$ cups   7. 95¢

8a. $28.80   b. $960   9. 85¢   10a. $32.90   b. $7

11a. $14   b. $13.99
12a. $1.85   b. $28.33   c. no   d. $4   e. $2.67
13. 25 ft   14. 8%   15. 39 600 kg   16. 21 120 bushels

PERSPECTIVES

ANGLES
CONSTRUCTING AND MEASURING ANGLES TUTORIAL 1
Inv: (page 296)
1a. 180^0 b. 90^0 2a. 45^0 c. 135^0 e. 315^0
Inv: (page 299)
1a,b. 80^0 c. 180^0 2a,b. 40^0 c. 180^0
3e. sum of angles of a triangle is 180^0
PIP: (page 301)
1a. acute   b. obtuse   c. acute   d. acute   e. reflex   f. right   g. obtuse

ANGLE RELATIONSHIPS   TUTORIAL 2
Inv: (page 302)
1a. 90^0 b. 180^0 c. 45^0 d. 45^0 d. 135^0 2. 45^0
Inv: (page 304)
1. They are equal   2c. $\angle$ PEC $=\angle$ LEN, $\angle$ PEL $= \angle$ CEN   e. equal
3ai,ii,iii,iv. 180^0 b. always 180^0 cii. $\angle$ CEL iii.   PEN
iv. $\angle$ CEL
PIP: (page 306)
1a. $\angle^s$ AMD, BMC or $\angle^s$ AMB, DMC   b. $\angle$ DMC = 121^0, $\angle$ AMD = $\angle$ BMC =59^0
2. Boris 130^0, Cheriane 50^0 3a. a = 67^0 b. c = 58^0, d = 90^0
4a. e = 35^0, f = 100^0 b. e = 58^0, f = 32^0, g = 148^0 c. i = 95^0
5ai. 180^0 ii. 270^0 b. 270^0, $\frac{3}{4}$ c. 45^0

ANGLES IN NAVIGATION   TUTORIAL 3
PIP: (page 308)
1b. 80^0, 260^0 2b. 170^0, 350^0 3a. 100^0, 190^0
4a. 7, 25   b. 7, 25   c. 15 , 33   d. 15 , 33
5f. 6.5 km   6f. Finish should be close to O.

CIRCLES
CIRCUMFERENCE OF CIRCLES   TUTORIAL 1
PIP: (page 312)
1. Diameter is twice the radius.
2a. 6340 km   b. 6320 km;   c. very close to spherical
3. 3000 m

Inv: (page 313)

a. slightly more than 3   b. 3
2. Multiply diameter by 3   3. 19

Inv: (page 315)

d. approximately 3 each time

PIP: (page 316)

4ci. 18 cm   ii. 18.8   5a. 25.8 cm   b. 31 m
6a. 911 m   b. 1759 m   c. 2.84 lira/m
7a. 23 m   b. 884   c. 531
8a. 5 cm   b. 31.4 cm
9a. 18 cm × 3.6 cm × 3.6 cm   c. 18 cm × 10.8 cm × 7.2 cm
10a. 39835   b. 1660 km/h or 461 m/s   c. 39835 (also)

AREA OF A CIRCLE   TUTORIAL 2

Inv 1: (page 319)

1a. 8 cm   b. 64 cm^2 c. less than 64 cm^2 2. 48 cm^2

PIP: (page 321)

1. 27 172 m^2 2. 31416 km^2

3a. Square the radius then multiply by π

 b. Divide the diameter by 2, then square the radius and multiply by π
4. 254 m^2 5a. 11 cm^2 b. 3300   c. no (she has 39.6 kg)
6a. 0.79 ft^2 (or 113 in^2)   b. 11.78 ft^2 c. 37.70 ft^2 d. 62.83 ft^2

7.

Radius (nearest 0.1 cm)	Diameter (nearest 0.1 cm)	Area (nearest cm^2)
2.9 cm	5.8 cm	26 cm²
1.3 cm	2.6 cm	5 cm²
5.0 cm	10.0 cm	78 cm²

8a. 28.5 cm   b. 42   9. 70 m^2 10g. 3π:50 or 0.188:1
11. 531 cm^2 12. 32 cm
13ai. 25 cm   ii. 50cm^2 b. 45 cm^3 c. $4032, $62.50   d. 0.41 cm^3

REVIEW

(page 327)

1a. acute   b. reflex   c. obtuse   d. acute   e. obtuse   f. acute   g. right
 h. reflex   i. straight   j. obtuse   k. reflex   l. obtuse
2a. 48°   b. $n = 70°, p = 110°$ c. $q = 10°, r = 80°$
 d. $t = 50°, u = 70°, v = 110°$
3c. 360°

4a. $C = 18.84$ cm, $A = 28.27$ cm^2 b. $C = 75.40$ m, $A = 452.39$ m^2

  c. $C = 201.06$ mm, $A = 3216.99$ mm^2 d. $C = 47.12$ cm, $A = 176.71$ cm^2

5. $d = 16.0$ cm, $r = 8.0$ cm.

6. $d = 14.0$ m, $r = 7$ m.

7. 15.71 cm^2 8. 41 540 m^2 9a. 38 m   b.113 m^2

SPORTS

CENTRAL TENDENCIES

SPORTS STATISTICS   TUTORIAL 1

PIP: (page 336)

1a. 15   b,c,d. 20

2a. Add all the numbers together and divide by the number of numbers

b. Arrange the numbers in increasing or decreasing order. If there is an even number of numbers, select the middle number. If there is an odd number of numbers take the average of the middle two numbers.

c. Select the number that occurs most often

d. Find the difference between the highest and lowest numbers

3a. 14   b. 18   c. 20   d. 15

4.

Player	Mean	Median	Mode	Range
Tomson	19	20	20	12
Cameron	15	20	20	17
Buffey	14	18	20	15

5ai. 12.6   ii. 12   iii. none   iv. 14

  bi. 4.3   ii. 4   iii. 6   iv. 7

  ci. 5.6   ii. 6   iii. 7   iv. 7

  6. $2000   7ai. 19   ii,iii. 20   iv. 12

MEAN, MEDIAN, MODE, RANGE   TUTORIAL 2

Inv: (page 339)

ai.Tomson 19.7, Cameron 17.7, Buffey 14.9

ii. Tomson 20, Cameron 16, Buffey 14

iii.Tomson 20, Cameron 15, Buffey 21

iv.Tomson 4, Cameron 16, Buffey 11

PIP: (page 339)

1a. 8   b. 6   c. 5   d. 13

2. Mean: 5.8, Med: 5.9, Mode: 8.2, Range: 9.8

3. $2713   4a. 159.6cm   b. 160 cm   c. 160 cm

MEAN, MEDIAN OR MODE?   TUTORIAL 3

PIP: (page 342)

2a. the average of the numbers   b. the middle number   c. the number that occurs most often
  d. the difference between the highest and lowest numbers

CENTRAL TENDENCIES IN SPORTS   TUTORIAL 4

PIP: (page 343)

1a. 28.4 b. 28   c. about 28 points per game

2a $60 429   b. $45 288   3a. 3   b,c. 0   4. 80

5. 16 987   6a. 5.5   b. 5.4   c. 5.4, 5.4, 5.5

8. 14.5   12a. 5 yd

12b,c.

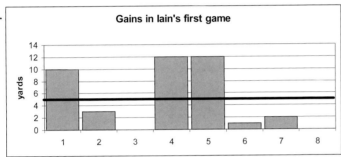

Gains in Iain's first game

TRACK TIMES   TUTORIAL 5

PIP: (page 346)

1a. Estevez: 3 min 32.4 s, Brunner: 3 min 8.58 s   b. wheelchair

2a. 2.22 s, 0.33 s   b. non-amputees   c. 1.9 s   d. 3.3 s.

PLUS/MINUS STATISTIC   TUTORIAL 6

PIP: (page 349)

1a.

Player	+/– Number
Micaela	–6
Darren	+27
Dan	+23
Brad	+23
Janet	+21
Tina	–18
Keith	–2

d. 5.3, 9.5, +23

2a.

Player	+/– Number
Marlene	+75
Sandy	+49
Mike	+48
Shannon	+47
Iain	+29
Wade	+15
Randa	+14
Rob	+4
Jennifer	0
Jay	–11
Allan	–21
Chris	–22
Bryan	–31

THEOREM OF PYTHAGORAS

SQUARE ROOTS   TUTORIAL 1

PIP: (page 352)

1.

Number	1	2	3	4	5	6	7	8	9	10	11	12
Number^2	1	4	9	16	25	36	49	64	81	100	121	144

2a. 4   b. 5   c. 6   d. 7   e. 12   f. 8   g. 10   h. 11
  i. 9

4a. 3.__   b. 5. __   c. 7. __   d. 8. __   e. 9. __   f. 10. __

5a. 3.317   b. 5.831   c. 7.071   d. 8.832   e. 9.747   f. 10.954

6a. 4.2426407   b. 7.0710678   c. 9.2736185   d. 9.7467943

THEOREM OF PYTHAGORAS   TUTORIAL 2

Inv: (page 354)

1. $e^2 = d^2 + c^2$.   2.

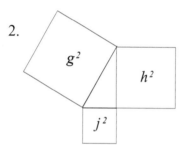

APPLYING THE PYTHAGOREAN THEOREM   TUTORIAL 3

PIP: (page 355)

1. 25   2. 16   3. AB = 5, RT = 5

4. CJ   J   C   11 236   11 236

5. 6 cm.   6a. 58.3 cm   b. 135 cm   c. 72 cm

7b. 23.2 ft   8b. diagonal   c. 80 yd

10. 250 yd   11. 38.7 m   12. 23 m   13. 38 yd

REVIEW

(page 361)

1a. 3   b. –7   c. –1   d. 9   e. –14   f. –2

2a. 11, 10, 9, 5   b. 9, 8, 7, 10   c. 7, 7, 7, 6

3a. Mean: 5.5 yd, Med: 4 yd, Mode: none   4. 72.8 kg   5. 5

6a. 179 cm   b. no change 7. 4   8. 262 m

9. 192 m   10. 13 m   11. 39 m

12a. 10 cm   b. 24 cm   c. 24 cm^2 d. same

ADVERTISING

CONSUMER CHOICES

PIZZA   TUTORIAL 1

PIP: (page 371)
1a. $48.98   b. $40.10   c. $43.15   d. 452 in^2 e. 603 in^2
2a. Enzo: $37.18, Bernie: $32.80

CELLULAR PHONES   TUTORIAL 2

Inv: (page 3
4)

1a.

	Callus	Bing	Coggers	Bowser
Approx Cost ($)	380	385	375 or 365	290

1c. about $3

PIP: (page 376)
1a. Callus: $1611.70, Bing: $1544, Coggers: $1276, Bowser: $1217.70
1c. Callus: $45, Bing: $36, Coggers: $27, Bowser: $18
2a. I: $170, II,III: $190, IV: $195

PERCENTS   TUTORIAL 3

PIP: (page 378)
1a. $12.8   b. $35   c. $158   2a. 15%   b. 20%

3. Product	a. (%)	c. ($)
Miranda	60	148.50
Metro	62	157.50
Astoria	65	127.50
Boulevard	53	127.50
Village	66	148.50
Explorer	62	178.50

BEST BUY   TUTORIAL 4

PIP: (page 379)
1. No
4a. $21.11   b. $44.87 less
7a. $21.40   b. $60.63
9. $1.15, $1.77

2a. $0.79/lb, $1.74/kg   b. Gala
6a. Either   b. Bruno's
8a,b. Zaba's
10.a The Shop   b. $100

11. Mean: $369.28, Med: $394.99, Mode: $399.99, Range: $450

REVIEW
(page 384)

3a. 33¢   b. 8   4. Yes

Index

SYMBOLS

+/- Statistic. *See* Central Tendencies

A

Aboriginal 101, 231, 329
Acute angle 298
Acute triangle 305
Algebra Tiles
    19, 24, 32, 55, 60, 213, 226
Altitude   *See* Height
Angles 296
  acute 298
  adjacent 303
  bisector 302
  common arm 303
  constructing 296
  measuring 296
  naming 298
  obtuse 298
  opposite 303
  right 298
  reflex 298
  straight 298
Area 176, 319 *See also* Measurement: linear measure
  breaking into smaller shapes 185
  octagon 188
  parallelogram 179
  rectangle 179
  trapezoid 184
  triangle 182
  circle 319
  ring 322
Arithmetic mean 335
Average 335

B

Bar graph 112
Base
  rectangle 177
  parallelogram 177
  triangle 183
Bearing 308
BEDMAS 4
Bisector 302
Broken-line graph 115

C

Calculator 6, 23, 352
Calendar 63
Capacity 195
  volume 192
Cartesian coordinates 45
Central Tendencies 334
  +/- Statistic 348
  mean 335
  median: 335
  mode 335
  range 335
Circle 312
  area 319
  circumference 312
  diameter 312
  Pi 314
  radius 312
  graph 97
Circumference 312
Conducting a survey 101
Conversion tables; metric and Imperial 204
  length 171 *See also* Imperial units
  mass, weight 198
  volume 192
Coordinate plane 45
  horizontal axis 45, 101
  ordered pairs 45
  origin 45
  vertical axis 45
  x-axis 45
  y-axis 45

D

Decimal 72
  adding 76
  multiplying 83
  rounding 72
  subtracting 76
Denominator 124
Diameter 312
Division 33
Divisor 155. *See also* Fractions: Dividing

E

Equation 212
  one-Step 219
    verifying 223
  two-Step 224
    verifying 232
Equivalent fractions 133
Equivalent ratios 239, 279
Estimation 353

F

Fahler 289
Fraction 122. *See also* Imperial units; Percent
  adding 139
  comparing 123
  dividing 150
  equivalent 133
  improper fraction 126
  mixed number 127
    multiplying 149
  multiplying 144
  proper fractions 126
  simplest form 136
  subtracting 139
Frequency 99

G

GST 274
Glendon 288
Graph
  bar graph 112
  broken-line graph 115
  circle graph 97, 102, 109, 110
  double bar graph 107
  histogram 107, 111
  horizontal axis 45, 101
  points on a line 49, 51
  vertical axis 45

H

Height 177, 181, 183
Hexagon 125
Histogram 101
Horizontal axis 45, 101
Hypotenuse 354

I

IAAF 346
Imperial units 158, 192. *See also* Fractions; Conversion tables
  adding and subtracting. *See* Fractions: Adding
Improper fraction 126
  change to a mixed number 132
Integer 8
  adding 17
  comparing 11
  dividing 34
  multiplying 24
  subtracting 19
  zero principle 13
Interior angles. *See* Triangles
Intersecting lines 304

M

Magic squares 52
Mass 199
Mean 335
Measurement 158
  linear measure 158
Median 335
Metric units 158, 192. *See also* Measurement, Conversion tables
Mixed number 127
Mode 335
Multiplication 33
  powers of 10
Mundare 289

N

Navigation 308. *See also* Angles
Number line 9. *See also* Imperial units: adding and subtracting
Number tricks 58
Numerator 124

O

Obtuse angle 298
Obtuse triangle 305
Olympic 325
Opposite angles 304
Order of operations 4
Orienteering 311
Origin 45

P

Parallelogram
  area 179
  perimeter 174
Pattern Blocks 125
Patterning relationship 45
Patterns 39
  calendar 63
  graphing 47
Percent 261
  discount 376
Perimeter 173 *See also* Circumference; Measurement: linear measure
  circle 312
  parallelogram 174
  rectangle 175
  triangle 173
  polygon 173
Pi 314
Pictograph 105
Place value 77, 85, 91
Plans, drawing 208
Product 35
Proper fraction 126
Proportion 279. *See also* Ratio
Protractor 296
Puzzles 53
Pythagoream theorem 351

Q

Quotient 35

R

Radius 312
Range 335
Rate 255
  unit 255
Ratio 238
  equivalent 239, 279
Reflex angle 298
Rectangle
  area 179
  perimeter 175
Rhombus 125
Right angle 298
Right Triangle 354
Rounding 72
Runway names 310

S

Square Roots 350
Statistics 334
Straight angle 298
Survey 246
  conducting a 365

T

Taber 289
Table of values 46
Tally 98
The King's Chessboard 39
Tipi rings 329
Transit 330
Trapezoid 125
Triangle
  acute-angled 305
  area 182
  constructing 299
  hypotenuse 354
  interior angles 305
  obtuse-angled 305
  perimeter 173
  right-angled 355
  right 354
Trundle wheel 330

U

Unit rate 255

V

Variable 218
Vertical axis 45
Volume 192
  Capacity 195
  formula 195
  medal (cylinder) 327

W

Weight 199
Wheelchair athletics 346

X

x–axis 45

Y

y-axis 45

Z

Zero principle 13

We would especially like to thank those who have given us permission to use their images in this publication.

Unit/Pic	Photo Credit
Puzzles	
• Intro pic (pg2)	Carla Belanger (CB)
Entertainment	
• Intro pic (pg 70)	Singer Laurie Church at the Canadian Aboriginal Festival
• Odd Job (pg 80)	"Odd Job", http://62.20.89.46/dreamtest/mera/index.htm
• Ribbon (pg89)	CB
• Stage (pg 98, 117)	"Glenns Orkester", http://www.glennsorkester.com/
• Tickets (pg 100)	CB
• Stage (pg 103)	Canadian Aboriginal Festival
• Concert (pg 114)	Sean Bettam & Stewart Whitehead from "Talladega"
Home	
• Intro pic (pg 120)	Signature Suites, Barrie ON, photos by Marianne Strasser
• Poster pics (pg 122, 123)	Comstock Images
• 110 sign (pg 172)	Highway #2, Southern Alberta CB
• Tools (pg 208)	CB
Food	
• Intro pic (pg 210)	Getty Images (The Image Bank)
• Pyrogy (pg 288)	David Yanciw , bigthings.com
• Bee (pg 289)	Town of Fahler
• Sausage (pg 289)	George Babak, Edmonton AB
• Cornstalk (pg 289)	David Yanciw, bigthings.com
• Group shot (pg 293)	Rikk Belanger
Perspectives	
• Intro pic (pg 294)	US National Oceanic and Atmospheric Administration
• Plane air (pg 308)	NASA
• Sexton (pg 309)	US National Oceanic and Atmospheric Administration
• Jet air (pg 309)	NASA
• Landing (pg 310)	NASA
• Earth (pg 312)	NASA
• Earth 2 (pg 318)	NASA
• Irrigation (pg 321)	Southern Alberta; CB
Sports	
• Intro pic (pg 333)	Comstock Images
• Hurdles (pg 334)	Comstock Images
• Hockey (pg 337)	Comstock Images
• Baseball (pg 343)	Comstock Images
• Football (pg 345)	Comstock Images
• Diamond (pg360)	CB
• Stadium (pg364)	Neil Hallsworth
• Volleyball girl (pg 367)	Comstock Images
Advertising	
• Intro pic (pg 368)	"The Blue Bottle", Barrie ON, photo by Marianne Strasser
• Cell phones (pg 373)	CB
• Girl w phone (pg 375)	Heather Rose Johnson; CB
• Window display (pg 377)	"Artifact", Barrie ON, photo by Marianne Strasser